Poverty, Politics, and Health Care

Richard A. Couto

The Praeger Special Studies program—utilizing the most modern and efficient book production techniques and a selective worldwide distribution network—makes available to the academic, government, and business communities significant, timely research in U.S. and international economic, social, and political development.

Poverty, Politics, and Health Care

An Appalachian Experience

PRAEGER SPECIAL STUDIES IN U.S. ECONOMIC, SOCIAL, AND POLITICAL ISSUES

Praeger Publishers   New York   Washington   London

Library of Congress Cataloging in Publication Data

Couto, Richard A
    Poverty, politics, and health care.

    (Praeger special studies in U.S. economic, social,
and political issues)
    Bibliography: p.
    1. Community health services—Kentucky—Floyd Co.
2. Poor—Medical care—United States. 3. Economic
assistance, Domestic—United States. I. Title.
[DNLM: 1. Delivery of health care—Appalachian
region—Politics—Appalachian region. 2. Poverty—
Appalachian region. 4. Quality of health care—
Appalachian region. WA30 C871p]
RA395.A4K43   362.5   74-14041
ISBN 0-275-09850-8

PRAEGER PUBLISHERS
111 Fourth Avenue, New York, N.Y. 10003, U.S.A.
5, Cromwell Place, London SW7 2JL, England

Published in the United States of America in 1975
by Praeger Publishers, Inc.

Among the more pleasant tasks of preparing this work is taking stock of the debts I have incurred. First, I must acknowledge my father and mother and family—their influence and sensitivity to human beings pervades this work and it is hoped that this study is an indication their efforts and love have borne some fruit.

Second, I am deeply grateful to the people of Floyd County who, through interviews, led me through the labyrinth of kinship ties and social and economic arrangements. Discretion suggests that they remain unidentified; but, without their generous efforts in recounting events, this study would be devoid of substantiating human experience. One person may be named for his part: to Father William Poole I am grateful for friendship, advice, an isolated cabin, and an introduction to the finest and most generous neighbors one could hope for.

The debts I amassed in Lexington are legion and for fear of adding to an already lengthy study I hope my friends will realize my gratefulness incorporates them all. Four people must be singled out: Gene Mason first encouraged me in an Appalachian study by refusing to accept numerous difficulties I suggested as prohibitive; Malcolm Jewell has set a standard of scholarship that greatly influenced my writing as I anticipated his examination; Ernest Yanarella encouraged me to stop writing about critical social science and to try doing it; finally, Herbert Reid's influence is such that, literally, without his scholarship and seminars this study would not have been possible. I also am grateful to the University of Kentucky Fellowship Office and the Northern Kentucky State College Faculty Grant Program, for travel funds, and to Sherry Stortz for her typing.

Having acknowledged substantial indebtedness it would be convenient to shift blame for any shortcomings; but while the merits may be shared, the shortcomings are entirely my own.

My wife Took not only helped prepare earlier manuscripts of this study but also managed to maintain an interest in the project and a belief that it was a worthwhile and finite task. Her participation and encouragement are much appreciated as are the unique contributions of Nathan and Jason.

CONTENTS

LIST OF TABLES

LIST OF ABBREVIATIONS

ARH	Appalachian Regional Hospitals
AV	Appalachian Volunteers
CAA	Community Action Agency
CAP	Community Action Program
CDGM	Child Development Group of Mississippi
EKWRO	Eastern Kentucky Welfare Rights Organization
FCCHSP	Floyd County Comprehensive Health Services Program
HEW	Department of Health, Education and Welfare
MFY	Mobilization for Youth
OEO	Office of Economic Opportunity
OHA	Office of Health Affairs
PCJD	President's Commission on Juvenile Delinquency
TVA	Tennessee Valley Authority
UMW	United Mine Workers

THEORETICAL PREMISES

Culture, we are informed by Max Weber, is

a finite segment of the meaningless infinity of the world
process, a segment on which <u>human beings</u> confer meaning and significance.[1]

It is, in this sense, a combination of possibility and socially constructed limitations; and, most important, from a phenomenological
viewpoint, culture is not only an inalienable presence but also a
human construction necessarily rooted in a taken-for-granted attitude.[2]
While culture may appear as "a ready made set of solutions for human
problems,"[3] this appearance masks important social and political
arrangements from which culture stems, and which are in turn sus-
tained by culture. The finite segment of possibility on which human
beings confer meaning and significance is not arbitrarily chosen;
nor is it a fixed moment in human experience. It is contingent upon
social, economic, and political arrangements and maintains its relevance and meaningfulness because of its dialectical relationship with
those arrangements. Culture is a contingent ongoing human process
manifest in institutional arrangements.

This theoretical premise, which underlies this work, is not
new to political science; the dialectical relationship between culture
and politics is implicit in much of the pluralist critique. Peter
Bachrach and Morton S. Baratz, for example, speak of the unconscious
ability of a person, or group, to create or reinforce barriers to the
public airing of policy conflict. This is a nondecision making process,
characterized not by the power A has over B but in the power that
the same values, attitudes, and institutions have over both. Bachrach
and Baratz quote E. E. Schattschneider approvingly when he points
out that all political organization has a bias in favor of the exploitation of some issues and the suppression of others. Thus, "some
issues are organized into politics and others are organized out."[4]
The shortcoming of the pluralists, according to Bachrach and Baratz,
is that they limit themselves to "issues" rather than the values and
biases underlying the issues that give them their fuller political
dimensions.[5] In so doing, the pluralists take for granted, or assume
the cultural values that inform and select the issues: culture is relegated to a "natural" or "given" condition.[6] To a phenomenologist

this means reducing the realm of meaning and limiting oneself to the study of acts, or in another context, "behavior."[7] Equally important, acceptance of culture as "given" renders culture apolitical, which is tantamount to the legitimation of existing values and structures of power and influence: a very political act. In other words, pluralism becomes the "ready made solution" of political problems.

This study in focusing on the values and biases of the actors hopes to reclaim culture as political. This is not a pioneering effort in this regard as will be indicated. Murray Edelman has pointed out that, because of cultural factors, the American poor have required less coercion and less in social security guarantees to maintain their quiescence than in any other developed country.[8] In a similar vein, Paulo Freire points out that given a commonality of beliefs, the self-perception of the poor as opposites of the nonpoor,

> does not yet signify engagement in a struggle to overcome
> the contradiction; the one pole aspires not to liberation
> but to identification with its opposite pole.[9]

The commonality of beliefs among poor and nonpoor explains why some social, economic, and political inequities remain nonissues rather than sources of conflict. But when beliefs are shattered and culture is recognized as a finite segment of the possible, then human responsibility for social, economic, and political arrangements must be recognized—hence, culture becomes politicized. It becomes politicized also because it must be defended against those who seek to make others accountable for allegedly inequitable arrangements and those who seek radical change to redress their grievance. Cultural values become politicized when the ambiguity they seemingly resolved reappears and the values, previously culturally imposed as "obvious," become contingent upon the power of the advantaged to defend them and modify or restore their "natural" appearance.

In this study, three concepts are employed to invoke the ambiguity hidden beneath cultural attitudes: poverty, health care, and maximum feasible participation of the poor. These concepts will allow us, it is premised, a glimpse of the social and economic arrangements that ordinarily hold the ambiguity and political nature of these terms in abeyance. The critical examination of these terms, as embodied in the conflict surrounding the Floyd County Comprehensive Health Services Program (FCCHSP), will, it is hoped, approach the goal set for philosophy and the sociology of knowledge by Richard Lichtman: to illuminate the social relations constitutive of the social world in the service of "a revolutionary self-awareness for those who would otherwise be the unwitting victims of social power."[10] Or, as C. Wright Mills has put it, a critical social science enables us to understand the larger historical scene in terms of its meanings for the inner life and the external career of a variety of individuals. It enables [us] to take into account how individuals in the welter of their daily experience, often become falsely conscious of their social position. Within that welter, the framework of modern society is sought, and within that framework the psychologies of a variety of men and women are formulated. By such means the personal uneasiness of individuals is focused upon explicit troubles and the indifference of publics is transformed into involvement with public issues.[11]

HYPOTHESES AND ASPIRATIONS

Stemming from these considerations of culture, this study has two basic hypotheses. The first is based on the view articulated most prominently by Louis Hartz and recently corroborated by Donald Devine[12] that a broad consensus of political principles and views prevail among Americans. This consensus, Lockian liberalism, is the finite segment of the possible within which poverty and health care are defined and political participation is devised.

The second hypothesis is related directly to the central fact of this study: an OEO health program initiated in 1967 to provide health care for the poor of Floyd County in eastern Kentucky ground to a halt in 1971. It was not a success in terms of its stated goal; there are still poor people in Floyd County in need of medical assistance. But, as we hope to show, the program did not cease merely because it failed to achieve its stated goals. The reason this federally funded program of health care for poor people was suspended is that it could not pursue its stated aim and support existing economic, social, and political arrangements in Floyd County. What this study hopes to illustrate is that this poverty program had only one chance to continue: that is, if it served to maintain or increase the privileged position of some in Floyd County. When it became impossible to serve both the stated goals specified by OEO regulations and the goals of the powerful, also articulated in the lexicon of the public good, the program could not continue. It was at once failure and success, and its inability to serve two masters incurred the wrath and sanctions of both.

Conflict over the nature of comprehensive health care ensued when it was defined as the establishment of clinics outside the control of the medical practitioners of the county. Once this division over comprehensive health care was established, differences in the interpretation of participation, health care, and even poverty followed, and

xiii

each side sought to legitimate its views and provide grounds for a consensus.

Both hypotheses this study seeks to illustrate imply that policy in pursuit of public goals is more clearly a mediation between existing institutions and values and public needs than merely a means to redress need. It is a mediation in that it legitimates existing arrangements by expressing their concern for a public need and addresses those needs in terms consistent with the existing distribution of economic, social, and political power—as if these arrangements were sufficient for the task of amelioration. Simply put, public policy follows existing distributions of power, not public need, and is shaped by the relation of existing power to the public need. Tom Bethell has shown how this is so in the administration of the U.S. Bureau of Mines;[13] while Edelman, citing several other studies of regulatory agencies, has stated the following:

> All conclude that few regulatory policies have been pursued unless they proved acceptable to the regulated groups or served the interests of these groups.[14]

The significance of the present study is that when the goals of the health program under examination were consistent with elite interests a segment of the program's clients demonstrated their awareness of their deprivation and demanded that another version of public need, inconsistent with elite interest or support, be instated as the program's goal. This has not been common in the experience of policy enforcing agencies;[15] the Eastern Kentucky Welfare Rights Organization (EKWRO) conjured up the ideals with which the program was conceived and graphically portrayed the distance the program remained from those ideals.

In addition to these hypotheses, this study has several other important concerns. It is a study of a poverty program in Appalachia; as such it entails an examination of the politics of a county in the region. No county is typically Appalachian and some caution should be exercised in making generalizations. Nonetheless, an attempt has been made, primarily by footnotes, to show similarities between the events in Floyd County and events elsewhere in Appalachia so that, hopefully, this study will be a useful examination of the political and cultural values of the Appalachian region, as well as testimony to another awakening minority, the Appalachian poor—symbolized in EKWRO.

The Appalachian context of this study should not preclude some larger generalizations. This study was undertaken with the conviction that the values and issues involved were not atypical or sectional, but were American values and issues writ large. Typified as "yesterday's people," Appalachians are dealing with the problems of today and tomorrow: poverty in a postindustrial state; technological unemployment; and, in this particular case, improved health care arrangements and their management. These are not only Appalachian problems but also American problems, prevalent and focused in Appalachia, with bearing for the ghettoes, the assembly lines, and the medically indigent. What happens to people when they no longer are needed by a postindustrial society? This is a question pertinent to this study and to people within or without Appalachia. Floyd County, like most of Appalachia and other minority groups, has had to deal with the question earlier than most members of the affluent society. Particularly pertinent are the lessons derived from an attempt at medical reform that was premised on greater utilization of existing medical facilities, just as are Medicare, Medicaid, and various proposed national health insurance plans.

Two other concerns pervade the study. The first is to write the history of a war on poverty effort—an urgent need according to Moynihan[16] and, fortunately, one that has been partly answered.[17] The second is to modify pluralist assumptions of adequate participatory mechanisms for an allegedly sufficient number of competitive interest groups. The elites under study here should not be taken as one monolithic power structure; important differences among them have been mentioned but not underscored. On the other hand, pluralism is also an inadequate portrayal of the nature of the elites encountered in this book.

The elites of this study shall be taken to be those groups and individuals whose power, status, and privilege are in dialectical relationship with Lockian liberal culture. This culture circumscribes the differences of elites as evidenced by the unity among elites when is necessary. Differences among elites are not denied, but they are limited to differences in appraising the need for change and the extent of change possible without damage to cultural values.[18] When debate extends beyond these limits to demands for change with uncertain or threatening implications for existing social, economic, and/or political arrangements, differences among elites are, by and large, forgotten in order to prepare a defense of common cultural assumptions. A study of such an extended debate must be willing to incorporate the nonelites or the "illegitimate" groups within its considerations. Fortunately for this study, EKWRO is of central importance in forcing an issue from nondecision to decision making status. As a critique of pluralism, this study hopes to dispel the happy Madisonian optimism of pluralism that sees progress in homeostasis, democracy in elitism, public good emerging from competing self-interests, and social change as a nonconstant-sum game in which everyone wins.

METHODOLOGY

The conflict over the Floyd County Comprehensive Health Services Program is most meaningful within the context of American conceptions of poverty and antipoverty strategies. Accordingly, chapters 1 and 2 develop this context by locating the cultural premises of poverty and antipoverty strategies within social, economic, and political values and arrangements and by contrasting these premises with alternative views and interpretations.

Chapter 3 offers an examination of the early operation of the health program, its context, and criticisms and evaluations of the program. Chapter 4 details the actors of the conflict and their opposing views, while Chapter 5 describes the extent and nature of the conflict, the defense of elite control of the program, and the apparent resolution of the conflict. Chapter 6 attempts to generalize from the experience of Floyd County to a discussion of conflict in terms of the interaction of cultural values and power.

Originally this study sought to reconstruct the controversy around the belief and symbols connected with poverty, health care, and participation. It seemed such a reconstruction would be valuable because it would yield a symbolic network unique and interpenetrating for each side of the conflict. This is still held to be a valuable part of the study because only by examining the belief systems pervading the symbols can we gauge the deeper issues and values being contested. However, it became clear during the course of the study that the pre-existing balance of power among the contenders predisposed the triumph and legitimation of one set of interpretive beliefs and symbols. The cultural determinants of the legitimacy of the actors and the supportive role culture played for the existing distribution of power impart the fullest understanding to the resolution of the conflict and the selection of one set of beliefs and symbols.

To uncover the issues, values, and beliefs, interviews were held with several of the actors in the controversy. The interviews included members of the Office of Health Affairs (OHA), a member of Representative Carl Perkins' office—though not Perkins himself, unfortunately—and persons involved on the periphery by connections with the governor's office or the Kentucky Economic Opportunity Office. The interviews also included a majority of the members of the Board of Directors of the health program, as well as spokesmen for both groups involved in the controversy. All interviews, but one, were conducted in a five-month period, from March to August 1972, with part of that time spent in residence in Floyd County. The interviews were open-ended but with a similar format. The interviewed person was asked about poverty, the poor, health care, and participation and was allowed to formulate his/her own answer. The interviews, when casual, would range over an array of related, and sometimes not so related, topics. But in this manner the issues were reconstructed in the perspective of the actors and not that of the investigator.

The value and validity of this approach to data gathering is its potential for uncovering the values and symbols that are taken for fact and the facts that are valued. A doctor who declared "I'm not going to answer any of your questions because they're just matters of opinion" actually evidenced the importance of this approach. Rather than risk the exposition of his opinion he stuck to the "facts"— which, of course, legitimated his critical attitude of the program. Only his political position and especially his role in the medical organization of the county—past, present, and future—explained both the "facts" he valued and his actions. A few important actors in the conflict refused interviews, explicitly or implicitly, possibly because as Steinbeck pointed out, "A question is a trap and an answer is your foot in it."[19] Fortunately, other sources of information were available to enable an accurate reconstruction of the views of the two central figures in the controversy who were not interviewed. The unavailability of the county judge led to an addition to the study not originally seen but emphasized time and again by those interviewed: namely, the machinelike characteristics of Floyd County politics.

The conflict in Floyd County over the health program was divisive and penetrated deeply into the feelings and thoughts of those concerned. A year after the controversy some participants were reluctant to talk about the program or the controversy; some relished the opportunity; some adamantly refused; no one was indifferent. Even after 12 months, conversations were held with precautions to avoid eavesdropping or incrimination. Because of this atmosphere confidentiality was promised to most interviewees. Their remarks, when included in the text, will appear without citation. All other comments, when part of the public record, gathered from newspaper accounts, or of special relevance because of their source, will be cited.

It should be obvious that a controversy so divisive and so enduring involved more than administrative or procedural questions. Each side in the controversy was identified by a set of views on the causes of poverty, the poor, health care for the poor, and the Office of Economic Opportunity mandate of "maximum feasible participation." To oversimplify by way of illustration: the poor were oppressed or lazy; poverty was social or individual in its origins; health care was a right of the person or a moral obligation of the provider; and maximum feasible participation was democracy or disorder. Before the conflict had run its course it appeared to many that fundamental concerns such as majority rule, electoral politics, the doctor-patient relationship—and the implications this had for the quality of care—

as well as an orderly, rewarding local life style were under attack.

The people interviewed were people who lived in direct contact with the program and the problems it entailed. Their lives, their attitudes, and their opinions were the program and its controversy. These are the people who literally spent the sleepless nights, suffered the nervous conditions and heart attacks, feared physical harm in reprisal for their position; who threatened others or were threatened; and who were moved to anger, incoherence, or tears. To neglect them is to raise politics to an abstract and rarified level beyond the lived world, and it would be a distortion of the reality as they lived it.

Participation in this study was the expression and recounting of a level of experienced politics few others reach. The hesitancy of some of those interviewed and the unwillingness of others to be interviewed may be taken as expression of that experience. What emerges is not the neat model of politics constructed for civics classes for purposes of socialization rather than education but, hopefully, a view of the lived substance behind the image.

The people interviewed oftentimes expressed their honesty, integrity, and sincerity in phrases that disarm the sophisticated social scientist or the cynic: "I would stake my life on it," or "I sure wouldn't want to lie." The truth is the truth as far as they are concerned, and the memory of conversations held in their homes, in remote "hollers" in some instances, is ample motivation to be faithful to them and their experience.

NOTES

1. Max Weber, The Methodology of the Social Sciences, translated by Edward A. Shils and Henry A. Finch (New York: The Free Press, 1949), p. 81.

2. Maurice Merleau-Ponty gives a short, concise discussion of phenomenology in Phenomenology of Perception, translated by Colin Smith (New York: The Humanities Press, 1962), pp. vii-xxi.

3. Oscar Lewis quoted in Charles Valentine, Culture and Poverty: Critique and Counter-Proposals (Chicago: University of Chicago Press, 1968), p. 116.

4. Peter Bachrach and Morton S. Baratz, Power and Poverty: Theory and Practice (New York: Oxford University Press, 1970), pp. 8-9.

5. Ibid., p. 11.

6. Donald J. Devine, The Political Culture of the United States: The Influence of Member Values on Regime Maintenance, (Boston: Little, Brown and Company, 1972), p. 3.

7. Contrasted with this emphasis on "behavior," which presumes the context and meaning of an act, is the phenomenological concern with "action." This concern is manifested by the attempt to arrive at the meanings of acts, that is, the realm of intention that inspires actors and that provides the ultimate explanation of their action. See Harold Garfinkel, Studies in Ethnomethodology (Englewood Cliffs, N.J.: Prentice-Hall, 1967); Alfred Schutz, The Phenomenology of the Social World (Evanston, Ill.: Northwestern University Press, 1967); George Psathas, "Ethnomethodology and Phenomenology," Social Research 35, no. 3 (1968): 500-17; Maurice Natanson, "Alfred Schutz on Social Reality and Social Science," Social Research 35, no. 2 (1968): 217-45; and John Gunnell, "Social Science and Political Reality: The Problem of Explanation," Social Research 35, no. 1 (1968): 159-201. Hwa Yol Jung, ed. Existential Phenomenology and Political Theory: A Reader, (Chicago: Henry Regnery Company, 1972).

8. Murray Edelman, Politics as Symbolic Action: Mass Arousal and Quiescence (Chicago: Markham Publishing Co., 1971), pp. 55-56.

9. Paulo Freire, Pedagogy of the Oppressed (New York: Herder and Herder, 1970), p. 30.

10. Richard Lichtman, "Symbolic Interactionism and Social Reality: Some Marxist Queries," Berkeley Journal of Sociology 15 (1970): 92.

11. C. Wright Mills, The Sociological Imagination (New York: Oxford University Press, 1959), p. 5.

12. Louis Hartz, The Liberal Tradition in America: An Interpretation of American Political Thought Since the Revolution (New York: Harcourt, Brace and World, 1955); Devine, The Political Culture of the United States.

13. Tom Bethell, The Hurricane Creek Massacre (New York: Harper & Row, 1972).

14. Murray Edelman, The Symbolic Uses of Politics (Urbana: University of Illinois Press, 1967), p. 24.

15. Ibid., p. 25.

16. Daniel P. Moynihan, Maximum Feasible Misunderstanding: Community Action in the War on Poverty (New York: The Free Press, 1970) p. 167

17. Huey Perry, "They'll Cut off Your Project": A Mingo County Chronicle (New York: Praeger Publishers, 1972); Polly Greenberg, The Devil Has Slippery Shoes: A Biased Biography of the Child Development Group of Mississippi (London: Macmillan, 1969); and Kenneth B. Clark and Jeannette Hopkins, A Relevant War Against Poverty: A Study of Community Action Programs and Observable Social Change (New York: Harper & Row, 1968).

18. Devine, The Political Culture of the United States, pp. 255-60.

19. John Steinbeck, Travels With Charley: In Search of America (New York: Bantam Books, 1963), p. 263.

Poverty, Politics, and Health Care

EARLY EXPERIENCE AND VIEWS

Benjamin Franklin's Conventional Wisdom

Poverty, while no stranger in America, has never been made to feel at home. There is something in the American belief system that seems to deny that poverty is natural, inevitable, or that it belongs in the American experience. From the start, the abundance of the new continent seemingly provided every man the means to sufficiency, if not abundance. True, some individuals were unable to acquire or provide for themselves because of sickness, physical handicaps, widowhood and dependent children, mental illness, and so on, and these were to be provided for; but poverty was the exception not the rule and before providing for a poor person it seemed wise to determine if that person was voluntarily or involuntarily poor. Relief in the latter instance was necessary and humane, but in the former case relief was debilitating. Perhaps the common sense of this latter observation was best articulated by America's foremost dispenser of conventional wisdom, Benjamin Franklin.

> I am for doing good to the poor, but I differ about the means. I think the best way of doing good to the poor, is not making them easy in poverty but leading or driving them out of it. In my youth I travelled much and I observed in different countries that the more public provisions were made for the poor, the less they provided for themselves, and of course became poor. And, on the contrary, the less that was done for them, the more they did for themselves, and became richer.[1]

The curious aspect of Franklin's view is that it evolved from a radically liberating view to an oppressive one, from an incentive to a burden. If poverty was not natural or inevitable, it was because every person had in his/her power the ability to achieve prosperity. But this belief had a darker side to it; if a person without an extenuating handicap did not achieve sufficiency or abundance, it was his/her own fault. Thus, "The entire American creed of individualism and self-help was based on the assumption that earnest seekers could always find honest employment."[2] Abundance was available for all who would make the effort. Franklin's view logically led to social and government inaction in creating equality and economic security because poverty, as an individual problem, was overcome by time, the opportunities prevailing, and personal initiative—which never goes unrewarded. The best support in old age or sickness, according to Franklin, was "industry and frugality during youth and health"; anything else "tends to flatter our natural indolence, to encourage idleness and prodigality, and thereby to promote and increase poverty. . . ."[3]

Government and social inaction to redress poverty and inequality was consistent with the laissez-faire capitalism that marked the 19th century in the United States. One observer notes that before the end of the 19th century the individuation of poverty "had been converted into a formidable bulwark of that strange brand of conservatism espoused by the dominant business class."[4] This strange brand of conservatism enjoyed a seemingly scientific foundation in the social Darwinism provided by Herbert Spencer, and manifested itself in philanthropy.[5] Even religion and morality became infused with this view. If sufficiency was available to all, those who did not achieve it did not make the effort. The gradation in sufficiency, or lack of it, and the degrees of abundance were correlates of the exercise of God-given abilities—especially initiative—and reflected a divine plan. Franklin had pointed out earlier that relief for the misfortunes of people was itself Godlike, but that relief should not be a reward for laziness and folly. If, as Franklin suspected, providence "has appointed Want and Misery as the proper Punishments for, and Cautions against as well as necessary consequences of Idleness and Extravagancy," relief would then be an "attempt to mend the scheme of Providence and to interfere in the Government of the World, and likely to do more harm than Good."[6]

Lockian Liberalism: Roots of the
Conventional Wisdom

Franklin was more a reflection and spokesman for the thought of his time than its source. His views on poverty—and other political,

2

social, and economic conditions—were part of a consensus of liberal political thought best articulated by John Locke and deeply embedded in the whole of the American experience.[7] Three central points of Locke's analysis are of especial importance for the American view of poverty: they are liberty, equality, and property.[8]

The essential characteristic of liberty, according to Locke, is freedom from external restraints, a characteristic very important for an understanding of political power. In the state of nature all men are in a perfect state of freedom "to order their actions, and dispose of their possessions and persons, as they think fit, within the bounds of the law of nature."[9] This freedom, while limited by the law of nature, is true liberty because man in the state of nature is not dependent on the will of any other man. Society is a contrivance to assure the protection of property and differs from the state of nature by the erection of rules and agreements among members of society. These covenants represent a limitation of liberty as man trades off as much of his natural liberty "as the good, prosperity, and safety of the society shall require" in exchange for freedom from arbitrary force that exists in the state of nature.[10]

Equality is also a characteristic of the state of nature insofar as "all the power and jurisdiction is reciprocal, no one having more than another."[11] In other respects men may not be equal because of age, birth, strength, and so on; but in respect to their natural freedoms, including liberty and property, all men are equal in that they are restricted only by nature. Equality prevails in civil society as well, but it is modeled upon the equality of the state of nature; indeed, Locke's entire purpose is to make civil society and government consistent with the state of nature. Civil society does not provide perfect equality but political equality; all men are subject to the same laws and are to be treated equally by the government.

The last important concept to examine is property, which includes not only land but also labor, personal and real property, and everything man has control over.[12] More important than what it is, is what property does; that is, it makes a person human by guaranteeing his liberty and by releasing him from dependence on others. Liberty is a function of property; a threat to one is a threat to both—which is the very reason that Locke gives for the development of civil society.

> The great and chief end therefore, of man's uniting into commonwealth, and putting themselves under government, is the preservation of their property; to which in the state of nature, there are many things wanting.[13]

If property is essential to liberty and liberty is essential to being human, civil society guarantees this last only when it protects

3

individual property. This duty of government precludes action to achieve equality in economic or social terms. In fact, the first duty of government—according to James Madison, who depended on Locke— is to protect inequality of property among men, who, though politically equal, are different in their capacities to accumulate property. When property accumulates in differing proportions among men it is a function of differing faculties, assuming they have not violated another's natural freedoms and the free exercise of those faculties.[14] For another person or government to interfere with that free exercise and consequent accumulation of property is a violation of the natural and civil rights of liberty.

There are several important aspects of Locke's liberal theory that are important to make clear. First, the rights of liberty, equality, and property are presocial and are rooted in the individual, who is the center of liberal thought,[15] so much so that his capacity to possess is an imposing limitation on all legitimate liberal political power.[16] Society and government were to function to perfect the individual's pre-existing rights and were not to redress inequalities arising from the exercise of these rights. Instead, differences among men with varying amounts of property and between men with and without property were acknowledged and perpetuated in the Lockian scheme.

In fact, although all men were equally subject to the same rules, only the men of property were permitted to make the rules.[17] Adam Smith noted the special relationship between government and inequalities of wealth.

> The subjects of every state ought to contribute towards the support of the government, as nearly as possible, in proportion to their respective abilities; that is, in proportion to the revenue which they respectively enjoy under the protection of the state. The expense of government to the individuals of a great nation, is like the expense of management to the joint tenants of a great estate, who are all obliged to contribute in proportion to their respective interests in the estate.[18]

Second, the market became the hallmark of Lockian liberalism. Government was presumed to be part of the market[19] and important for the supply of political goods such as taxes, tariffs, laws and regulations, stability, education, military protection and expansion, and other factors thought necessary to make the market system run smoothly and efficiently.[20] Men and society were transformed by the precedence of the market. Men in C.B. Macpherson's terms became possessive individuals and society became "a lot of free and equal individuals related to each other as proprietors of their own capacities and of what they have acquired by their exercise. Society consists of relations of exchange between proprietors."[21]

Given a tradition of feudalism, Lockian liberalism and the market relations of men are radical departures from relations of tradition and authority.[22] Despite this liberating aspect there were several severely limiting aspects to the view of man entailed in Locke's analysis and developed by others. Man was supposed to be "a Middling creature of limited possibilities"[23] more given to indolence than to excellence. The range of possibility was lowered to man's level in such a way as to emphasize negative characteristics rather than positive accomplishment: activity became overcoming indolence; pleasure was the absence of pain; health the absence of illness; good government was the lack of arbitrary government; and achievement was providing against scarcity. Sheldon S. Wolin, commenting on the negative characteristics of liberal man, says, "In reality the homo economicus of liberal theory was a creature not so much obsessed by the quest of gain as one frightened by the ever-present prospect of loss."[24]

One may search Adam Smith's writings and find nowhere a discussion of action intended to advance the good of society as a whole. Instead, one finds that men individually seeking the satisfaction of necessary passions and appetites, assumedly instilled by nature, bring about the moral good and material well-being of society by an invisible hand.[25]

Another severe limitation of liberalism's view of man was the creation and justification of distinctions among people. If liberty was the essence of being human and if liberty depended on property, then those without property could not be fully human—as evidenced by their limited participation in civil society. Macpherson makes the case even stronger.

> In choosing to make the essence of man the striving for possessions, we make it impossible for many men to be fully human. By defining man as an infinite appropriator, we make it impossible for many men to qualify as men.[26]

Macpherson also points out that property alone was not a sufficient guarantee of liberty, that is, freedom from dependence or external restraint. A man's labor is his property, but to be a liberating power he must not only have the capacity to labor but also access to the means of labor. Capitalism, however, following liberal tenets, allows for the private ownership of the means of production as part of the inequality among men. Since in order to gain access to that which is privately owned the user must exchange a desired value or power in his property, capitalist and laborer are in a market relationship. There is not free and equal access to the means of production and/or labor and without that access a person loses freedom.[27] It should be pointed out that this arrangement of access and exchange most singly undergirds American medicine.

In the last analysis, Locke's articulation of the natural rights of liberty and property and the limits they implied for equality, as well as his explanation of society in view of them, permitted him to provide a moral basis for a class state.[28] Locke must be understood, then, not only as a break from the traditional bonds of feudalism but also as a defense against radical democracy.[29]

Americans stood in a very special relationship with Lockian theory since the basic social norm of Locke, free individuals in a state of nature, was the apparent factual premise of the inception of their country.[30] Lockian theory and American practice seemed the perfect blend as the settlers of the new world wrote compacts constructing civil and political society and seemed to have before them endless abundance to guarantee the liberty of all but the most indolent.

This special blend of theory and practice contributed to an absolutism in the American mind and the "sober faith that its norms are self-evident."[31] Louis Hartz maintains that atomistic individualism, inherited from Locke, was "instinctive" to the American mind and the master assumption of American political thought.

> History was on a lark, out to tease men, not by shattering
> their dreams, but by fulfilling them with a sort of satiric
> accuracy. In America one not only found a society suf-
> ficiently fluid to give a touch of meaning to the individu-
> alist norms of Locke, but one also found letter-perfect
> replicas of the very images he used.[32]

America appeared as a tabula rasa, a manipulable environment, separate from a feudal past and devoid of social traditions to overcome. In such a setting Lockian principles did not appear radical, indeed they seemed so eminently suited to the American situation that they have contributed to the profound conservatism of American politics and certainly our conservatism toward poverty.

Satire was present early in the American experience, but few recognized it because they were unable to comprehend that the Indians violated the liberal assumption of a tabula rasa.[33] Further, the satiric accuracy of possessive or atomistic individualism as the expression of American liberty and higher human purpose is related to the individuation of poverty. This view, which Franklin exemplifies, was a radical view in its inception; it presumed some degree of prosperity was available to every person, given the equality and liberty of the market relations among men that replaced the far more rigid class structure of the world left behind. The new world offered every person—except slaves and women—the equal and recognized right to pursue life, liberty, and happiness through property as well as an abundant continent as a means to achieve those rights. With these conditions failure to achieve prosperity seemed to spring from individual deficiency or inability of a voluntary or involuntary kind. This view of poverty commanded as large a consensus as its inverse, the liberty of the possessive individual of Lockian liberalism.[34]

Thomas Paine and an Alternative View

Consensus is not unanimity, and there were dissenters from the view of individuated poverty. Herman Melville summarized his feelings about rich men who speak about poor men in a word he could not print in Harper's in 1854.[35] But more clearly he did say,

> Of all the preposterous assumptions of humanity over humanity—nothing exceeds most of the criticisms made on the habits of the poor by the well-honored, well-warmed and well-fed.[36]

Very clearly Melville indicated that symbols and culture shared by poor and rich alike, such as Lockian liberalism, enhanced the latter while degrading the former and added a peculiar and painful responsibility to the poor for their poverty.

> The native American poor never lose their delicacy or pride, hence, though unreduced to the physical degradation of the European pauper, they yet suffer more in mind than the poor of any other nation in the world. Those peculiar social sensibilities nourished by our own peculiar political principles, while they enhance the true dignity of a prosperous American, do but minister to the added wretchedness of the unfortunates first, by prohibiting their acceptance of what little random relief charity may offer; and second, by furnishing them with the keenest appreciation of the distinction between the ideal of universal equality and their grindstone experience of the practical misery and infamy of poverty—a misery and infamy which is, ever has been, and ever will be, precisely the same in India, England and America.[37]

Another dissenter, Henry David Thoreau, offered his contemporaries a view of the inextricable links between the pursuit of commerce, the transfer of powers within the capitalist system, and the inequalities found among men. Using the railroad as his symbol of American commerce, Thoreau observed:

> We do not ride on the railroad; it rides upon us. Did you ever think what those sleepers are that underlie the rail-road? Each one is a man, an Irishman, or a Yankee man. The rails are laid on them, and they are covered with sand, and the cars run smoothly over them. They are sound sleepers, I assure you. And every few years a new lot is laid down and run over; so that, if some have the pleasure of riding on a rail, others have the misfortune to be ridden upon.[38]

The views of Melville and Thoreau and later Henry George, Henry Demarest Lloyd, Edward Bellamy, William Dean Howells, Jane Addams, Lincoln Steffens, and Theodore Dreiser, while important, were snippets of dissent from the consensus of Americans on the Lockian liberal philosophy that provided a moral and legal basis for the tolerance of inequality and poverty. The only clear articulation of an alternative view of inequality and poverty was provided by Thomas Paine.

Paine was spokesman for the nation, most effectively, during the nation's pains of revolutionary birth when promise not policy was accentuated. His political and humanitarian views extended beyond those of his contemporaries; and, because of this distance, as well as the difference between the ideals that encourage men to fight and the practical concerns that are the object of liberal govern-ment, he was repudiated when the affairs of the nation were turned over to practical men.

In Paine's scheme of political arrangements there were three social groups: the state of nature, civilization, and government. Property is created in civil society and like all other social inventions, in Paine's mind, it was intended to perfect natural rights, the means of livelihood, and provide for the necessities and/or wants of men, freedom and security, that are less perfect in the state of nature. However, no social arrangement is perfect, and an observed con-sequence of property and society's management of it is the affluence of some and the deprivation of others. The earth, in its original state, was the property of all, and each person had access to economic se-curity because of that right. If social arrangements denied someone economic security, the government was to remedy this dysfunction of society by fulfilling and restoring a natural right.[39]

8

What is important for our analysis is that Paine supplies us with an alternative explanation of property and poverty, in that property is not rooted in the individual but is a social arrangement. Some people may lose rights and opportunities that other people have or may possess them imperfectly because of social arrangements. Thus, the prosperity of some and nonprosperity of others might have explanations beyond mere individual ability. The access people have to the avenues of success because of social arrangements—religion, education, labor, and so on—might also explain how they finish. Slavery was, of course, obvious evidence of the validity of Paine's view, which offers a far-ranging critique of social constructs—for example, slave, savage, poor—that establish and maintain distinctions among people. It is not surprising, then, that Paine was an advocate of the poor, was an abolitionist, and, almost 200 years ago, even made references to the oppressed state of women.[40]

The difference between Franklin and Paine is linked in important ways with the difference between Locke and Jean Jacques Rousseau with regard to equality. Rousseau acknowledged the differences among men in the state of nature based on "age, health, bodily strength, and the qualities of mind and soul."[41] These were both inevitable and necessary; however, political differences of riches, rank, power, and personal merit were not. They were all reducible to inequalities of wealth, and where Locke saw these inequalities stemming from liberty and conducive to the productivity and moral good of society, Rousseau saw dangers to other forms of equality, especially political equality and democratic values.[42]

Paine's concern for equality as well as liberty had important implications for his view of society and government. The persistent and serious inequities of wealth were sufficient proof of the necessity of wealth's redistribution, especially if one presumed social, not merely individual or "natural," causes for the inequities. Paine's works, Rights of Man and Agrarian Justice, contained meticulous empirical accountings of redistributive spending to alleviate the needs of the poor. This work had several important premises: the first that the right of all persons to livelihood may be denied by social arrangements and the second that of the role of government to redress these arrangements and to restore the natural rights of people. For Paine, equality in society was important and necessary for political equality, just as social and civil inequality were linked in Lockian liberalism—observations shared with both men by Alexis de Tocqueville.

> Those who believe that complete equality can be established in a permanent way in the political world without introducing at the same time a certain equality in civil society seem to me to commit a great error.[43]

9

Social and political equality were the only guarantees of democracy and continued equality, according to Paine. In his essay, "A Serious Address to the People of Pennsylvania on the Present Situation of their Affairs," he pointed out that only equality between rich and poor in the participation of government could serve to remove the distinctions among them.

The point of this historical account is to illustrate two important points: first, poverty in America has been recognized as an aberration; second, the aberration of poverty had two explanations, exemplified by Franklin and Paine. By his analysis Paine placed between individual effort and natural abundance institutional arrangements and values. He did not presume the adequacy of institutional arrangements to promote the natural condition of sufficiency and posited the necessity of government action to redress social inequities. On the other hand, Franklin shared the Lockian-inspired optimism that the United States offered to all its citizens the opportunity to attain sufficiency and permitted the acceptance of poverty as the consequences of individual inability or indolence.

THE REDISCOVERY OF POVERTY AND 20th CENTURY VIEWS

The New Deal and the Affluent Society

The Depression afforded many citizens a more familiar acquaintance with poverty and a different national experience. Poverty might still seem an aberration, but it was also, in 1930, beyond the control of individual effort alone. The Depression called forth government effort, not wholesale social, economic, and political reform but sufficient intervention to guarantee security and participation in the economy.

While some have seen the New Deal as the contradiction of Lockian liberalism it is clear to others that the New Deal stayed well within liberal principles.[44] Government was acting not to alter the market relations among men but to preserve them by restoring the acquisitive capacity for many who had lost it. The emphasis throughout the New Deal was on change through and for growth, not redistribution. The redistribution that did take place was for the purpose of restoring the economy; it never violated the principle of proportionate costs and benefits between social arrangements and government effort.[45] Like the franchise before it, the New Deal and the emergence of the welfare state were government outputs designed to preserve essential market relations by attending to discontent and

10

malfunctions that the unattended capitalist system had created; in so doing Roosevelt simultaneously removed a threat to the continuation of capitalism and "primed the pump" of economic recovery. Liberal economic and social thought certainly were reformed, but not without reform being "liberalized."[46]

The New Deal and the new war seemed to justify Lockian liberal assumptions and the American faith in them. Unemployment dropped from 23.6 percent of 16.9 percent during Franklin Delano Roosevelt's first term. It persisted at that level and increased for two years of his second term; but eventually unemployment dropped from 14.6 percent to 1.2 percent from 1940 to 1944. This figure of 1.2 percent has not been approached since then.[47]

There was very little in the 1950s and the afterglow of the New Deal to indicate this nation was so close to rediscovering its own poor. The decade seemed to belong to the "affluent society." It had "become evident to conservatives and liberals alike that increasing aggregate output was an alternative to redistribution of wealth or even to the reduction of inequality."[48] Thus, inequality, "the oldest and most agitated of social issues," was in abeyance; so too was the fear of economic insecurity.

"Production" was the new justification of Lockian optimism and could function as a symbol that all classes, poor and nonpoor, could share. It promised gains for everyone while dealing with poverty as a matter of course. Indeed, excesses of wealth could be explained as necessary for production—investment, savings, new business, and so on—and the redistributive mechanism that production represented. In classic liberal terms a social problem was best treated by economics; and efficiency, to foster growth, was the politics of equality.

Yet, John Kenneth Galbraith himself very clearly retracted from Lockian optimism, for if poverty could be solved by merely increasing production, "no one would be called upon to write at such length."[49] The real point of Galbraith's analysis was the imbalance between affluent private consumption and the neglected public sector, of which the poor were part.[50] Poverty continues, Galbraith lamented, because Americans choose to ignore it.

If it was Galbraith's intention to bring poverty to the attention of the American people and to call forth hard answers for hard questions, he was less than successful. The American preference to contemplate wealth, not poverty, and to assume opportunity, rather than deny it, made the affluent society a one-dimensional concept. The contrast of poverty and affluence added another reason to the plethora that Benjamin Franklin saw "to bless Divine Providence for the evident and great Difference in our Favour, and be convinced that no Nation that is known to us enjoys a greater Share of human

Felicity."[51] Similarly there seemed to be little urgency to the question of poverty. It was a "disgrace" not an injustice; and if the forces of American production could produce affluence for the many, with redirection, greater efficiency, and maximization of utilities, those forces could produce sufficiency for all.

The Pejorative Tradition: Lockian
Liberalism Updated

The important question implicit in this renewed interest in poverty was the implications for antipoverty strategies. Did the conceptualization of poverty imply institutional sufficiency or institutional change? There is little evidence that the new works on poverty did much to shake the optimism of Americans, implicit in Galbraith, that time and the adequacy of their institutions would solve their problems.

Some observers have attributed inequality among people to conditions of nature: inherent genetic limitations may be responsible for factors, such as intelligence, that greatly influence the position of a person, or all the members of that genetic pool, in the socio-economic pyramid.[52]

Far more widespread has been the explanation of inequality, and particularly poverty, in terms of society—not the society of rich and poor, but the society of poor. This form of explanation focuses on the culture of the poor for an understanding of their inequality. According to Oscar Lewis, the culture of poverty is

> a label for a specific conceptual model that describes in
> positive terms a subculture of Western society with its
> own structure and rationale, a way of life handed on from
> generation to generation along family lines. . . . It is a
> culture in the traditional anthropological sense in that it
> provides human beings with a design for living, with a
> ready-made set of solutions for human problems and so
> serves a significant adaptive function.[53]

According to some, this culture is poverty inducing and replete with "pathological" characteristics that conspire to keep people poor. Analysts with this view are frequently referred to as part of the pejorative tradition. They resemble Franklin in that they divide the poor into categories of competent and incompetent; but, unlike Franklin, they admit the culture of the poor among the factors that disable the poor and reduce their competence.[54]

They also differ from Franklin in that they admit the possibility that the characteristics of the poor were induced by social injustice,

12

such as slavery. But the consequence of the analysis is the same as Franklin's: the poor must be driven or changed and poverty has no links to ongoing institutionalized inequality.

> What then is the problem? We feel that the answer is clear enough. Three centuries of injustice have brought about deep-seated structural distortions in the life of the Negro American. At this point, the present pathology is capable of perpetuating itself without assistance from the white world. The cycle can be broken only if these distortions are set right.[55]

The inescapable conclusion of the pejorative tradition is that the poverty of some is inwardly caused by culturally induced characteristics that differentiate the poor from the "normal."[56] Hence, poverty is perpetuated by one generation acculturating the next into pathological characteristics that guarantee incompetence in dealing with the prevailing opportunities to escape poverty.

The literature on Appalachian poverty is permeated with elements of the pejorative tradition. The clearest statement of the responsibility of the Appalachian poor for their poverty came from Arnold Toynbee.

> The modern Appalachian has . . . failed to hold his own ground and has gone downhill in a most disconcerting fashion. In fact, the Appalachian "mountain people" today are no better than barbarians. They have relapsed into illiteracy and witchcraft. They suffer from poverty, squalor and ill-health. . . . The Appalachians present the melancholy spectacle of a people who have acquired civilization and then lost it.[57]

Most authors do not posit Appalachian culture as a regression; rather, it is "arrested," "dormant," or "analgesic" and the area's people are "our contemporary ancestors." In an appendix to Yesterday's People, Jack Weller compares traits attributed to the middle class and those of the southern Appalachian as well as value orientations of the southern Appalachian and the professional class.[58] The conclusion stemming from the difference in value systems seems inevitable: the root cause of Appalachian poverty is the characteristics of the Appalachian poor. Hence, despite its humane purpose, the consequence of this work is the disparagement of the Appalachian poor—and their psychology, which is considered abnormal or pathological—because they differ from some proposed norm. As Rupert Vance makes clear in an introduction to Weller's book, an emphasis on people as they are and not the forces that shape them makes it inevitable that a change in poverty must be a change of the poor. "The crux of the problem is clear. To change the mountains is to change the mountain personality."[59] This is the essence of the pejorative aspect of the culture of poverty and its closest kinship with Franklin: its premises lead us to conclude that nothing can be done against poverty without first changing the poor. If the subsistence of the poor is guaranteed, it is not necessary to do anything against poverty because it appears as a self-imposed condition of the poor and efforts of relief or change always run the danger of making conditions worse by disrupting "things as they are."

Yesterday's People is by no means the only pejorative comment on Appalachia, as Mike Maloney and Ben Huelsman make clear in an excellent bibliographical essay;[60] but it is symptomatic of works within the pejorative tradition. First, it accepts cultural values as a given, and the premises of, behavior. Such an acceptance leaves unexamined the liberal assumption beneath inequality and is tantamount to a reification of those assumptions. This, according to Peter Berger and Thomas Luckman, is a characteristic of much of American social science.[61] Second, this uncritical acceptance of liberal assumptions misconstrues "all important aspects of the culture concept."[62] Rather than an adaptive or defense mechanism integrally related to a preceding and ongoing set of institutions, culture is construed as a causal factor. This misconstruction and attendant reification has important policy implications for poverty programs, rural or urban. As Edward Banfield points out, "Facts are facts, however unpleasant, and they have to be faced unblinkingly by anyone who really wants to improve matters in the city."[63] One of these facts for the pejorative tradition is "the large numbers of people emerging in modern society who are irresponsible and depraved,"[64] the unworthy poor.

The consequence of social science's reifying perspective has been to narrow the channels of change to those that do not endanger liberal assumptions. Most concisely put, much of social science approximates a defense of the unique liberal conception of equality and its corresponding social and economic inequality. Even Franklin, while professing to oppose oppressing the poor, lamented writers who incite the poor by criticizing the rich as well as political arrangements and wished that the "true state of things" were better understood and the poor not made more uneasy and unhappy "than their situation subjects to be."[65]

14

Exonerating the Victim: Another Cultural View
of Poverty

Other commentators on poverty, while recognizing differences in behavior and attitudes between poor and nonpoor, hesitate to devise cultural explanations for these differences. As Lee Rainwater points out, discussions of a poverty culture in isolation from the social, economic, and ecological setting to which the culture is an adaptation are misleading.[66] It is not sufficient merely to explain that past institutional arrangements or values, like slavery, underlie the adaptation of lower-class culture, if that culture is then presumed to perpetuate itself; this would be an ahistorical view of culture. If culture is an adaptation to existential conditions, as Charles Valentine insists[67] and Oscar Lewis implied earlier, its continuation is possible only if the formative conditions are still felt to exist.[68] Thus, culture cannot be perpetuated merely by values being passed on to a younger generation; those values must be tested against contemporary conditions and experience gathered to validate their wisdom and applicability.

This view of culture incorporates poor and nonpoor alike in explaining poverty and is related to Paine's views that premised institutional and systemic causes as the origins and sustenance of poverty. Poverty is an ongoing process not because of the culture of the poor but because the poor are impeded from eliminating their own poverty by economic and social situations beyond their control. Their culture is a response to this powerlessness.

The pejorative tradition does not emphasize the adaptive function of culture and almost totally ignores the existential setting necessary for a culture's renewal.[69] The consequence of this ommission is to open the arsenal of social science to the defenders of a stratified social class system and institutional arrangements that perpetuate poverty. As Valentine observed, "These formulations support the long-established rationalization of blaming poverty on the poor."[70] As such, William Ryan points out, the pejorative tradition of "blaming the victim" takes its place in a long series of American ideologies that have rationalized injustice and cruelty.[71]

It should be evident that the pejorative use of the culture of poverty concept is itself an external influence in perpetuating the institution of poverty.[72] By distracting "attention from crucial structural characteristics of the stratified social system as a whole"[73] the culture of poverty concept helps keep them intact so that alternative explanations, such as the culture of poverty, remain necessary. In other words, social problems are defined in such a way as to circumvent the need for political action and to require either incremental liberal policies of welfare or stringent measures against the poor.[74]

Critics of this pejorative use of the culture of poverty offer alternative systemic explanations of poverty. These views focus on external, societal features that interact with the poor and overcome "the almost total unwillingness of conventional society to admit its complicity in the suffering and exclusion that lower-class people experience."[75] This is important because the analysis of poverty greatly influences the envisioned requirements and nature of political remedies. A systemic analysis of poverty leads to a need for more drastic political action than analyses that individuate poverty. In the light of systemic analyses,

> "thinking people" will stop deluding themselves that the underclass is other than product of an economic system so designed that it generates a destructive amount of income inequality and face the fact that the only solution of the problem of the underclass is to change that economic system accordingly.[76]

A brief but important systemic analysis of Appalachian poverty, replete with implications for political action, has been offered by Helen Lewis. She reviews the pejorative tradition and recalls the portrayal of Appalachians as the passive and apathetic carriers of the destructive traits of their culture—such as traditionalism and fatalism. This pejorative view, Lewis alleges, has been passed into public policy by change agents who,

> although they will reject this contention . . . are themselves culturally isolated in a middle class and/or bureaucratic institutional culture and . . . are ethnocentric about their values. They are upholding their particular subculture which is dominant.[77]

The view they bring

> assumes that the Appalachian culture is not only distinct but pathogenic; there is no recognition that mainstream institutions might be pathogenic and responsible for the Appalachian problems, rather, the difficulty must be within the family or the non-institutional community. It becomes a way of blaming poverty on the poor.[78]

In contrast to this pejorative analysis Lewis suggests Appalachia may be viewed

> as a subsociety structurally alienated and lacking resources due to processes of colonialism and exploitation.

16

Those who control the resources preserve their advantage by discrimination. The people are not essentially passive but these "subcultural" traits of fatalism, passivity, etc., are adjustive techniques of the powerless; ways in which people protect their way of life from new economic modes and the concomitant alien culture. These values are re-actions to powerlessness.[79]

She goes on to explain the poverty of the region by the region's similarities with a colony, defined as "domination over a geographically external political unit most often inhabited by people of a different race and culture, when this domination is political and economic, the colony exists subordinated to and dependent upon to mother country."[80] While some characteristics of colonies seem inapplicable to Appalachia, the history of the region seems to conform to the process of colonization offered by Lewis. This includes: first, forced or involuntary entry; second, rapid modification of culture and social organization of the colonized; third, control by the dominant group; and, finally, a condition of racism, social domination by which the colonized are defined as inferior or different and that rationalizes the exploitation, control, and oppression by the superordinate group.

Even granting the colonial analogy is not complete, Lewis points to a factor, coal, that is part of the larger culture, of which the poor are part, and shows that factor to be a former and ongoing contributive factor to Appalachian poverty. If her suggested interpretation is substantially correct, then it is obvious that "changing the values of Appalachians will not change the system of colonialism."[81] This conclusion is substantially different from the one Weller leads us to in Yesterday's People.[82] To change this system of colonialism may be much more difficult than changing Appalanchian people because of the warp and woof of American and Appalachian economic and social structures. As one coal company executive put it, "If there is something wrong with what we are doing in Eastern Kentucky, then, there is something wrong with the country."[83]

POVERTY DEFINITIONS AND ANTIPOVERTY
STRATEGIES

Defining Poverty and Imposing Scarcity

These contending conceptualizations of poverty, pejorative and systemic, have important ramifications for the definition of poverty. The U.S. Bureau of Labor Statistics had devised a budget describing

17

a standard of living as early as 1946. This budget was inadequate to serve as a standard for poverty, however, because it described the "moderate but adequate" standard of living for an urban worker's family of four and was "too high to be consistent with the objectives of public assistance funds or with the funds available to administer such programs."[84]

The inadequacy of the "moderate but adequate" budget suggests that there are important social determinants for an appropriate standard for poverty. Any standard of poverty has to consider the number of people it would encompass. A number that is too large not only forecasts an expensive poverty program but also suggests a defect in the function of the American economy and society.[85]

It was possible, of course, merely to adopt an already calculated standard of living lower than the modest but adequate standard. However, that standard was above subsistence, and the poverty standard was to be "the sine qua non of goods and services," a floor of services, a minimum standard.[86]

The core of the poverty budget was a food plan devised by the U.S. Department of Agriculture; adequacy of food was taken as a generally acceptable standard of overall adequacy. The Department of Agriculture's food plans were guides to estimating costs of adequate diets and extrapolated to family incomes. Mollie Orshansky comments:

> All the plans, if strictly followed, can provide an acceptable and adequate diet, but—generally speaking—the lower the level of cost, the more restricted the kinds and qualities for food must be and the more skill in marketing and food preparation that is required.[87]

In January 1964, the Department of Agriculture initiated an emergency food plan that was 75 to 80 percent of the low-cost plan used for the lower budget of the Bureau of Labor Statistics. This food plan was devised for "temporary or emergency use when funds are low." The budget provided $4.60 weekly for each person for food, or 22¢ a meal; the weekly food budget for a family of four amounted to $18.40. Table 1 gives the results of the extrapolations from this food budget by family size for selected years 1964-72.

The stringency of this definition has critics among those most familiar with it and even those responsible for it. Orshanksy, in discussing the formulation of the definition of poverty, explains in equal detail a level she calls low income. For every table concerned with the poverty level based on the economy food budget, she includes corresponding figures for a low-income level, 100 to 125 percent of poverty. This level more closely resembles the lower budget of the Bureau of Labor Statistics and approximates perhaps relative poverty in contrast to the other figure of absolute poverty.[88]

18

TABLE 1

OEO Poverty Levels for Select Years 1964-72
(in dollars)

| Family | Farm | | | Nonfarm | | |
Size	1964	1970	1972	1964	1970	1972
1	1,080	1,500	1,700	1,540	1,800	2,000
2	1,390	2,000	2,100	1,990	2,400	2,600
3	1,710	2,500	2,800	2,440	3,000	3,300
4	2,190	3,000	3,400	3,130	3,600	4,000
5	2,580	3,500	4,000	3,685	4,200	4,700
6	2,895	4,000	4,500	4,135	4,800	5,300
7	3,245	4,500	5,000	4,635	5,400	5,900

Sources: Figures for 1970, Office of Economic Opportunity, Guideline: Healthright Programs, (Washington, D.C., U.S. Government Printing Office, 1970), Appendix C, p. 13; figures for 1964, Office of Economic Opportunity, Dimensions of Poverty in 1964, (Washington, D.C.: U.S. Government Printing Office, 1965), p. 8.

In 1970 there were 25.6 million poor persons, by definition, in the United States; an additional 10.2 million persons were within a range of 100 to 125 percent of the poverty levels. These numbers, when added, equal 18 per cent of the total population of the United States and are greater than the population of Canada; the combined population of Illinois, Pennsylvania, and Ohio; or three times the population of New England.

The poverty definition in use distorts several aspects of the poverty problem. The emphasis on subsistence ignores the question of the equality of those who are poor and those who are not. This emphasis also underestimates the number of poor, which is perhaps a prerequisite for congressional approval of limited funds for antipoverty measures. Finally, the definition distorts the efforts to combat poverty. When Sargent Shriver boasted of raising 4.5 million Americans out of poverty in the first five years of the War on Poverty, he actually was saying a number of people had moved from being categorically poor to being "near-poor"; the significance of this change was possibly more statistical than experiential for the persons involved.

A related point to be made is the adequacy of the definition for subsistence. It should be remembered that the poverty thresholds resolve about the Department of Agriculture's "economy" food plan. Orshansky writes:

> Assuming the homemaker is a good manager and has the
> time and skill to shop wisely, she must prepare nutriti-
> ous, palatable meals on a budget that for herself, a hus-
> band and two young children—an average family—would
> not come to about 70 cents a day per person. [89]

The assumption is a large one, as Orshansky realizes. The Bureau of Labor Statistics has documented the merely theoretical adequacy of this diet and also the imposition of demands it makes on the poor,

> Although families can achieve nutritional adequacy from
> the low-cost plan, it has been estimated that only one-
> fourth of those who spend amounts equivalent to the cost
> of the plan actually have nutritionally adequate diets.
> Menus based on this plan will include foods requiring a
> considerable amount of home preparation, as well as
> skill in cooking to make varied and appetizing meals.[90]

It should be pointed out that the low-cost plan just under discussion is between 20 and 25 percent higher than the economy plan used in devising the poverty threshold. The statement has stark implications: only one-fourth of those spending 20 to 25 percent more than the amount allotted the poor for food achieve nutritionally adequate diets.

Remedial Implications of Scarcity

It is reasonable to assume that Franklin's fear of making the poor comfortable in their poverty was embodied in the definition of poverty as a minimum standard. Franklin felt that the difficulty of gaining relief, the possible shame attached to it, as well as the hand-to-mouth existence it provided were important safeguards against indolence;[91] a subsistence definition of poverty contains these safeguards.

Scarcity, imposed on the poor, also serves several important functions for the larger society. It provides a training ground for the values of hard work, frugality, and all the other characteristics that supposedly separate those who suffer scarcity from those who do not.[92] Conformity of the poor to society's standard is fostered by the dependence on bureaucratic standards and conditions inculated by the need to remain eligible for levels of relief that are at best commensurate with expenditures for subsistence.

The "scientific judgments" behind the poverty definition approximate Jurgen Habermas' conception of publicly administered definitions "which extend to what we want for our lives, but not how we would like to live if we could find out, with regard to attainable potentials, how we could live."[93] They are negatively designed to describe the extent of the intolerable and to delineate all else as tolerable. These scientific judgments are ideological devices—inadvertently perhaps, but nonetheless inevitably—to convey society's attitude toward the poor.

An essential implication of the definition of poverty is the benign optimism of Benjamin Franklin; as Paul Jacobs put it, "America is potentially affluent for all those who want affluence."[94] The values of liberalism go untested by the conditions of poverty because those values serve as its premise: for example, central to the thought of both Adam Smith and the punitive nature of imposed scarcity is the premise that a proportion should exist between the economic benefits derived and the economic contribution made by an individual. Related to this belief is the view of the political system as evolving from the natural state through society and a corresponding fear that political action to remedy or change an existing condition may result in greater harm than good. Banfield, well within the pejorative tradition and an advocate of absolute standards of poverty, also feels that "to meddle with the structures and operations of a successful political system . . . is the greatest foolishness men are capable of."[95]

Redefining Poverty: Systemic Characteristics

The liberal assumptions behind imposed scarcity—namely, its remedial nature and system—related necessity—occur to the American mind, it may be surmised, with the same "given" quality that Louis Hartz assured us marks the liberal tradition in America. The scarcity imposed by defined poverty also is justified by comparing the American poor vis-à-vis the poor of other societies, or the past conditions of the poor. Thus, Franklin observed:

> To those indeed who have been educated in elegant plenty,
> even the provision made for the poor may appear misery,
> but to those who have scarce ever been better provided
> for, such provision may seem quite good and sufficient,
> these latter have then nothing to fear worse than their
> present condition, and scarce hope for anything better than
> a Parish maintainance.[96]

There is far less room for complacency if American poverty is understood in terms of equality rather than absolute deprivation.

While it is patently obvious that the poor are not equal in social and economic terms with those who are not poor, the reasons for their inequality must be examined, unless it is to be assumed that the poverty of some is the "natural" consequence of indolence or in some other manner their private problem, such as genetics or "culture."

Just as the pejorative tradition of the culture of poverty may be recast by examining the relation of that culture with the larger culture of which it is a part, so too the characteristics of the poor assume greater explanatory power in relation to the economic system.[97] As Orshansky suggests, "in our work-oriented society, those who cannot or do not work must expect to be poorer than those who do."[98] Just how much poorer is established by a definition of need based on subsistence. It is clear, however, that it is not merely a matter of employment or unemployment that determines poverty or nonpoverty; more than half of the heads of poor families report having a job and 30 percent of all heads of poor families have been employed at a full-time job for at least one year.[99]

Several studies have made clear that individuals with specified characteristics of age, sex, race, and education are more often poor than other individuals with different characteristics and that employment does not alter this distribution automatically.[100] Table 2 selects three factors—age, education, and sex—and relates them to poverty. The index of poverty given is the quotient of the percentage of a group with a specified characteristic in the total population, divided by the percentage of that same group among the poor. If poverty were distributed randomly, as it apparently would be in an egalitarian society, the percentages would be the same and their quotient would be one (1). But like analysts before us, we see some indexes are considerably higher than one (1), indicating that some demographic characteristics have a higher incidence in the poverty population than in the entire population. It is understandable that levels of education should correspond to levels of wealth in an acquisitive and elitist society; we also might expect those who work to have different levels of income from those who do not. What is not so easily explained is that only 4.9 percent of the male heads of poor families were unemployed while 52 percent were employed and 5.5 percent of the female heads of families were unemployed, compared with 29 percent employed. It is also paradoxical to accept poverty as a consequence of unemployment in a society that accepts unemployment as inevitable by defining full employment as 4 percent or even 5 percent unemployment.[101] Equally incongruous to a view of poverty as the consequence of personal characteristics is the greater incidence of poverty among persons over 65 years of age and under six. Likewise, the higher incidence of women among the poor than men, in every category, is difficult to explain. Table 3 illustrates that the incidence of poverty

TABLE 2

The Occurrence of Poverty by Sex, Age, Education, and
Employment Status

	Total Population		Population below Poverty		Poverty Index
	(1)	(2)	(3)	(4)	(5)
	Total (in 1,000's)	Percent of Total	Total (in 1,000's)	Percent of Total	(4) ÷ (2)
Total	202,489	100	25,522	100	1.0
Sex					
Male	98,228	48.5	10,879	42.6	.88
Female	104,248	51.5	14,643	57.4	1.11
Age					
Under 6	21,395	10.6	3,561	14.0	1.32
6-15	40,936	20.2	6,106	23.9	1.18
16-21	21,275	10.5	2,581	10.1	.96
22-64	99,629	49.2	8,653	33.9	.69
65 and over	19,254	9.5	4,709	18.5	1.95
Male	8,165	42.4	1,552	33.0	.78
Female	11,090	57.6	3,157	67.0	1.16
Education					
All persons over 14 years completed	148,241	100	16,981	100	1.0
None	1,328	.9	521	3.1	3.44
Eight or less	34,789	23.5	7,719	45.5	1.94
Twelve or less	80,370	54.2	7,062	41.6	.77
More than twelve	31,754	21.4	1,679	9.8	.46
Family Heads					
Total	51,948	100	5,214	100	1.0
Male	45,998	88.5	3,280	62.9	.71
Employed	37,015	71.3	1,697	32.5	.46
Unemployed	1,390	2.7	162	3.1	1.15
Not in labor force	6,590	12.7	1,365	26.2	2.06
Female	5,950	11.5	1,934	37.1	3.27
Employed	2,989	5.8	556	10.7	1.84
Unemployed	229	.4	107	2.1	5.25
Not in labor force	2,732	5.3	1,270	24.4	4.60

Source: U.S. Department of Commerce, Bureau of the Census, Current Population Reports, Series P-60, No. 81, "Characteristics of the Low-Income Population, 1970" (Washington, D.C.: U.S. Government Printing Office, 1971).

TABLE 3

The Occurrence of Poverty According to Race by Sex, Age,
Education, and Employment

	White Population			Black Population		
	Percent of Total (1)	Percent below Poverty (2)	Index (2) ÷ (1) (3)	Percent of Total (4)	Percent below Poverty (5)	Index (5) ÷ (4) (6)
Total	87.6	68.5	.78	11.2	30.0	2.68
Sex						
Male	87.8	67.6	.77	10.9	30.5	2.80
Female	87.4	69.2	.79	11.5	29.5	2.57
Age						
Under 6	82.9	58.8	.71	15.5	39.4	2.54
6-15	84.9	59.9	.71	13.8	38.3	2.78
16-21	86.3	64.8	.75	12.5	33.9	2.71
22-64	89.1	71.0	.80	9.7	27.4	2.82
65 and over	91.8	84.6	.92	7.4	14.5	1.96
Male	91.5	82.0	.90	7.5	16.3	2.18
Female	92.1	85.8	.93	7.3	13.6	1.86
Education						
All persons over 14 years completed	88.9	73.0	.82	10.0	25.6	2.56
None	73.1	76.6	1.05	21.9	29.6	1.35
Eight or less	84.0	71.5	.85	14.6	27.5	1.88
Twelve or less	89.3	72.0	.81	9.8	26.7	2.72
More than twelve	93.5	85.9	.92	5.1	11.0	2.16
Family Heads						
Total	89.2	71.0	.80	9.5	27.7	2.92
Male	91.6	79.4	.87	7.4	19.1	2.58
Employed	91.9	78.4	.85	7.2	20.2	2.81
Unemployed	88.6	78.4	.88	10.1	21.0	2.08
Not in labor force	90.9	80.7	.89	8.1	17.8	2.20
Female	73.7	56.7	.77	25.3	42.4	1.68
Employed	75.4	54.3	.72	23.6	44.8	1.90
Unemployed	63.8	53.3	.84	34.1	47.7	1.40
Not in labor force	72.7	58.2	.80	26.5	40.9	1.54

Source: U.S. Department of Commerce, Bureau of the Census, Current Population Reports, Series P-60, No. 81, "Characteristics of the Low-Income Population, 1970" (Washington, D.C.: U.S. Government Printing Office, 1971).

in every category of the black population is greater than that of the corresponding white population.

It is possible, of course, to attribute the higher incidence of poverty among populations with certain characteristics to those unique characteristics. This is Social Darwinism applied to the unsuccessful to explain their lack. If genetics and biology seem too blatant a Social Darwinistic explanation of poverty, then "The culture of poverty" may explain the same groups' poverty in light of different characteristics, but importantly, characteristics that are still their own. All of this exonerates systemic characteristics or institutional values as responsible for the higher incidence of poverty or illness among some populations.

The very definition of poverty as described earlier is an exoneration of all but the individuals. Poverty is defined in terms of sufficiency without reference to other groups as if the wealth of some had no bearing on the poverty of others. Likewise, the definition concerns itself with income levels and not institutional arrangements that explain why certain groups fall more frequently below the level of poverty. The only bearing equality has on poverty, by this definition, is to see that no one suffers deprivation according to an absolute standard establishing a tolerable level of poverty. As such, the definition is a compromise. On one hand, it admits that some might suffer deprivation without public assistance; on the other, the level of assistance is at a level low enough to remind the poor that only their own effort can bring more than subsistence.

NOTES

1. Benjamin Franklin, "On the Price of Corn and the Management of the Poor," in Essays on General Politics, Commerce and Political Economy (New York: Augustus M. Kelley Publishers, 1971), pp. 358-59.

2. Robert H. Bremner, From the Depths: The Discovery of Poverty in America (New York: New York University Press, 1965), p. 15.

3. Benjamin Franklin, "On the Labouring Poor," in The Political Thought of Benjamin Franklin, edited by Ralph L. Ketcham (New York: Bobbs-Merrill Company, 1965), p. 220.

4. Bremner, From the Depths, p. 17.

5. Robert H. Bremner, American Philanthropy (Chicago: University of Chicago Press, 1960).

6. Franklin, "Poverty and the Effects of German Immigration to Pennsylvania," in The Political Thought of Benjamin Franklin, p. 73.

7. Ketcham emphasizes that Franklin absorbed John Locke's philosophy without formal study, indicating the "natural" appearance of Locke's ideas. See Franklin, The Political Thought of Benjamin Franklin, pp. xxxii and xxxvii. On the other hand, Carl Van Doren mentions Franklin's intellectual debt to Locke. Compare Carl Van Doren, Benjamin Franklin (New York: Garden City Publishing Co., 1938), pp. 14, 190, and 192.

8. These concepts most recently have been reconstructed in Donald J. Devine, The Political Culture of the United States: The Influence of Member Values on Regime Maintenance (Boston: Little, Brown and Company, 1972), pp. 135-230.

9. Ibid., p. 190.

10. Ibid., p. 190.

11. Ibid., p. 201.

12. Ibid., p. 206

13. Ibid., p. 206.

14. Ibid., p. 207. For a full discussion of government's relation to the diversity of wealth according to Madison see The Federalist Papers, No. 10.

15. C. B. Macpherson, The Political Theory of Possessive Individualism: Hobbes to Locke (New York: Oxford University Press, 1962), p. 1.

16. Sheldon S. Wolin, Politics and Vision: Continuity and Innovation in Western Political Thought, (Boston: Little, Brown and Company, 1960), p. 310.

17. Macpherson, The Political Theory of Possessive Individualism, pp. 247-48.

18. Adam Smith cited by Richard Lichtman, "The Political Economy of Medical Care," in The Social Organization of Health: Recent Sociology No. 3 edited by Hans Peter Dreitzel (New York: Macmillan, 1971), p. 268.

19. Ibid., p. 268; also C. B. Macpherson, The Real World of Democracy (New York: Oxford University Press, 1972), p. 8.

20. Macpherson, Real World of Democracy, p. 8.

21. Macpherson, The Political Theory of Possessive Individualism, p. 3.

22. Macpherson, Real World of Democracy, p. 41.

23. Wolin, Politics and Vision, pp. 296-97; see also p. 327 for Franklin's views.

24. Ibid., p. 328.

25. Ibid., p. 333.

26. Macpherson, Real World of Democracy, p. 54.

27. Ibid., p. 43.

28. Macpherson, The Political Theory of Possessive Individualism, pp. 250 and 269.

29. Wolin, Politics and Vision, p. 294.

30. Devine, The Political Culture of the United States, p. 60.

31. Louis Hartz, The Liberal Tradition in America: An Interpretation of American Political Thought Since the Revolution (New York: Harcourt, Brace and World, 1955), p. 58.

32. Hartz, Liberal Tradition in America, pp. 60-62.

33. Franklin, The Political Thought of Benjamin Franklin, pp. 74-75. See also Michael Rogin, "Liberal Society and the Indian Question," Politics and Society 1, no. 3 (May 1971): 269-312.

34. Richard Parker, The Myth of the Middle Class: Notes on Affluence and Equality (New York: Liveright, 1972), pp. 51-91, gives a historical account of attitudes toward poverty since colonial times, indicative of their Lockian influence.

35. Herman Melville, "Poor Man's Pudding and Rich Man's Crumbs," in Great Short Works of Herman Melville, ed. by Warner Berthoff, (New York: Harper & Row, 1970), p. 173.

36. Ibid., p. 172

37. Ibid.

38. Henry David Thoreau, "Where I Lived and What I Lived For," in Walden or, Life in the Woods (New York: New American Library, 1960), p. 67.

39. Thomas Paine, The Complete Writings of Thomas Paine, edited by Philip S. Foner (New York: Citadel Press, 1945), vol. 1, pp. 4, 275-76, 357, and 610; vol. 2, pp. 274 and 286.

40. The range of views held by Paine are perhaps indicative of the fact that no one is able to take a radical stance on only one issue in America, because the political beliefs and social institutions of the United States are so interwoven that to pull out a thread is to threaten to unravel the whole fabric. References to the abolitionist and feminist positions of Paine may be found in The Complete Writings of Thomas Paine, vol. 2, pp. 16, 19, 21, and 24.

41. Parker, The Myth of the Middle Class, p. 190.

42. Ibid., pp. 186-95.

43. Cited in Parker, The Myth of the Middle Class, p. 186.

44. Hartz, Liberal Tradition in America, pp. 259-83.

45. Macpherson, Real World of Democracy, pp. 57-58.

46. Ibid., pp. 9-11.

47. U.S. Department of Commerce, Bureau of the Census, Statistical Abstract of the United States, 1960 (Washington, D.C.: U.S. Government Printing Office, 1960), Table 263, p. 205.

48. John Kenneth Galbraith, The Affluent Society (New York: New American Library, 1958), p. 83.

49. Ibid., p. 257.

50. Stephan Thernstrom, "The Myth of American Affluence," Commentary 48, no. 4 (October 1969): 74.

51. Franklin, The Political Thought of Benjamin Franklin, p. 385.

52. For a discussion of attempts to "explain" inequality see S. M. Miller and Ronnie Steinberg Ratner, "The American Resignation: The New Assault on Equality," Social Policy 3, no. 1 (May/June 1972): 5-15.

53. Oscar Lewis, "The Culture of Poverty," Scientific American 215, no. 4 (October 1966): 19.

54. Edward C. Banfield, The Unheavenly City: The Nature and Future of Our Urban Crisis (Boston: Little, Brown and Company, 1968), p. 245.

55. Daniel R. Moynihan, The Negro Family: The Case for National Action (Washington, D.C.: U.S. Department of Labor, 1965), p. 47.

56. Banfield, The Unheavenly City, p. 126. For an excellent discussion of American ethnocentrism and poverty see Dorothy B. James, Poverty, Politics and Change (Englewood Cliffs, N.J.: Prentice-Hall, 1972), pp. 32-44.

57. Cited by Harry M. Caudill in Jack Weller, Yesterday's People: Life in Contemporary Appalachia (Lexington: University of Kentucky Press, 1965), pp. xiii-xiv.

58. This comparison was prepared by Marion Pearsall. See Weller, Yesterday's People, pp. 161-66.

59. Rupert Vance in ibid., p. vii.

60. Mike Maloney and Ben Huelsman, "Humanism, Scientism and Southern Mountaineers: A Review," People's Appalachia 2, no. 3, (July 1972): 24-27.

61. Peter Berger and Thomas Luckman, The Social Construction of Reality: A Treatise in the Sociology of Knowledge (Garden City, N.Y.: Doubleday Anchor Books, 1967), p. 198.

62. Charles Valentine, Culture and Poverty: Critique and Counter-Proposals (Chicago: University of Chicago Press, 1968), p. 15.

63. Banfield, The Unheavenly City, p. vii.

64. Nathan Glazer cited in Valentine, Culture and Poverty, p. 26.

65. Franklin, "On the Labouring Poor," p. 220. Despite the protests of writers of the pejorative tradition, Wiley concluded that they provide the rationale for policies" that are extremely oppressive and repressive to large numbers of people." George Wiley, "Masking Repression as Reform," Social Policy 3, no. 1 (May/June 1972): 16.

66. Lee Rainwater, "The Problem of Lower-Class Culture and Poverty-War Strategy," in Daniel R. Moynihan, ed., On Understanding Poverty: Perspectives from the Social Sciences (New York: Basic Books, 1969).

67. Valentine, Culture and Poverty, p. 5.

68. Herbert J. Gans, "Culture and Class in the Study of Poverty: An Approach to Anti-Poverty, Research," in Moynihan, On Understanding Poverty, p. 210; also Rainwater, "The Problem of Lower-Class Culture and Poverty-War Strategy," p. 250.

69. Valentine, Culture and Poverty, p. 15; Eleanor Burke Leacock, ed., The Culture of Poverty: A Critique (New York: Simon and Schuster, 1971), p. 8, writes that the volume is an edited work that contains articles concerned, "that a too hastily conceived concept of a 'poverty of culture' has been widely applied and misused," p. 8.

70. Valentine, Culture and Poverty, p. 15. Also Leacock, The Culture of Poverty, pp. 10-11.

71. William Ryan, Blaming the Victim (New York: Random House, 1971).

72. Oscar Lewis in Leacock, The Culture of Poverty, p. 35.

73. Valentine, Culture and Poverty, p. 17.

74. For the importance of the analysis of a problem for determining necessary policy measures see James B. Rule, "The Problem with Social Problems," Politics and Society 2, no. 1 (Fall 1971): 47-56; and also C. Wright Mills, "The Professional Ideology of Social Pathologists," in American Journal of Sociology 49, no. 2, (September 1943): 165-80. See also Frances Fox Piven and Richard Cloward, Regulating the Poor: The Functions of Public Welfare (New York: Random House, 1971).

75. Rainwater, "The Problem of Lower-Class Culture and Poverty-War Strategy," p. 251.

76. Lee Rainwater in Leacock, The Culture of Poverty, p. 36.

77. Helen Lewis, "Fatalism or the Coal Industry? Contrasting Views of Appalachian Problems," Mountain Life and Work 46, no. 11, (December 1970) 5.

78. Ibid., p. 6.

79. Ibid., p. 6. It should be noted that Lewis sees a struggle between "their way of life" and an alien culture. This would seem to signify that Appalachians share the values of other Americans, or at least are aware of them, but have distinct values as well. See also Helen Lewis, Sue Kobak, Linda Johnson, "Family, Religion and Colonialism in Central Appalachia or: Bury My Rifle at Big Stone Gap," in Jim Axelrod, ed., Growin' Up Country (Clintwood, Va: Council of the Southern Mountains, 1973), pp. 131-56.

80. Helen Lewis, "Fatalism or the Coal Industry?" p. 7.

81. Ibid., p. 12.

82. Weller seems to have come to a more systemic interpretation of Appalachian poverty. See Jack Weller, "Appalachia: America's Mineral Colony," Vantage Point 1 no. 2 (1974): 2-3.

83. Helen Lewis, "Fatalism or the Coal Industry?" p. 10. Related to Lewis' analysis is Oscar Lewis' suspicion that the poverty of culture may be endemic to the early free enterprise stage of capitalism. Compare Oscar Lewis, "The Culture of Poverty," p. 24. It may be argued that, if not a colony, Appalachia is in the throes of an early stage of capitalism. Bethell gives evidence of very punitive capitalist behavior unchecked by government regulatory agencies. See Tom Bethell, The Hurricane Creek Massacre (New York: Harper & Row, 1972).

84. U.S. Department of Labor, Bureau of Labor Statistics, 3 Standards of Living for an Urban Family of Four Persons Spring, 1967 (Washington, D.C.: U.S. Government Printing Office, 1969), p. vii.

85. Parker, The Myth of the Middle Class, pp. 94-95 and 151.

86. Mollie Orshansky, "Counting the Poor: Another Look at the Poverty Profile," Social Security Bulletin 28, no. 1 (January 1965), p. 5.

87. Orshansky, "Counting the Poor," p. 5.

88. For discussions of the poverty definition see James, Poverty, Politics and Change, pp. 2-8; also Joseph A. Kershaw, Government Against Poverty (Chicago: Markham Publishing Co., 1970), pp. 7-14.

89. Orshansky, "Counting the Poor," p. 10.

90. U.S. Department of Labor, Bureau of Labor Statistics, Standards of Living, p. 9.

91. Franklin, The Political Thought of Benjamin Franklin, p. 74.

92. See Herbert J. Gans, More Equality (New York: Pantheon Books, 1973), pp. 102-27.

93. Jurgen Habermas, Toward a Rational Society: Student Protest, Science and Politics (Boston: Beacon Press, 1968), p. 120.

94. Paul Jacobs, "Our Permanent Paupers," The New Leader 47 (March 30, 1964): 7ff. The roots of this belief, it should be clear and as Devine points out, are in the Lockian premise of economic abundance for free men in a manipulable environment. Devine, The Political Culture of the United States, p. 47.

95. Banfield cited in Sheldon S. Wolin, "Political Theory as a Vocation," American Political Science Review 63, no. 4 (December 1969): 1069. It is the satire of history, which Hartz alluded to, that Banfield should recently suggest the elimination of minimum wage laws for the very same reasons Franklin suggested; namely, the price of labor is subject to supply and demand and artificial limitations imposed by government may bring the wages above the level employers can afford to pay without suffering loss. Franklin, The Political Thought of Benjamin Franklin, p. 223; Banfield, The Unheavenly City, p. 245.

96. Franklin, The Political Thought of Benjamin Franklin, p. 74.

97. Miller and Ratner, "The American Resignation," p. 7.

98. Orshansky, "Counting the Poor," p. 5.

99. Ibid., p. 5.

100. Oscar Ornati, Poverty Amid Affluence (New York: Twentieth Century Fund, 1966), pp. 38 and 50. In regard to the connection between poverty and racial discrimination, see Lester C. Thurow, Poverty and Discrimination (Washington, D.C.: The Brookings Institution, 1969).

101. Miller and Ratner point out the paradox of the severe emphasis on unemployment in a society dominated by a work ethic. In particular they point out the importance of high unemployment in controlling inflation. "The poor, as economist Garth Mangrum has said, have become, the price stabilizers of the economy, suffering for the benefit of other groups in society. Then they are charged with an unwillingness to work or with having an appetite for jobs above their appropriate station in life." Miller and Ratner, "The American Resignation," pp. 12—13. See also, John C. Donovan, The Politics of Poverty, 2d ed. (New York: Pegasus Press, 1967), pp. 116-17.

2

"TRICKLE DOWN" AND PROPORTIONAL
STRATEGIES

Preserving Inequality

When inequality is given serious consideration in a definition of poverty, the complexity and cost of the problem are compounded immeasurably. The difficulty with a definition of poverty in these terms is in the implications for antipoverty strategies. The costs of eradicating relative poverty by cash transfer payments, even if economically possible,[1] cannot be legitimated within the Lockian liberal purview of the state. The intervention of government into the economy with antipoverty programs aimed at the relatively poor extends beyond the function of the state, which is foremost to make people secure in their property and to preserve the distinctions of wealth among them. This belief has led to opposition to a progressive income tax in the past and presently helps maintain a tax structure that emphasizes growth and development rather than redistribution.[2]

A definition of poverty that includes equality runs counter to several other beliefs in the American political culture. De Toqueville, commenting on America, said that he knew of no other country "where a profounder contempt is expressed for the theory of the permanent equality of property."[3] The possibility of unlimited acquisition is held more precious than leveling the differences among social and economic classes, and therefore government functions sufficiently when it provides equal opportunity for all to gain affluence. Even though unlimited acquisition is beyond the experience of most persons, its surrogate, the apparent security and affluence of the middle class, functions to forestall radical social and economic change. Not only does the large, seemingly homogeneous middle class legitimate the social and economic sufficiency of existing arrangements for a vast majority; it also levels the differences among socioeconomic groups. Richard Parker maintains that the myth of a homogeneous, secure, affluent, and majoritarian middle class holds the promise of a conflict-free society, the end of ideology and acquiescence to existing arrangements.[4] Poverty, after all, is not the problem of the many, nor the visible, nor the educated or powerful.[5]

This end of conflict, lack of ideology, and the corresponding assumptions of opportunity play an important part in establishing what Orshansky, borrowing from Gunnar Myrdal, calls an American "underclass": a group for many of whom "poverty is neither a sometimes nor a one-time thing."[6] They do so by the benign neglect implicit in the belief that conditions may be bad but they have been worse and are getting better; by the fear of meddling with basically satisfactory conditions; and by the optimism that abundance within a stratified society is distributed more or less proportionate to ability. Few would ascribe to this "trickle down" theory as just outlined, yet the "lingering myth of the invisible hand" has consistently circumscribed antipoverty measures.

Never very popular with some poor, the "trickle down" theory has been compared to feeding the horse extra hay to fatten the sparrows. Evidence has been increasing to demonstrate the limitations, if not the untruth, of this theory. W. H. Locke Anderson offered statistical evidence, in 1964, that the elimination of poverty through "trickle down" methods was likely to be slower and more uncertain in the future than it had been in the past, because some groups of poor people were "relatively untouchable by changes in the general level of income."[7]

The effectiveness of the "trickle down" theory as an antipoverty strategy may be assessed by examining changes in the distribution of wealth, a measure that combines scarcity with equality. Dividing the nation's wage earners into fifths, we can assess the ceiling of earnings for each group and the proportion of the total income each group receives. Two papers presented before the Congressional Joint Economic Committee in January 1972 give us a very clear picture of the recent distribution of personal income. Lester Thurow made the point that while the incomes of everyone—male and female, rich and poor, majority and minority member—had risen from 1947 to 1969, they rose at about the same rate. Even where the ratios of incomes had decreased—the average income of the richest 20 percent of all families fell from 8.6 to 7.3 times that of the poorest 20 percent of all families—the average difference between these groups increased from $10,565 to $19,071 (in 1969 dollars).[8] Thus, while some equalization was occurring it was consistent with giving more to those who had much already.

The second paper of importance to this question was prepared by Josephy A. Pechman and Benjamin A. Okner of The Brookings Institution. The figures they used were from a sample of 30,000 taken from the 1967 Survey of Economic Opportunity conducted by the U.S. Bureau of the Census for OEO and other figures taken from 90,000 income tax returns for 1966. Pechman and Okner's study points out the disparity of income distribution and the effects of taxation that is illustrated in Table 4.

Before adjustment, via the tax structure, the top 1 percent receive more income than the entire bottom 20 percent. Pechman and Okner adjust these income figures by correcting for nonreporting and underreporting in tax returns and by imputing additional income such as rent on owner-occupied homes; employer supplements to wage and salary incomes; tax-exempt interest on state and local bonds; accrued

TABLE 4

The Effects of Taxation on Income Distribution
(in dollars)

Quantile Ranking	Income before Adjustment	Percent of Total	Income before Adjustment	Percent of Total
Lowest Fifth	2,762	4.1	3,261	3.4
Second Fifth	2,762- 5,381	10.8	3,261- 6,057	10.7
Middle Fifth	5,381- 7,852	17.5	6,057- 8,747	17.0
Fourth Fifth	7,852-10,982	24.9	8,747-12,500	23.8
Highest Fifth	10,982-16,933	42.7	12,500-20,227	45.1
Top 5 percent	16,933-33,333	16.0	20,227-44,792	19.1
Top 1 percent	33,333 and up	4.8	44,792 and up	6.8

Source: Joseph A. Pechman and Benjamin A. Okner," Individual Income Tax Erosion by Income Classes," Prepared for the U.S. Joint Economic Committee Compendium of Paper on the Economics of Federal Subsidy Programs, mimeo. (Washington D.C.: The Brookings Institution, 1972) p. 7.

gains on capital assets; and transfer payments. In other words, the adjustment sought to modify incomes in line with the workings of the tax system; obviously, the greatest benefit goes to the rich. The discrepancy between the very rich and the bottom 20 percent after taxes is doubled. The significance of this adjustment is to show a "trickle up" mechanism in the tax structure.[9]

Further significance of the distribution of income in promoting equality is seen in Table 5. A comparison of income distribution over a span of 34 years shows that the greatest redistribution of income occurred during 1935 to 1947—most especially during the war years 1941-47, when unemployment was lowest.

Thurow, Pechman and Okner, and the figures on income distribution all indicate that the "trickle down" approach has slowed considerably in recent years. Even when it has worked it has not meant a reduction in the distance of the poor and the nonpoor; it has been

TABLE 5

Income Distribution for Selected Years 1935-69
(in percent)

Family Personal Income	1935	1941	1947	1953	1959	1965	1967	1969
Lowest fifth	4.1	4.1	5.0	4.9	4.5	5.3	5.4	5.6
Second fifth	9.2	9.5	11.8	11.3	10.9	12.2	12.2	12.3
Third fifth	14.1	15.3	17.0	16.6	16.2	17.6	17.5	17.6
Fourth fifth	20.9	22.3	23.1	22.5	22.7	23.7	23.7	23.4
Highest fifth	51.7	48.8	43.0	44.7	45.7	41.3	41.2	41.0
Top 5 per- cent	26.5	24.0	17.2	19.9	19.9	15.8	15.3	14.7

Source: Information compiled from U.S. Department of Commerce, Bureau of the Census, Statistical Abstract of the United States, 1972, 93rd ed. (Washington, D.C.: U.S. Government Printing Office, 1972).

35

what David Potter called a "leveling up" approach rather than a social revolution. The wealthiest of Americans saw their share of income decline but not their wealth, a comparatively small price to pay for avoiding the radical redistribution of wealth other nations were undergoing while America went through her much milder New Deal.[10] The trickle down approach is premised on "new factors," something in which everyone can share. Without new factors, redistribution would be a sum-difference game with winners and losers rather than a non-constant-sum, where everyone gains or at least no one loses. Some social reformers have based their demand for radical social and political action on an analysis of the factors given; but such action has been avoided by introducing a new factor such as "the frontier," "nature's abundance," or technology. Thus, Henry Demarest Lloyd could anguish, even before the beginning of this century, "Our young men can no longer go west, they must go up or down."[11] Yet, with almost three-quarters of the 20th century completed, America still displays a genius for maintaining everyone in their place—while providing mobility and relief for the lowest places—by dividing up the benefits of some new factor proportionately or even regressively. Because of new factors the poor need not go up or down; they can merely stand still, in an absolute and a relative sense.

When the American government has intervened to prevent poverty, its intervention has been consistent with Lockian liberal principles. Social security, for example, was relief on an apparently proportionate basis. Far from being redistributive, social security was described as an insurance mechanism and in fact has important regressive features about it. Since it was cast in the mold of an insurance program in which people transfer their earnings from one point in time to another it was a variant on Franklin's opinion that frugality and industry in youth is the best provision for old age and infirmity.[12] Likewise, welfare provides relief payments only for the "worthy poor" and even then grants only a percentage of the amount for subsistence. Thus, welfare was premised on a belief of individual effort to overcome poverty and is designed to provide relief and incentive simultaneously, or at least alternately.[13] Such interventions have been initiated hesistantly and begrudgingly because of the unique confluence of opportunity, poverty, and moral worth in the American mind.

THE WAR ON POVERTY

The Executive Declaration of War

The early efforts of the Kennedy administration to deal with poverty, especially Appalachian poverty,[14] exemplified the belief found in Galbraith that better management and administration of existing economic and social institutions were adequate to deal with the problems of poverty. This attitude was explicit in Kennedy's Yale Commencement Address of 1962.

> The fact of the matter is that most of the problems, or
> at least many of them, that we now face are technical
> problems, are administrative problems. They are very
> sophisticated judgments which do not lend themselves
> to the great sort of "passionate movements" which have
> stirred this country so often in the past.[15]

It is important to realize that Kennedy could reduce problems like poverty to the "technical" level only because he too held fast to the beliefs of his forebears. Sheldon S. Wolin clearly points out that the modern attempt to substitute administration for politics is rooted in the Lockian notion of society "as a self-subsistent entity"[16] with, we must not forget, important "natural" correlates—for example, the achievement of property and the inequality among persons. This convenient optimism in the capacity of administration to deal with social and political problems[17] not only stems from the same Lockian premises of the conservative faith in laissez-faire but also illustrates the conceptual framework of an apparently contradictory policy:[18] advocacy for change without challenging the liberal premises behind social arrangements.

The genesis of OEO illustrates the influence of the mentality of administrative amelioration. The War on Poverty was initiated not because of the uprising of the poor or labor radicalism but because members of the executive branch decided poverty could and should be eliminated or at least reduced. It is significant that of the 137 persons consulted by Shriver in the formative period from February 2 to March 16, 1964, except for a few civil rights spokesmen, none were poor.[19] While it is not unusual for the poor not to be consulted on legislation, it is important to realize, as Daniel Moynihan points out, "the main pressure for a massive government assault on poverty developed within the Kennedy-Johnson administration, among officials whose responsibilities were to think about just such matters." Consequently, poverty problems were submitted to "a type of decision-making that is suited to the techniques of modern organizations, and which ends up in the hands of persons who make a profession of it."[20]

The lessons gained by the experience of the Grey Areas Program of the Ford Foundation and the President's Commission on Juvenile Delinquency (PCJD) gave the OEO planners their major insights and premise for poverty strategies. Among the lessons

gained were the inability of voluntary agencies to reach the poor
or the inappropriateness of their services when they did reach them.
It also was felt that public agencies offered fragmented and unrelated
services and limited understanding of the problems of the poor. In
addition, little political leadership was exercised by or on behalf of
the poor; most programs were conducted with a minimum of participation of the program's beneficiaries.[21] The dissatisfaction with existing arrangements led the OEO planners to incorporate into OEO what
had been unique in the previous Grey Areas and PCJD programs.

> Maximum feasible participation proceeded from observa-
> tions and concerns about the failure of the white middle
> class to provide a service structure to alleviate pover-
> ty or the intellectual and personal leadership which
> would bring about the institutional change in concert with
> interests and concerns of people in the ghetto, barrio,
> and generally speaking rural America, the poor there.
>   The assumption was that with whatever resources
> that the government had to offer, it probably couldn't do
> any worse than it had been doing by supporting service
> bureaucracy.[22]

Maximum feasible participation was vague enough for some to
see implications the government could not live up to, while others
found it to be at heart a return to our soundest democratic traditions.
As it turned out, the two views were related. In any event, Lyndon
Baines Johnson offers us one view prevalent at the time.

> Basically the idea was this: Local organizations would
> be formed in the neighborhoods and communities where
> the poor people themselves lived, and programs to help
> the poor would be channeled through organizations on the
> scene. This plan had the sound of something brand new
> and even faintly radical. Actually, it was based on one of
> the oldest ideas of our democracy, as old as the New
> England town meeting—self determination at the local
> level.[23]

The task of the antipoverty program was based on the opportunity hypothesis of Richard Cloward and Lloyd Ohlin[24] and was intended
to open "legitimate avenues" to "conventional goals." It is very important to realize that it was presumed by many that opportunity and
participation of the poor would yield their pursuit of conventional
goals, a testimony to the abiding apparent "givenness" of these goals.

Just as important to realize however is that community action agencies evolved with a variety of interpretations. According to Kenneth B. Clark and Jeannette Hopkins these meanings fell between community organizing and community action. Community organizing involved the instrumental role of professionals or other middle-class agents in directing the energies of the poor into nonabrasive activities consistent with the expectations of others; while in community action the poor acted on their own behalf and for their own ends.[25]

An important question arises at this juncture; namely, which of the ambiguous meanings of community action agencies are consistent with the Lockian liberal tradition? To put the question another way, which government interventions were consistent with Lockian views of the state? The equality of opportunity and participation imparted by government interventions were orthodox with Lockian liberal principles if sufficiently circumscribed.[26] As Richard Parker points out, the new class belief in democratic elitism was just such a circumscription. It assumed that

the nature of American life is a technological world requiring a kind of decision-making that relies exclusively on specialists. It seeks to define and deal with America's problems, as President Kennedy put it, in terms of "technical problems, administrative problems . . . which do not lend themselves to the great sort of 'passionate movements.' "[27]

Organization of or by the poor for pursuit of conventional goals was consistent with the social cohesion required to maintain the political consensus toward existing socioeconomic differences. But the implicit threat of organizing the poor for action that was not explicitly directed to achieving conventional goals was very early recognized. The HARYOU study, "Youth in the Ghetto," was denounced by a New York City councilman for containing "radical sociological ideas, which might allow professional agitators to bring about an economic-social revolution in our city." Likewise on August 16, 1964, four days before the signing of the Economic Opportunity Act, the New York Daily News informed New Yorkers that Mobilization for Youth, a program jointly sponsored by Grey Areas and PCJD, had become infested with "Commies and Commie sympathizers."[28]

The question was raised: Were the poor to conform to structures and expectations or change them? More fundamental, did the institutional and social arrangements of America have the capacity to eliminate poverty without reconstruction? The question of strategy reflected the differing concepts of poverty: Was the target in the War on Poverty the individual (a pejorative view) or the community (a systemic view)? But even in this latter view there were differences as to the sufficiency of the institutions to handle the new demands the elimination of poverty would make on them and their culpability in the maintenance of poverty. Here the question appeared to be: Could sufficient reform be brought about without conflict among classes and/or between the poor and the institutions serving them?[29]

In its inception the poverty program seemed to say yes and no to all these questions. On the one hand, it created a new set of institutions—community Action Agencies (CAA's)—to handle the specific needs of the poor, but with the ambiguity of the service- and conformity-oriented community organizing and the potentially much more politically unsettling community action. On the other hand, the poverty program, by rejecting a program of public employment, trusted existing economic arrangements to provide the essential factor in eliminating poverty by self-help and employment. Perhaps some of the confusion stemmed from the hurried preparation of the poverty program. The emphasis on planning, while evident in the four and one-half years of preparation for the Mobilization for Youth program, was jettisoned by President Johnson's insistence on impact—quick and immediate and bold new learning experiences—and reduced to a period of 44 days. Johnson's decisions narrowed the strategies—as it increased the ambiguities.

The Ambiguous Assault on Poverty

On August 20, 1964, President Johnson signed the Economic Opportunity Act into law. Not since Theodore Roosevelt had there been so much anticipation of a splendid little war.

> Today for the first time in all the history of the human race, a great nation is able to make and is willing to make a commitment to eradicate poverty among its people.[30]

But in the haste to mobilize, certain features of the war remained unclear. The War on Poverty was a symbol of purpose and challenge by which a nation could memorialize an admired and slain president. It was also a program that permitted a new president to place his stamp on his office and fulfill his conception of his public self as another Franklin Delano Roosevelt. What was not clear was the commitment to eradicate poverty and to absorb the costs implied in such a task.

Frances Fox Piven insists, and it is an underlying assumption of this study, that "public goals are a political resource more than a set of first principles guiding action."

> The concrete programs and structures launched under the
> banner of lofty public goals are in fact formed to deal with
> the various political circumstances of any agency and to
> suit the political leadership on which the agency depends.
> . . . The motivating force in government-action, the
> force which shapes public goals and the programs and
> structures created in their name, reflects . . . the adap-
> tive rationalism through which a political system and its
> member parts are maintained.[31]

The subsequent history of OEO was to verify the truth of this
observation time and again. The single most important question later
asked of poverty measures was the relation of antipoverty measures
to existing institutional structures. In their haste to approve the measure Congress did not envision its implications and to some extent
was not concerned with them. It was the day of congressional activism.
Kennedy's assassination and an election year had swept away the
equilibrium of Congress and its normal deliberative manner. The
Economic Opportunity Act "was reviewed by the Congress with the
minimum of care, in the shortest period of time, and with the least
understanding of what was about to happen."[32]

There were precursors of what was about to happen. The
Tennessee Valley Authority (TVA) was an undertaking similar to OEO
in regards to its "grass roots" participation policy. It is true that
TVA brought about participation without conflict, but Philip Selznick
has pointed out the ambiguity of this success. In fact, the grass roots
policy of TVA was manipulated to serve its organizational needs by
concessions with local and national interests and restricted the authority's policy and behavior.[33] The grass roots policy became co-
optation, which is to say "the process of absorbing new elements into
the leadership or policy-determining structure of an organization
as a means of averting threats to its stability or existence."[34] The
primary consequence of co-optation was not democratic. In fact,
wherever possible, co-optation was only formal, sharing public symbols,
administrative burdens, and appearances of power without the substance.[35] The purpose of informal co-optation, on the other hand,
was to assimilate groups from the environment of the authority that
were necessary for its survival and often resulted in the formulation
of policy in line with the interests of the informally co-opted elements.[36] Thus, "close to the people" meant the co-optation of local
government and private associations.[37] The unavowed but real grass
roots policy was the full utilization of local institutional resources
and arrangements.[38] Co-optation meant not only adaptation to environmental pressures but also perpetuation of the status quo by legitimating already powerful institutions as sufficient for the "new" grass roots
participation policy of the authority.

41

The similarities and differences between TVA and OEO should be drawn out. There was little reason to doubt that OEO ran the danger of other bureaucracies of becoming introverted and concerned with its own maintenance. OEO might have to make concessions to local and national interests that determined its survival.[39] The poor were not among these interests. They were not part of OEO in the beginning and it was not of necessity to co-opt them informally later. All of which is to say that, if representation of the poor on poverty programs did not mean conflictless increase in services and benefits, the institutional needs of OEO perhaps could require the co-optation of the groups in conflict with the poor, or some other group of nonpoor. Or, to put it another way, if control by the poor of Community Action Programs (CAP's) meant conflict with local authorities and powers, survival for OEO might dictate abandoning the poor for the latter. In fact, throughout OEO's experience it meant exactly that.

The first and perhaps most dramatic instance of informal co-optation was the Child Development Group of Mississippi (CDGM). The real bone of contention were the millions of dollars going to poor blacks to finance a Head Start program beyond the control of the school system. In 1966 CDGM, despite congressional criticism and investigation, was granted $5.6 million for 175 centers serving 9,000 children in 28 Mississippi counties. Both John Stennis (Dem.-Miss.) and CDGM leaders realized the implications of these proportions: CDGM had taken "all the non-adrenaline, old fashioned, respectable implications of the term civil rights and put them to work in advanced Movement form: federal programs."[40] The day after the OEO approval of the grant, Stennis, Senator James Eastland and Republic John Bell Williams, all Democrats from Mississippi, joined in criticizing the "remarkably poor judgment" of OEO.[41]

Shriver was faced with powerful congressional opposition, on the one hand—Stennis being on the Senate Appropriations Committee—and a successful and controversial project, epitomizing poor people helping themselves, on the other. Thus, "Shriver couldn't come out and kill his most famous, most excellent project. Neither could he, for reasons of political precariousness, tolerate a controversial or successful project."[42] He resolved his difficulty by forming in August 1966 a coalition of reformed Democrats called Mississippi Action for Progress to replace CDGM; in October OEO gave this new group $2 million, without having received their application, and responsibility for the Head Start Program in Mississippi.

Perhaps the best portrayal of the importance of the CDGM experience was given by a mother within the organization.

It didn't take them long to figure out we was up to no good at all. We was being 'uppity'. . . . It was the way they went about doing this that got us feeling drawn to it. I'd say. They made us feel it was ours, and we were somebody, and not people they'd throw us something, so that they could go home and feel better. . . .

They probably saw that they got us going too fast, and that we'd be real honest to goodness practicing citizens of the USA and they never allowed that here, and, maybe up in Washington they're not ready for it either.[43]

CDGM was not an isolated experience. Its experience was prevalent among antipoverty programs and illustrated that the closer a CAP was tied to local institutional and political arrangements the less successful they were in eliminating structural and systemic causes of poverty, but the greater were their chances of continuation. On the other hand, the further a program was from local control the more controversial it was and the more perilous its existence no matter how successful. A conflictless poverty strategy would pay a price in effectiveness, while an effective poverty program would pay its price in survival. This in part was the lesson of TVA according to Philip Selznick. It was also "the most general important conclusion" of a study of social reforms prior to OEO, "no movement of reform in American society can hope to supplant the conflict of interest from which policy evolves."[44] Part of that conflict is rooted in the apparent "given" nature of middle-class values, beliefs, and arrangements. "Even without conscious collusion or naked self-interest, the values, tastes and distastes of middle class America naturally conspire to render as little to the less fortunate as its own security and conscience will allow."[45] The definition of poverty and the degree of scarcity and inequality imposed bear this observation out as well as the restrictions on the meaning of maximum feasible participation and the scope of the CAA's.

What became apparent with the experience of CAA's and especially some manifestations of maximum feasible participation was that middle-class America had a stake in the present institutional arrangement, both because of the roles and status conferred by this arrangement and because the service strategy seemed adequate to Americans.

The strength and pervasiveness of resistance suggests that once teachers [administrators, doctors, judges, police, social workers, bureaucrats, Presidents] are established in their profession they may be unable to assimilate changes which disrupt the beliefs by which they structure their roles.[46]

When poverty efforts entailed suggested threats to the existing distribution of wealth or power, and conflict ensued, it was inevitable that demands for institutional change on behalf of the poor would be relegated to lesser importance. As Sundquist put it,

> The affluent majority will not be persuaded that tranquility is not an important objective of society—and one superior, if a choice had to be made, to the elimination of poverty itself.[47]

Lockian liberalism after all looks to society for change and to government for stability.[48] The ambiguity within maximum feasible participation was short-lived because no government will finance conflict with itself and OEO's continuation depended upon congressional and public co-optation.

In hindsight it is clear that by 1967,

> as the Economic Opportunity programs, one by one,
> gained broad congressional acceptance, became en-
> meshed in the incremental process of budget making,
> and were increasingly institutionalized within the depart-
> mental bureaucratic structures, they were "tamed" politi-
> cally and administratively. The process of homogeniza-
> tion rendered the antipoverty programs more "acceptable"
> in the circles of orthodoxy.[49]

The ability of OEO to adapt to "circles of orthodoxy" was demonstrated by its ability to win congressional and local political support and even more so by its willingness to extinguish itself when it fell into presidential disfavor. Howard Phillips, director and dismantler of OEO, complained that OEO had operated on the premise "that people overcome poverty collectively, not individually."[50] Later his successor was also to defend the dismantling of OEO. "I'm convinced what we're doing here is in the interest of the poor people of this country."[51]

Another aspect of the ambiguity of OEO to emphasize here is that the conflicts over antipoverty strategies on the local level had direct repercussions on the national level via the institutional links, very importantly the party links, that connected local and national officials. When the mayor of Syracuse said, "If we can't have the program the way we want, we'll have none at all,"[52] one can safely assume he would test his leverage for change in Washington before settling for nothing. Legislators were relatively easy to pry loose from the Economic Opportunity Act given the measure was not theirs; that executive pressure for support of OEO had disappeared by 1967;

44

and that no groups of poor or others effectively countered the mounting pressure for withdrawal and cease-fire in the War on Poverty.

Just as important, the re-election of representatives and senators depended on the support of party officials in their districts and states, and the support of a big-city mayor or governor was an asset. But it was exactly this group of officials and party leaders who were voicing the greatest criticism of the poverty programs. Congress proved itself to be highly susceptible to their critical pressure, exactly because each of its members stood in very similar relationships with mayors, governors, county judges, and numerous interest groups. The import of this situation was a fresh discovery to those within OEO, including John Wofford, Deputy Director of CAP.

> One of the lessons of the first four years of the program is that local politics turned out to be of acute interest and impact at the national level.[53]

In a very important passage James L. Sundquist brings together several important elements of our study thus far—namely, the conceptualization of poverty, poverty strategy, and conflict. If the task of OEO was to change the poor, as individuals,

> then what was called for was community organization for the provision of individual services, in better but essentially traditional ways, an approach acceptable to the power structure of most communities. . . . But if the problem is in the social setting rather than the individual, then the remedies are not so clear or so simple. Correction of personal deficiencies on the part of the poor must be accompanied—indeed preceded by changes in community behavior, both by the community of the poor and by the larger community. These ends inevitably involve the organization of the poor under their own leadership for their own ends, and also inevitably, some degree of challenge to and confrontation with, the larger community. But can a national government maintain for long a program that sets minorities against majorities in communities throughout the land?[54]

Maximum feasible participation, as it evolved in practice, placed this question squarely before the country, and circumstances such as budget considerations, the Vietnam War, the waning of executive support, and congressional co-optation would coalesce to bring about a revision of antipoverty strategies.[55]

HEALTH CARE AND POVERTY

Crisis in Health Care

By 1967 OEO was being criticized for the apparent premise of many of its programs that institutional arrangements had failed to meet or were incapable of meeting the needs of the poor. Indeed, its continuation in 1967 was possible only because of the Green Amendment, which legislated a definition of maximum feasible participation that assumed the capacity of existing political and institutional arrangements to deal adequately with poverty. [56] Yet, the premise of the Neighborhood Health Centers, a new front in the War on Poverty that opened in 1967, was the necessity of constructing an alternative set of institutions.

> The health care that has been offered these people [the poor] has missed its mark; the rate of disease, disability, and premature death has been higher for the poor than for the rest of the population. [57]

The inadequacy of health care for the poor had been carefully detailed in November 1965 at a White House Conference on Health by Alonzo S. Yerby. Yerby concluded that characteristics of health care for poor people were not true for other Americans and referred to our system of medicine as a "two-class system of medicine, separate and unequal—a system where poor must barter dignity for health." [58]

Joseph English, Acting Assistant Director of the U.S. Office of Health Affairs, gave an indication of the second-class system of medicine among the poor. According to his testimony before the House Committee on Education and Labor in 1967, poor families have three times more disabling heart disease; seven times more visual impairments; three times more conditions of arthritis and rheumatism; and four times more incidence of high blood pressure. In addition, dreaded and often fatal diseases of the poor are tuberculosis, influenza, and pneumonia—diseases that the more economically fortunate had not suffered unduly for a generation. Among the poor who are employed, one-third have a chronic illness that severely limits their ability to work. [59]

The inadequacies of health care for the poor articulated the failure of a system that seemed inadequate in other respects as well. When President Johnson named an Advisory Commission on Health Manpower in the summer of 1966, it was felt that a crisis was impending. The report of this commission confirmed this feeling.

"There is a crisis, the intuition of the average citizen has foundation in fact."[60] The feeling of crisis came on with the spiraling cost of medical care. Assuming that the health care trend from 1965 to 1975 would continue as the previous 10 years, projections were made for the future. Total expenditures for health care were seen to increase by 140 percent; the cost of physician-directed services would increase, it was estimated, by more than 160 percent; short-term general hospital services would increase by more than 250 percent; dentist-directed services would about double; expenditures on drugs would rise about 65 percent. This compares with a projected increase of 20 percent in the general price level. The cost of health services per person would nearly double to a sum greater than $400 a year and would result in a national expenditure approaching some $100 billion. Little promise of greater benefits accompanies these spiraling costs. In terms of cost-benefit analysis, "the wisdom of continuing expenditures for health services at the projected rates" was questioned.[61]

Some analysts have minimized the crisis of American health care, using the "culture of poverty" to explain the apparent inadequacy of health care for the poor. Nathan Glazer, for example, finds that culture "operating through socio-psychological factors, is . . . clearly one element determining the health of a population." Further, varying degrees of health among different groups are attributable to "varied origins and distinct subcultures" of a population.[62] The import of Glazer's analysis is to forestall any fundamental change of the American health system. What seems called for is the reorganization and better utilization of existing arrangements; but such reorganization must be careful to preserve the principle of proprietorship, that is, "what people do and don't do, to and for themselves." Glazer, citing Victor Fuchs, concludes,

> With so much attention given to medical care, and so
> little to health education and individual responsibility
> for personal health, we run the danger of pandering to
> the understandable urge to buy a quick solution to a
> difficult problem.[63]

Glazer's analysis neglects the socioeconomic correlates of health[64] but is consistent with the existing American health care system.

> Care for the poor was a residual of the entire system;
> care for the paying patient was the dominant characteris-
> tic, a characteristic that has had a powerful influence on
> the structure and ownership of personal health services
> in the United States.[65]

47

When efforts to change the American health system have been discussed or initiated, their prime concern has been "making health services easier to finance on the part of the general population by insurance."[66] The prevailing structure of health services has been and continues to be accepted as a given. Doctors are accepted as private entrepreneurs who up until recently controlled their own price mechanisms; indeed, government laissez-faire toward doctors seemed constitutive of the doctor-patient relationship. The pivotal conflict of the various recent health insurance proposals still appears to be the amount and form of government regulation of a private industry.[67]

The effect of payment mechanisms has been to bolster this system, while mitigating some of its excesses but exacerbating others. Thus, while access is provided some individuals, questions of control, accountability, accessibility, and priorities, have not been addressed—government regulation not withstanding.[68] Most important, payment mechanisms have accelerated the spiraling costs of medical care without yielding any consequent increase in quality.[69]

Social and Political Implication of OEO
Health Standards

In contrast with other government efforts, OEO's health program was accompanied by rhetorical flourishes that invoked the early ambiguity of OEO and institutional change. English in his testimony invoked no one less than Aristotle in establishing not only the importance of health care but also the right that people have to the best form of health care that society may provide.

> Health of mind and body is so fundamental to the good
> life that if we believe that men have any personal rights
> at all, as human beings, then they have an absolute right
> to such a measure of good health as society and society
> alone is able to give them.[70]

The claim to a moral right to society's best efforts to provide good health was in serious contradiction with Lockian liberal premises. Rights, in the Lockian view, were presocial, rooted in the state of nature and limited to life, liberty, and property. This last natural right included labor, which could be viewed as a commodity sold for a wage or purchased for its product.[71] No matter how sacred its appearance, the doctor-patient relationship was a market relationship bound by contractual agreements regarding the transfer of labor and wages. Government is required to protect the right of contract and perhaps assure patients access to medical labor by means of payment mechanisms; but to state health care as a right is to neglect the important Lockian liberal premise that society is a series of contractual relationships. Further, rights are possessed by the individual and not imparted by society in the Lockian analysis. Yet, it is possible for liberal society to construct rights and impart them, such as the franchise or minimum wage laws, to protect political cohesion and unrest.[72] These rights are mechanisms of equality—not absolute equality, but remedies to inequality that threatens the liberty of some.[73]

The cost and access to health care represented just such a threat for the poor as well as for others. The first response of government was a payment mechanism that assured access to medical service without altering the market premises of medicine even though regulating it. Medicare and Medicaid have undergone several re-evaluations and restructurings of eligibility in light of their costs demonstrating that transfer payment schemes are not based on the right to medical care but on a hierarchy of need and the acceptable cost of the program, measures determined by others.

Richard Lichtman contends that health care is a test of the moral limitations of the Lockian liberalism embodied in welfare capitalism because it contests the moral basis of the right to health care—community—with the liberal model of all social relations—the market.[74] The true moral justification for a social program of medical care lies in the fact that health is a fundamental constituent of a fully realized human life and that each of us is responsible to each for the highest development of that life.[75] Opposed to this view was the "liberal's willingness to permit a commercial institution established for profit to shape his conception of a communal institution designed for the public welfare."[76]

OEO, in its health programs and its consideration of health care as a right, resurrected a fundamental question in relation to rights and social forms, with roots in the difference between Franklin and Paine and with bearing on its conflicts of the preceding few years. When society has the ability to provide a service to each of its members and the only obstacle to such provision is the continuation of the existing arrangements with their inequity, is such a service deemed a right of the members of that society, to be further realized in sufficient forms of quantity and quality by political action, or is such a service to be considered as a privilege until such time as the obstacles to its equitable distribution are removed by those in control of the service? More simply put: Is health care as a right to be realized by those who want more of it and better quality or is it to be granted by those who provide it as a safeguard of providers' rights?

It is not surprising that English did not address himself to this question. However, elements of the programs a Neighborhood Health

Centers that he outlined raised other important questions. First, there was the relation of health rights and inadequate care.

> When the Declaration of Independence was framed and when there was language in there talking about the rights of life, it might have meant one thing back in the 17th and 18th century. Today, we wonder, as far as the poor are concerned, if that statement doesn't have something to do with their right not to have their lives whittled away by illness.[77]

Rights evidently may come to encompass aspects of life that at an earlier time were considered the privilege of a few or the responsibility of the individual, when means became sufficient to provide these services or goods to the many.

Second, there was the question of participation. OEO had been committed to expanding participation in decision making to the poor via CAA's, but, while that commitment was reassessed in 1967 by the Green Amendment, English was committing OEO to explicit and extensive consumer participation.

> These services should be derived from the needs of the people to be served, not just what we as physicians think is right or what is convenient for us but that in these programs a primary emphasis be the needs of the people to be served and that it be with their participation.
> That is part of the way that the community action spirit is represented in this program.[78]

Shriver then extolled the health program as one of the programs "which constitute in their entirety community action."[79]

In sum, the establishment of a health program within OEO was based on: first, criticism of existing facilities and their attempts to deal with the health needs of the poor; second, the need for constructive alternatives to the existing institutional arrangements; and, third, the people who were clients of such a health program were to participate in the policy making and evaluation of the program. All of which was in contradiction to the view of the sufficiency and adequacy of the American medical system or the adequacy of reforms limited to insurance arrangements.

EPILOGUE AND FOREWARD

One aspect of the health program was uncertain, and this related to the fundamental ambiguity of OEO: namely, how far could the health

programs go in the creation of new forms of health care? This was
the central question of antipoverty strategy from the beginning. Could
poverty be eliminated within the institutional and service structure
already existing by the better organization of poor people for better
efficiency? How much opposition and prodding of the service structures and existing political and social arrangements by the mobilized
poor could be justified or tolerated? OEO did not, and probably could
not, decide these questions centrally and definitively. OEO, after all,
was part of that structure, supposedly committed to change but required to respond to the demands of others in order to survive. What
is essential to this study is that the rhetoric of officials, elected and
appointed, and the ambiguity of OEO strategy and programs offered
to some groups of poor people the hope for change while at the same
time creating a threat to local political and economic elites. The
resolution of this threatening ambiguity was achieved primarily on
the local level. The experience there demonstrated the importance
of local politics to a degree that had heretofore been unnoticed. The
resolution of this ambiguity oftentimes pitted new forms of poor people
peoples' organizations against established, as well as elected, authorities. But, more than this, ambiguity pitted conflicting views of
government, poverty, politics, strategies of change, and the status
quo against each other and touched very deeply into the belief systems
of those involved in resolving that conflict.

Floyd County, Kentucky was not exceptional in this regard. On
the contrary, it was typical of the stage upon which poverty strategies
were acted out and involved elements of the conflict that had been
seen previously in Syracuse, Chicago, New York, Oregon, Mississippi,
as well as Kentucky. The conflict that ensued was not unique to Floyd
County entirely. It is unique only in that it was much more visible
and had a specific cast. Yet, these actors played roles and represented
interest that were pervasive and ubiquitous: established and insurgent
power; the performance of the past and the promise of the future; the
adequacy and the inadequacy of the present; the values of ascribed
versus achieved status; primary relationships and contractual obliga-
tions; the dispensation of privileges or the achievement of rights; the
traditional mores and the encroachments of the outside, and so on.
All of these and more were the conflicts that surfaced in Floyd County
in resolving the strategy of its Comprehensive Health Services Program. These conflicts were not entirely new but became articulated,
recognizable, and divisive of a community and gave Floyd County a
look at itself that otherwise would have been avoided. Characteristics
of Floyd County, previously hidden, became revealed, and it is the
premise of this study that an examination of the conflict of Floyd
County will reveal to the nation lessons about herself hidden in the
"common sense," Lockian liberal American conception of poverty,

politics, and health. Aspects of present conditions become clearer sometimes when something great is attempted—such as the elimination of poverty—or when assumptions about the responsiveness of officials, the concern of authorities, and the adequacy of existing institutions are put to the test of democratic control and equality.

NOTES

1. Under the prevailing standards of poverty the cost of eliminating poverty in 1970 by direct cash payment to all those below the poverty level totaled $11.447 billion dollars. With a standard of $4,716.50, or one-half of the median income, it is reasonable to assume this cost would double or triple. See U.S. Bureau of the Census, Current Population Reports, Series P-60, No. 81 "Characteristics of the Low-Income Population, 1970" (U.S. Government Printing Office: Washington, D.C. 1971), Table K, p. 13. The calculation of this figure is a complicated task, which extends beyond the confines of this study. But a rudimentary calculation may be necessary to justify my assertion. The nonfarm figure of poverty for a family of four in 1970 was $3,600, some $1,116.50 below the suggested level of $4,716.50. The mean poverty family income deficit was $1,419 in 1970. By using a poverty standard of $4,716.50 the mean deficit becomes $2,535.50. This would increase the deficit for poor families from $7.85 billion to approximately $13.22 billion. The new figure for unrelated individuals would be roughly $6.5 billion. In addition to these increases, new deficits would be created by the increased number of poor people and the distance between their once not poor income and the new figure of $4,716.50. A rough approximation of this new deficit would be $4.6 billion. The aggregate of the amounts needed to eliminate gaps between incomes below $4,716.50 for a family of four or its equivalent would be roughly $24.32 billion, more than double the present figure of $11.447 billion.

2. Miller and Ratner describe how tax reforms could yield billions of additional dollars. See S. M. Miller and Ronnie Steinberg Ratner, "The American Resignation: The New Assault on Equality," Social Policy 3, no. 1 (May/June 1972): 11-12.

3. Donald J. Devine, The Political Culture of the United States: The Influence of Member Values on Regime Maintenance (Boston: Little, Brown and Company, 1972), p. 205.

4. Richard Parker, The Myth of the Middle Class: Notes on Affluence and Equality (New York: Liveright, 1972), pp. 10-14.

5. Ornati, in an early but still excellent study of poverty, developed this idea further. "To the extent that a little poverty is all right, so long as it happens to members—or even most members—of

certain groups, it reflects indifference. It may even reflect hypocrisy in people who with the next breath insist that America is a land of equal opportunity that any man can rise on his own." Oscar Ornati, Poverty Amid Affluence (New York: Twentieth Century Fund, 1966), p. 121.

6. Mollie Orshansky, "Who's Who Among the Poor: A Demographic View of Poverty," Social Security Bulletin 28, (July 1965): 26.

7. W. H. Locke Anderson, "Trickling Down: The Relationship Between Economic Growth and the Extent of Poverty Among American Families," The Quarterly Journal of Economics 78, no. 4, (November 1964): 512. See also Mollie Orshansky, "Counting the Poor: Another Look at the Poverty Profile," Social Security Bulletin 28, no. 1 (January 1965): 21.

8. Lester C. Thurow and Robert E. B. Lucas, The American Distribution of Income: A Structural Problem, a study prepared for the use of the Joint Economic Committee, Congress of the United States (Washington, D.C.: U.S. Government Printing Office, 1972), p. 7.

9. Joseph A. Pechman and Benjamin A. Okner, "Individual Income Tax Erosion by Income Class," mimeographed (Washington, D.C.: The Brookings Institution, 1972).

10. David M. Potter, People of Plenty: Economic Abundance and the American Character (Chicago: University of Chicago Press, 1954), p. 121. Also Louis Hartz, The Liberal Tradition in America: An Interpretation of American Political Thought Since the Revolution (New York: Harcourt, Brace and World, 1955), pp. 259-83.

11. Migration still is advocated as a "new factor" for Appalachians. Parker points out that the new factor responsible for the "affluence" of the middle class is indebtedness. Parker, The Myth of the Middle Class, pp. 4, 86, and 149. See also John Kenneth Galbraith, The Affluent Society, (New York: New American Library, 1958), p. 201.

12. Max J. Skidmore, Medicare and the American Rhetoric of Reconciliation (University: University of Alabama Press, 1970).

13. See Frances Fox Piven and Richard Cloward, Regulating the Poor: The Functions of Public Welfare (New York: Random House, 1971).

14. James L. Sundquist, Politics and Policy: The Eisenhower, Kennedy and Johnson Years (Washington, D.C.: The Brookings Institution, 1968), pp. 97-105.

15. Parker, The Myth of the Middle Class, p. 39.

16. Sheldon S. Wolin, Politics and Vision: Continuity and Innovation in Western Political Thought (Boston: Little, Brown and Company, 1960), p. 313.

17. Hans Peter Dreitzel, ed. Recent Sociology, No. 1: On the Social Basis of Politics (New York: Macmillan, 1969), p. xi.

18. Hartz makes the same point regarding apparent differences between the New Deal and its critics. Hartz, Liberal Tradition in America, pp. 259-83. See also Devine, The Political Culture of the United States, pp. ix, 62, and 231-86.

19. John C. Donovan, The Politics of Poverty, 2d ed. (New York: Pegasus Press, 1967), pp. 31-32. Moynihan calls the War on Poverty "a self-imposed concern and politically an optional one" for Kennedy. Daniel P. Moynihan, Maximum Feasible Misunderstanding: Community Action in the War on Poverty (New York: The Free Press, 1969), p. 24.

20. Parker, The Myth of the Middle Class, p. 47.

21. Kravitz, "The Community Action Program—Past, Present and Its Future," in James L. Sundquist, ed., On Fighting Poverty: Perspectives from Experience (New York: Basic Books, 1969).

22. Richard Boone, personal interview at Washington, D.C., March 31, 1972.

23. Lyndon Baines Johnson, The Vantage Point: Perspectives of the Presidency, 1963-1969 (New York: Holt, Rinehart and Winston, 1971), p. 74.

24. Richard Cloward and Lloyd Ohlin, Delinquency and Opportunity (New York: The Free Press, 1960), pp. 86 and 211.

25. Kenneth B. Clark and Jeannette Hopkins, A Relevant War Against Poverty: A Study of Community Action Programs and Observable Social Change (New York: Harper & Row, 1968), pp. 39 and 235.

26. C. B. Macpherson, The Political Theory of Possessive Individualism: Hobbes to Locke (New York: Oxford University Press, 1962), pp. 271-75.

27. Parker, The Myth of the Middle Class, p. 203.

28. Moynihan, Maximum Feasible Misunderstanding, pp. 102, 121-22.

29. For an earlier examination of this question see Peter Marris and Martin Rein, Dilemmas of Social Reform: Poverty and Community Action in the United States (New York: Atherton Press, 1967), especially pp. 52-54.

30. William Selover, "The View from Capitol Hill: Harassment and Survival," in Sundquist, On Fighting Poverty, p. 161.

31. Frances Fox Piven in Moynihan, Maximum Feasible Misunderstanding, p. xvi.

32. Sundquist, On Fighting Poverty, p. 3. For the history and formation of the OEO legislation, see Joseph A. Kershaw, Government Against Poverty (Chicago: Markham Publisher Co., 1970); Sar A. Levitan, The Great Society's Poor Law (Baltimore: Johns Hopkins University Press, 1969); Sundquist, On Fighting Poverty; and Donovan, The Politics of Poverty. For the shift in Congress see Sundquist, Politics and Policy.

33. Philip Selznick, TVA and the Grass Roots: A Study in the Sociology of Formal Organization (New York: Harper & Row, 1966), p. 2.

34. Ibid., p. 13.

35. Ibid., p. 261.

36. Ibid., p. 219. The transformation of TVA because of this informal co-optation has been described by James Bramscone in the pages of The Mountain Eagle. See for example, "TVA Says It May Own Its Own Strip Mines," The Mountain Eagle (Whitsburg, Ky) June 27, 1974, p. 1.

37. Ibid., pp. 63-64.

38. Ibid., p. 217.

39. The very genesis of OEO was marked by Johnson's compromises for congressional support, including top level personnel in OEO, grants for impoverished farmers, and granting the governors veto powers over OEO programs in their states. Compare Sundquist, Politics and Policy, p. 149; Moynihan, Maximum Feasible Misunderstanding, pp. 95-96; and Donovan, The Politics of Poverty, p. 36. Sundquist indicates that Yarmolinsky's racial policies earned him the animosity of the North Carolina delegation.

40. Polly Greenberg, The Devil Has Slippery Shoes: A Biased Biography of the Child Development Group of Mississippi (London: Macmillan, 1969), p. 28.

41. Donovan, The Politics of Poverty, p. 85.

42. Greenberg, The Devil Has Slippery Shoes, p. 603.

43. Robert Coles, "Rural Upheaval: Confrontation and Accommodation," in Sundquist, On Fighting Poverty, pp. 112-13.

44. Marris and Rein, Dilemmas of Social Reform, p. 230.

45. Idem.

46. Ibid., p. 69.

47. Sundquist, On Fighting Poverty, p. 152.

48. Devine, The Political Culture of the United States, p. 60.

49. Donovan, The Politics of Poverty, p. 146.

50. Louisville Courier-Journal, February 5, 1973, p. A-2.

51. Alvin J. Arnett in Bill Peterson, "Former Kentuckian Is Wielding the Ax on Poverty Programs," Louisville Courier-Journal and Times, February 25, 1973, p. E-1.

52. Selover, "The View from Capitol Hill," p. 180; Moynihan, Maximum Feasible Misunderstanding, pp. 132-35.

53. John Wofford, "Politics of Local Responsibility: Administration of CAP-1964-1966," in Sundquist, On Fighting Poverty, p. 98.

54. Sundquist, Politics and Policy, p. 152.

55. The legislative fate of OEO falls beyond the scope of this work. Excellent accounts may be found in Donovan, The Politics of Poverty; and Kershaw, Government Against Poverty.

56. See Moynihan, Maximum Feasible Misunderstanding, p. xix; and Edith Green, speech of November 7, 1967. (Mimeographed.)

57. Office of Economic Opportunity, Healthright Programs: The Neighborhood Health Center (Washington, D.C.: U.S. Government Printing Office, 1970), p. 1, also Hurley, "The Health Crisis of the Poor," in Hans Peter Dreitzel, ed. The Social Organization of Health: Recent Sociology No. 3 (New York: Macmillan 1971) p. 107.

58. Alonzo S. Yerby, "The Disadvantaged and Health Care," American Journal of Public Health 6, no. 1 (January 1966): 9.

59. U.S. Congress, House Committee on Education and Labor, Economic Opportunities Amendments of 1967, Hearings before an ad hoc task force of the Committee on Education and Labor, House of Representatives, on H.R. 513, 90th Cong., 1st sess., 1967, pp. 854-55. See also Hurley, "The Health Crisis of the Poor," p. 86.

60. Report of the National Advisory Commission on Health Manpower, vol. 1 (Washington, D.C.: U.S. Government Printing Office, 1967), p. 2.

61. Report of the National Advisory Commission on Health Manpower, vol. 2 (Washington, D.C.: U.S. Government Printing Office, 1967), pp. 34-36.

62. Nathan Glazer, "Paradoxes of Health Care," The Public Interest 22 (Winter 1971): 62-77.

63. Ibid., p. 77.

64. Hans Peter Dreitzel, ed., The Social Organization of Health: Recent Sociology No. 3 (New York: Macmillan, 1971) pp. vi-xiii.

65. Odin W. Anderson, Health Care: Can There Be Equity? The United States, Sweden and England (New York: John Wiley and Sons, 1972), p. 52.

66. Ibid., p. 65.

67. Clark C. Havighurst, ed., Health Care (Dobbs Ferry, N.Y.: Oceana Publications, 1972), p. viii. Theodore R. Marmor, The Politics of Medicare (Chicago: Aldine Publishing Company, 1973), passim.

68. Health Policy Advisory Center, The American Health Empire: A Report from the Health Policy Advisory Center (New York: Vintage Books, 1971), p. 189.

69. Marmor, The Politics of Medicare, pp. 86 and 90-93. Also Editors of Fortune, Our Ailing Medical Society: It's Time to Operate (New York: Harper & Row, 1969), p. 32. Anderson, Health Care, p. 98.

70. U.S. Congress, House Committee on Education and Labor, Economic Opportunities Amendments of 1967, Hearings, p. 849.

71. Macpherson, The Political Theory of Possessive Individualism, p. 220.

72. Ibid., pp. 272-76.

73. C. B. Macpherson, The Real World of Democracy (New York: Oxford University Press, 1972), p. 10.

74. Richard Lichtman, "The Political Economy of Medical Care," in Dreitzel, The Social Organization of Health pp. 265, 272, and 276.

75. Ibid., p. 267.

76. Ibid., p. 274 and also 272.

77. U.S. Congress, House Committee on Education and Labor, Economic Opportunities Amendments of 1967, Hearings, p. 849.

78. Ibid., p. 851.

79. Ibid., p. 848.

A NEW HEALTH PROGRAM FOR FLOYD COUNTY

Origins and Initial Planning

The initial development of the Floyd County Comprehensive
Health Services Program (FCCHSP) was, interestingly enough, outside of Floyd County. Early in 1967, John D. Whisman, Cochairman
of the Appalachian Regional Commission, called T. P. Hipkins, President of the Appalachian Regional Hospitals (ARH), and gave Hipkins
three pieces of information. First, OEO was looking for areas to
research and development health care techniques in rural settings.
Second, Floyd County, in Eastern Kentucky, was rural and certainly
disadvantaged enough to qualify for an OEO program. Third, there
was an underused Appalachian Regional Hospital at McDowell in the
south central portion of Floyd County.

After receiving Whisman's message, Hipkins enthusiastically
sketched a proposal for a program and submitted it to OEO, while
opening preliminary discussions with groups in Floyd County. As he
envisioned the program, it would be headquartered at the McDowell
hospital with outreach stations—at least three of them—in different
areas of the county. The program was to emphasize flexibility and
experimentation, as one of its subsidiary purposes was to test various
and new methods of health delivery systems. The keystone of the
proposal was the Patient Program Coordination Team, whose function
Hipkins put in these terms:

> The teams would provide early echelon service such as
> simple aid stations, family counseling, simple rehabil-
> itation counseling, simple screening, simple health

education, etc. at the outreach area. But perhaps more importantly, [the team] would serve as a referral and coordinating mechanism, and if you will, "interference runner" for the families for which they are responsible.[1]

What is important in terms of the future development of FCCHSP is that the team concept envisioned the provision of some medical care and especially the innovation of new services and arrangements, that is, outreach areas, to deal with the simple health needs of the poor. It was thought that these innovations would continue the ongoing evolution and development of new roles for health and health-related workers; because the proposal was tentative, the specifically envisioned developments and innovations were not enumerated. A budget of over $5 million for a five-year program was proposed.

One area that was not addressed at all was community involvement. Hipkins' proposal, submitted in March 1967, simply said of community involvement: "All items under the heading as listed in the Guidelines are being observed."[2] Actually, Hipkins tended to view the program proposed as an operation of the McDowell hospital, which had a citizen advisory committee that was sufficient, in Hipkins' estimation, to meet the requirements of community involvement. Floyd County residents, however, disagreed with him.

> When I had my public meeting in which I proposed this to what I thought was a representative group of citizens, they [the medical society members] were there and instead of shooting it down per se, I think they agreed that maybe some parts were good, but they didn't think the ARH should operate it; they thought the Health Department ought to operate it.[3]

Hipkins acquiesced in this request because to oppose it would be tantamount to confronting the Floyd County Medical Society, which held an indirect influence on the Health Department by approving the department's head and a direct one by the positions of several physicians on the Board of Health.

> I backed off and let it go to the Health Department rather than let it go down the drain completely. . . . I was trying to demonstrate I guess that I didn't have horns and I wasn't down there to change the world.[4]

Other Interventions into Health Care

Hipkins knew that as far as the medical society of Floyd County was concerned, he had some proving to do. "Our hospital and its physicians were kind of outsiders."[5] ARH was, in fact, the most recent of a series of incursions into the medical system of eastern Kentucky, and, as such, inherited the bitter opposition of the local physicians to the Miners Memorial Hospitals at McDowell—whose operation ARH had assumed after the United Mine Workers (UMW) had withdrawn.

The opposition of the local physicians to the UMW hospitals was reaction to the explicit criticism of the medicine practiced in Appalachia, which these hospitals represented. The Miners Memorial Hospitals were an attempt to provide the quality care that the Boone Report, conducted at the instigation of the UMW, had documented was not available in Appalachia.[6]

The immediate upshot of the Boone Report was to give John L. Lewis, UMW president, the momentum for achieving a Welfare and Retirement Fund in 1947 that tied UMW fortunes to the production of coal by assessing a levy of five cents for each ton of coal produced for the fund. A miner and his family could draw on the fund to acquire medical service and hospitalization without any cost to themselves. It was the belief of the fund's trustees that the infusion of money for health care would improve the facilities and attract new health professionals. But by 1952 it was obvious that the fund had aggravated the existing problem.

Despite the bellowing of the American Medical Association that the fund was a venture in "socialized medicine," many camp doctors promptly recognized the Welfare Fund as a gravy train. They climbed aboard with alacrity and plundered it with great skill. The empty rooms in their little hospitals were filled with beds and new cubicles were opened. Chronic ailments for which the patient had already taken bags of pills and gallons of tonics now required bed rest and hospitalization. Surgery was undertaken for trivial complaints. Bushels of tonsils, adenoids and appendices were removed. The "head nurse" at one of these establishments described the situation in her hospital in inelegant terms: "It's all a woman's sex life is worth to even walk through this place. It's got so the doctors spay every woman who comes in the door!" In their new found prosperity the overworked physicians had to find assistants. They cast about and came up with a motely assortment of doctors from other states and from foreign countries.[7]

The Boone Report had specified two problems that the fund had not remedied: the hospitals of the Appalachian area where by and large proprietary hospitals characterized by "small closed staffs" and inadequate facilities[8] and the area lacked new and young physicians. The problems were related:

> A primary barrier to young physicians is medical monopolies similar to those which tend to emerge in the coal-mining areas, especially where proprietary hospitals with closed staffs predominate.[9]

The UMW took direct action to remedy these problems in the early 1950s by constructing 10 hospitals—six in eastern Kentucky with one at McDowell—and recruiting personnel to staff them. The new facilities and staffs earned widespread praise and represented not only "the application of the principles of both modern business and medical science in the field of health care"[10] but also the failure of local physicians to do the same.

Local physicians also opposed the UMW hospitals because of the premise of the facilities regarding health care. As Harry M. Caudill states, it

> [The fund] presupposed that the industry should assume a moral responsibility for the men it maimed and the children of those it slew and attempt to maintain the health of miners and their families as a "fringe benefit".[11]

This presupposition ended a laissez-faire market attitude toward health care and inserted a third party into the traditional doctor-patient relationship. With some difficulty, physicians and health professionals were recruited from across the nation, resulting in an infusion of new professionals with a diversity of ideas. Their arrival cut off the local physicians from the fund and some former patients. Moreover, their presence represented a major innovation in health care in the mountains—the salaried physician. For these reasons, then,

> Many of the resident physicians deeply resented their new colleagues. Out of spite and envy they denounced the United Mine Workers' physicians as practitioners of "socialized" medicine, and in only one or two counties were they allowed to obtain membership in the county medical association.[12]

61

The UMW's medical effort lasted for less than a decade. Despite an increased levy of 20¢ a ton for the fund by 1952, the benefits accruing to miners were withdrawn slowly almost from the beginning. The disability pension was abolished in 1952 and by 1962 the UMW announced the closing of four of its hospitals in Eastern Kentucky, including the facility at McDowell. What had been such a promise of hope was now a bitter memory as the fund eliminated some benefits and tightly guarded the dispensation of others.[13]

The Floyd County Medical Society had long been antagonistic to the Miners Memorial Hospital at McDowell and had refused membership to hospital physicians. Even under ARH, the McDowell hospital physicians finally were allowed into the medical society only when they instituted a fee-for-service practice. This experience was not unusual in the experience of ARH, although the opposition in Floyd County was a bit more adamant.[14]

Floyd County's Needs

This was the historical context of Hipkins' meeting in Floyd County in April 1967 and the basis of his decision to back off rather than see his proposal abandoned. Hipkins accompanied Floyd County officials to Washington to signify his willingness to change the proposals and the grantee and delegate of the program. The group he accompanied included: Russell Hall, health officer for Floyd and Martin counties; Harry Eastburn, director of the Big Sandy CAP, which included Lawrence, Floyd, Martin, Johnson, Magoffin, and Pike counties; and Henry Stumbo, judge of Floyd County since 1949 and also a member of the Board of Health of Floyd County and the Big Sandy CAP. The group received assurances from OEO officials and Congressman Perkins that the changes in Hipkins' proposal that had been suggested by the medical society would be approved. Under the new arrangement the Big Sandy CAP was to be the grant's applicant, and its delegate ot administer the program would be the Floyd County Board of Health. ARH was now out of the program completely; the Board of Health proceeded to submit a proposal along the lines Hipkins had suggested within a three-week deadline, by May 1, 1967.

Along with this change of control in the program, the proposed budget was increased from $5.07 million to $6,842,663 and several changes of procedure were made as well. The Patient Program Coordinating Team was maintained, but the provision of even minimal primary service was no longer included among its tasks; instead,

the proposed project will simply make excellent health services more available to families in which the

motivation of the individuals to seek such services had
been diminished through cultural and educational circumstances, through social and economic misfortune,
and through having to use traditional or less than adequate services not designed to best meet needs of the
family.[15]

Devoid of outside influence, the program would seek to change the
motivation of the people of Floyd County and not its "excellent health
services."

There is little doubt that Floyd County qualified and still qualifies
in terms of poverty and health needs. According to the census of 1970,
34.9 percent of the families of Floyd County had incomes of less than
the poverty level. Of these families, 545 had incomes less than $1,000;
1,170 earned between $1,000 and $2,000; and 1,028 families earned
between $2,000 and $3,000. Unemployment was 10.2 percent; 46 percent of all persons over 25 had less than an eighth grade education;
and 55.7 percent of all housing in the county was termed substandard.[16]
These figures were all improvements over the 1960 statistics; yet,
in 1966, 465 of the 767 men examined by the Selective Service were
rejected, nearly 61 percent.[17]

The average infant mortality rate of Floyd County from 1965
to 1971 was 23.3; this compares with the Kentucky average of 22.2
and the national average of 21.8.[18] While the figure of infant mortality
does not tell all about a health system, the proposals for the first year
of the program assured OEO officials that the health care needs of
the poor in the county were much worse than even health professionals
knew. The proposal postulated that even the local health care personnel of long standing, "will be surprised by the true picture when all
the facts are uncovered about the real health status of indigents in
this county."[19]

Three central and unanswered questions still surrounded the
program. The first was the rationale of a health program as an antipoverty strategy. The proposal did not give a rationale for a health
program in combating poverty; it merely repeated some assumptions
that were considered self-evident and related health care to a market
model of maximum utilization.

It is proposed that health is one of the determinants of
poverty and that the improvements of the health status of
the family will be a major factor in permitting wage
earning individuals within the family unit to realize their
best potential for economic independence and social
growth. This assumption is considered self-evident.[20]

Exactly how health programs were to restore jobs to men who had been driven out of work by automation in the coal industry; how it was to provide skills and education to a population long devoted to an extractive economy no longer in need of their labor; how it was to attract industry to provide jobs—none of this was specified. It was assumed, however, that health programs would provide limited employment opportunities to some of the poor and training and career opportunities for others among the poor.

The second central question unresolved by the proposal concerned the adequacy of the program to meet the health needs of Floyd County's poor people. The proposal made very clear that part of the health problem was the inadequate service caused by the heavy case loads the doctors of the county already had and the time exacted from them due to their roles as community leaders.

> Often patients must wait for hours or even return another day in order to see a doctor. Many of our doctors see one hundred patients a day—can that be good service? This is in addition to their hospital case load of patients. Complicate this with lack of transportation, ignorance and inability to fill in medical forms and we find the poor very inadequately served on the whole.[21]

The proposed solutions to this already existing problem and to the yet unmet needs of the poor were transportation and education. People were to be brought to already overworked doctors, and they were to be educated as to the use of payment mechanisms such as Medicare and Medicaid. Similarly, education was to extend to the poor a recognition of the need for some medical attention regularly and on a preventive basis. In sum, the program was to teach the poor the need for medical care, how to pay for it, and then transport this newly created market to already overworked doctors. The program made no provision for direct medical services or recruitment of additional full-time physicians even though the proposal recognized a wide gap between need and services available in several specialities.

The final question unresolved by the proposal was the reason Floyd County was chosen. The number of doctors in Floyd County had fluctuated between 17 and 23 since 1967. This meant a ratio of 1:2,111 at worst and 1:1,560 at best, which is still twice as high as the national ratio of 1:750 but far better than some neighboring counties. Knott and Breathitt counties each had two doctors for populations larger than 14,000; Wolfe County had one physician for a population of 5,569. There was not one hospital in any of these three counties, while Floyd had three hospitals, 128 hospital beds, and one extended care facility.[22]

With these questions before it, it is probably with good reason that FCCHSP was funded as a research and development program. At the very least, it was in an ideal position to experiment in the formulation of health delivery techniques within areas with already existing facilities rather than in the creation of new facilities in other areas. Whatever the reasoning, the Big Sandy CAP received a grant of $469,715 for its delegate, the Floyd County Board of Health, during the first week of June, 1967, a short while after English's testimony outlining Neighborhood Health Centers before the House Committee on Education and Labor.

THE NATURE OF THE PROGRAM

Fulfilling Unmet Needs

FCCHSP was funded for three consecutive years with budgets amounting to $3,038,788. During the last year, 1971, the program received some additional $800,000 from OEO; but, two months after this grant, the program was suspended and much of the grant was frozen. At no time was any of the money spent for a one-stop, family-oriented health care center with the direct provision of medical care and from which outreach services such as nutrition, home nursing, and health education could be provided participants in the program. These kinds of services are what English described as comprehensive health in 1967, but OEO realized that rural areas might not have the facilities and services of urban areas and so "simpler, less comprehensive services" could be established at first, although even these rural programs "should be designed so that they may develop to provide full comprehensive services as resources and capabilities expand."[23] This development did not take place within FCCHSP and the program remained primarily a referral service.

Nurses working for FCCHSP were permitted to render very limited primary care. Upon written doctor's orders, nurses could change bandages, give certain injections, irrigate catheters, take blood pressures, give skin tests for tuberculosis, dispense worm medicine, and supervise bedfast paraplegics if seen regularly by a doctor. With their nursing duties specified and requiring written doctor's orders, nurses spent most of their time aiding the project's medical diector when clinics were held at the outposts and supervising aides who were enrolling eligible families and keeping records. The nurses also helped arrange appointments with the physicians of the county if a program participant was sick, eligible for treatment, and had some form of third-party payment. Requests for medical attention went to the central office and appointments with doctors were arranged there. If a person lacked a source of third-party payment, the program would pay the doctor's fee only on a "last dollar basis," that is, only in those cases where program participants had no other source of payment. In such a case the person was sent to the project's medical director or to the project director, who examined the person and decided whether the ailment was serious enough to warrant a doctor's appointment. In case of an emergency, this referral authority and authority to hospitalize were shared with the chief social worker and the field workers. Each subsequent appointment of the consumer required approval from the central office.

For those consumers unable to reach physicians for appointments due to a lack of transportation, transportation was made available by the program. As a local minister pointed out, transportation is a formidable barrier for many people in reaching medical services within the county.

> I think it's tragic that the program is now gone because
> it was ministering to many families that previously had
> only limited medical treatment. A lot of people in the
> hollers, for example, did not have transportation. . . .
> Sometimes if a man and his wife on a sixty or seventy
> dollar a month income, social security or something for
> example, they might have to pay twenty or twenty-five
> dollars for a visit to the doctor and medicine, plus trans-
> portation. Maybe a third or more of their income would
> be wiped out all at once. There are a lot of people who
> simply did not go to a doctor because of that, I'm con-
> vinced.[24]

It is common for a neighbor to charge holler residents without transportation five dollars for a round trip to the doctor within the county and more for trips of longer distance. FCCHSP saved participants this expense, as well as the fee for medical care and medicine. An important limitation placed on transportation provided by the program was that patients had to see a doctor in Floyd County. Patients had freedom of choice as long as the physician chosen was within the county. This was a problem for some of the people otherwise eligible for the program. These people lived closer to Pikeville than they did the towns of Floyd County, and consequently they always had "doctored" in Pikeville rather than with the more distant physicians of Floyd County. Because many poor persons preferred their physicians of long standing, they were ineligible for the program and its benefits. In addition to transportation within the county, free transportation also was arranged to special clinics and specialists in Lexington,

Lousiville, Ashland, and Huntington. Program participants also were provided transportation to the drug store of their choice in order to acquire whatever medicines might have been prescribed. OEO agreed to pay for medicine on a last dollar basis and provided $1.40 for the druggist for filling the prescription. Transportation had to be arranged by 3:00 p.m. the day before an appointment.

After a year of operation, the program acquired the services of one of the two proposed salaried dentists who provided direct dental service at the Mud Creek outpost. Previous to his arrival, all patients had been referred to local dentists; subsequent to his arrival, two-thirds of the program's participants continued to be referred and one-third of the participants were served directly by the program's dentist. Time and again the dental needs of the poor people were judged by members of the professional staff to be the most widespread of medical needs. Despite this, FCCHSP spent a year in recruiting a program dentist, and two additional years were spent in acquiring a second.

Aides at the outposts had a great deal of success in enrolling eligible families into the program considering the remoteness of some areas of the county and the problems of communication. By the end of the third year of the program, some 12,610 people out of a projected total of 20,000 eligible persons actually had been enrolled in the program. In addition to this effort, the aides made referrals for families to social and medical services; provided ancillary services such as conversation for the lonely and isolated; and often stretched the boundaries of the program to provide aid for distressed families.[25]

The outposts of the program hosted clinics on pediatrics, cardiac care, and maternal and infant care, as well as offering other services during the hours of 8:00 a.m. to 4:30 p.m. Emergency service was provided individually by a community aide, who acted as liaison with the team leader or the project's medical director to get approval for whatever transportation and medical care was needed.

The program also had other services that were incipient. Family planning and environmental health by the program's fourth year still were not fully implemented. On the other hand, nutrition lectures, homemaker services—women who would tend the home of a hospitalized wife or mother—and health education services were of limited scale and dubious value. The health educator, for example, focused on the drug problem in the area but did not mention the occurrence of intestinal parasites among residents of the county. One study revealed that 55.5 percent of 339 persons tested from a community of 375 had one to four intestinal parasites.[26]

One reason for this misemphasis, no doubt, was the experiential learning that the program's staff was undergoing regarding the nature and extent of the problems of people within their county. The first-year proposal had postulated that the true dimensions of Floyd County's health problems would surprise many people, even health professionals. As one aide who worked for the program commented:

> I lived here twenty-two years and I didn't know that there were that many crippled children. You don't know. You don't go up those hollers and cricks and so forth. I didn't know there were that many people in Floyd County in need of medical help. Course a lot of these hollers and cricks, I didn't know they existed. I knew the main highway, yes, but these other little places, I didn't know where they were, I didn't know where they're about.

Consumer input was supplied by the 12-member citizen advisory committee; four members of which were members of the Big Sandy CAP board and the remainder were representatives of the outposts. Official assessment of this board's functioning was lavish:

> The group is very good and we feel that community leadership is developing. It has been refreshing to observe their reasoning in making decisions and to note their keen insight into the problems faced.[27]

"Comprehensive Health Care" Redefined

At face value this board seemed a successful and necessary implementation of the spirit and letter of maximum feasible participation, but in other areas FCCHSP woefully lagged behind the requirements of a comprehensive health program. During the three years of operation there was very little evidence of any movement of the program toward the direct provision of medical care.

The problems that were discussed in subsequent program proposals and assessments portrayed the program as a referral mechanism. In this regard the program was afflicted with several shortcomings: a lack of adequate numbers of local providers of services, especially dentists and therapists; the lack of knowledge of health and welfare programs on the part of clients; the lack of adequate coverage by the state medical assistance program; the lack of sufficient methods of communication; and the lack of clients' ability to gain medical service unless covered by Title XVIII or XIX of the Social Security Adjustment of 1965.[28]

Other problems of the program were with the people it served. These problems necessitated a change in the people and the customs of the area. The isolation of the area, it was reasoned, fostered an attitude among the area's residents of fear of strange situations and also hindered the development of know-how in reaching needed services or programs. Likewise, illiteracy and the low educational attainment of the poor people prevented many of them from following through on methods of treatment or procedures to effect a cure or preserve health. That these latter two conditions should be mentioned as problems is evidence that the spirit of the Patient Program Coordination Team as an advocate on behalf of the patient had been lost. The standards of living and what seemed to be the unique values of the poor, rather than their unique needs, also seemed problematic as they supposedly contributed to an early acceptance of old age, the years of awaiting relief from life.

Some of the problems the program's administrators listed as handicaps were the very services they were supposed to be providing, a form of "blaming the victim." This list of problems included the poor personal and/or environmental health practices caused by lack of training and substandard environment; poor and meager nutrition; above-average birthrate; lack of preventive medicine; and even lack of comprehensive medical- and health-related services.[29]

None of the problems encountered and none of the weaknesses confessed reflected on the program itself. Some problems were attributed to OEO, such as the lack of a second dentist and of a sliding fee schedule to establish contractual arrangements with the local medical providers. Lack of such a schedule evidently led to great amounts of confusion in which doctors were being reimbursed with OEO funds on an "as charged" basis rather than a fee schedule as provided with other third-party payments. Because OEO offered reimbursements greater than other payment schedules for the same service, its funds soon lost "last dollar basis." Doctors, on the other hand, charged that despite the lack of a formal agreement OEO never paid more than 70 percent of a fee and, after the suspension of the program, settled its debts for services already provided for as low as 12¢ to the dollar. Despite its problems and some confusion the program was evidently quite satisfactory.

> We have as you may say "proved ourselves" and our
> program to our people. We feel this allows us to ask
> and expect even more cooperation. It also leads us to
> expect that we will have more success in health educa-
> tion with the indigent as we have their trust and confi-
> dence. There are many, many reasons to expect success
> during the coming year. WE ARE NEEDED—WE ARE
> WANTED—WE ARE DOING THE JOB.[30]

With great success pieces of existing facilities were being fitted into a network of services for the poor. OEO was functioning in much the same way as the UMW Welfare and Retirement Fund had functioned from 1947 until the construction of the Miners Memorial Hospitals, namely as an infusion of funds into a modified but unchanged medical system that qualified for the money because of its supposed short-comings. No competing facilities had been established, and criticism of the program remained unpublicized for two years. In other words, FCCHSP had become part of the "system," a term that Peter Schrag describes with specific meaning for Appalachia.

> [It is] a self-contained social mechanism isolated phys-
> ically and culturally form the outside world, although
> partially sustained by public funds for education and wel-
> fare that the outside world provides. Its elements in-
> clude chronic unemployment of an industrial population,
> a historic neglect of formal education, a lack of cultural
> capital, a political structure founded on family associa-
> tions and nepotism, an exploitative coal industry con-
> trolled by irresponsible absentee ownership, and increas-
> ingly, a tradition of dependence and helplessness . . .
> (A) "vast paleface reservation" . . . an area exhibiting all
> the signs of institutional dependency associated with peo-
> ple who have adjusted to a life where all decisions, and
> even identity itself, are determined by the keepers of
> the institutions.31

Indicative of much of the program's attitude was the observation regarding the reorganization of the hospital referral system, admit-tedly the weakest part of the program: "until we devise something better we must keep things status quo."

INTERVENING EVALUATIONS AND CRITICISMS
OF THE PROGRAM

An Outsider's View: The Sparer Report

OEO sent a site evaluation team to Floyd County in June 1968 to examine the program in its first minimal operations after nine months of existence. The evaluation team was made up of two expe-rienced medical audit members of the Columbia University School of Public Health and Administrative Medicine; a professor of surgery from New York University; and four OEO officials, two of them members of the Office of Health Affairs (OHA), a newly created branch of OEO. This team's criticisms, though couched in diplomatic terms, were very telling. The medical audit team surmised:

> This program is an opportunity to demonstrate the effectiveness of eliminating several of the major barriers to the receipt of services by needy persons in rural areas without making basic changes in the existing medical care system.[32]

Except for two surgeons in two different hospitals and occasional inpatient care, the quality of care provided was "very discouraging. . . It is difficult to concentrate on methods to increase the input into this system which has so little to offer."[33] The medical content of patient contact was reported as extremely poor with little effort given to a complete examination and minimum attention paid the attending complaint of the patient.

The appraisal team made clear that FCCHSP had not yet demonstrated its effectiveness. Part of the problem were the attitudes of those involved, including OEO—which was faulted for not making clear "the extent to which OEO grants can go in assuring the full continuous care of the patient."[34] The appraisal team also found confusion among the FCCHSP staff that paralleled the essential ambiguity of OEO, that is, the relationship of antipoverty measures and existing institutions and arrangements.

> The project staff does not appear to have a clear picture of what it wants to occur. Does it want to establish a focal point for the medical care processing for the poverty population of the community? If so, where does it want that focal point to be, at the project, at the nursing station, or at the office of the private practitioner? Does it want to provide more than episodic care for the patient and the family? If so, much more will need to be done in this area.[35]

Finally, the medical audit team cited the opinion of a Prestonsburg physician about the program, which the medical society largely had determined. Real progress in unfragmented health care would come, in his opinion, with the completion of the new Highlands Hospital, within which perhaps OEO doctors could be incorporated.[36] Obviously OEO was not viewed as a major innovator in health care but either as part of the old fragmented medical system or the "new" system that was still well within such traditional bounds as fee for payment, physician control, and episodic care.

In the opinion of the team the program was "quite short of expectations" in its purpose to treat sick persons who were poor.[37] For improvement the report urged a more flexible referral system and the direct communication between county physicians and project nurses. This would permit better information flow, it was assumed, and also break the monopoly of physician contact held by a few administrators in the central office.[38] The delivery system seemed unnecessarily complicated, overcentralized, and hindered by a lack of paramedical personnel who could deal with some of the ailments without a referral to a physician.

The evaluation team also recommended that the citizen advisory committee be given responsibility for hiring staff members in the future and that more attention be given hiring people from the target group of the program, since very few had been hired up to that time.[39] The citizen advisory committee was the vehicle of maximum feasible participation for the program, and, despite the program's intentions for this group and even the reports of its activities, the site evaluation team was dissatisfied with what they observed. One team member concluded: "It is readily obvious that there is no meaningful participation of the consumer in the conduct of the program.[40] As a matter of record, the committee had made two decisions in a nine-month period: to erect a sign directing patients to the Osborn outpost and to mandate that nurses should wear uniforms in the field.

One member of the evaluation team traced the cause of overcentralization to Helen Wells, program administrator. It was suggested her duties be specified and limited since so much of the dissatisfaction in the outposts stemmed from her exercise of regulatory control and discretion from the central office. Wells' part in the citizen advisory committee came under explicit criticism: "One has the feeling that she would not willingly give any real decision-making power to this group."[41]

This same evaluation team member also traced the lack of community participation to Harry Eastburn, director of the Big Sandy CAP. She reported a discussion with two members of the Appalachian Volunteers (AV's), a private antipoverty volunteer organization with some OEO funding, wherein the AV's suggested that effective community action had not and would not take place in Floyd County as long as Harry Eastburn controlled the poverty program of the area. This, according to the team member, was in part due to the personality of Eastburn: "Mr. Eastburn is an Alabaman, ex-army sergeant who runs his organization like a military unit, and also doesn't like to delegate authority to others."[42]

Observations such as these regarding Wells and Eastburn are indicative of what many local authorities in Floyd County and the Big Sandy CAP came to resent most about "outside" observers:

the length of their stay did not permit them to become sensitive to the source of their information. Comments often were made about the "Washington people" arriving in Floyd County in large rented cars; staying at the finest accommodations in the county; taking whirlwind tours of the project; sporting the very latest in eastern fashions; and then rushing out of the county to meet their plane back to Washington. This procedure kept them insulated from the problems of the programs and the county and offered little opportunity to understand the political nuances and intricacies of the county, Big Sandy CAP, or FCCHSP. Both sides of the conflict would criticize OHA for this.

In particular, their criticism of Helen Wells put the evaluation team on a collision course with FCCHSP because it viewed her as a dysfunctioning member of the program rather than the guardian of certain program objectives. Wells was literally present at the creation. The minutes of the Board of Health's April 11, 1967 meeting note that she took part in the explanation of the program to the people assembled, together with T. P. Hipkins and Harry Eastburn. Prior to FCCHSP, Wells had been involved with other antipoverty efforts, such as the VISTA program of the Big Sandy CAP. Although limited to Floyd County, the VISTA program ran into significant problems as the ban on communication between VISTA workers and AV's and the ban on community organizing in Mud Creek, a section of Floyd County, were not observed. The VISTA program soon lost favor and was dropped at about the time the health program was being initiated.

Despite the evaluators' criticism, by some standards Wells evidently was doing very well. Her position as program coordinator, which had not been mentioned in the first-year proposal, paid the highest salary of any full-time administrator. Both the executive director, Russell Hall, and his assistant devoted only 20 percent of their time to the project; therefore, for all practical purposes, Wells was in charge of the day-to-day running of the program. For her work during the three years of the project she drew an annual salary ranging from about $10,000 to a little more than $12,500. It would become evident later that an attack on Wells was an attack on the program's most powerful supporters and would precipitate a most bitter battle. The evaluation team, in its two-day visit, made the mistake of taking Wells as the root rather than the branch of the program's difficulties.

A Later Outsider's Appraisal: The Hentschel Report

Little less than two years after the evaluation team's visit, Glen Hentschel was sent from OHA to FCCHSP to provide technical assistance. His observations of the program in March 1970 indicate that the program had evolved solely into a referral agency, entirely within the ongoing medical practice of Floyd County.

Hentschel's report levied criticism on almost every conceivable aspect of the program, including its philosophy, which he interpretated as doing for the poor rather than the poor doing for themselves. As evidence he reported: no decision making board with any authority had representatives from the poor; the poor received little training except for nutrition classes—the health educators of the program spent little time working directly with the poor; and a lack of commitment to hire nonprofessionals from the target population was still obvious. In addition, the Board of Health had refused to listen to grievances of groups of poor people or their representatives—the CAA on Mud Creek, EKWRO, or VISTA. The hiring practices of the program were prejudicial not only to the groups of poor people but also to the achievement of the very services the program was established to provide. Only 20 of the nearly 100 employees of FCCHSP were from the low-income group, and, Hentschel reported, "there were reports that if a person wanted a job with FCCHSP, he had to have local political concurrence." This also applied to professional positions in the program left vacant as well: if "no persons with these specialities [were] available locally . . . the program management did not want to hire outsiders for the program."[43]

By this time, also, the circle of bureaucracy within the program was full-drawn: a program of public service became concerned with internal mechanism and devices and a confusion of goals was masked by tasks that consumed time but served little other purposes.[44] Evidence of this is in Hentschel's comments on the fetish the aides had for paper work and making out records—which took up two hours of their workday; however, "there were no apparent reasons for all the questions that had to be answered as the program was not utilizing the data collected."[45] Perhaps the paper work represented a goal displacement; while it increased, glaring irregularities of the program also increased or remained unabetted. One irregularity was the program's inclusion of people whose income made them ineligible for the program; a second irregularity was the continued reimbursement of physicians with OEO funds when patients were covered by other payment plans that paid less.[46]

Hentschel went on to point out several other shortcomings of the program in 1970. Little was done to affect the environmental conditions of the poor specifically because this was not felt to be part of the comprehensive health program. The location of some outposts were so remote as to make assess difficult. The family planning aspect of the program was very inadequate, featuring a practice unique in all of Kentucky: the project director required the signature of the husband of any woman who desired to participate in

the family planning program.[47] The Homemakers Service was likewise very poorly organized, and the very existence of the service
was unknown to many who could have used it. Indeed, the administrator in charge of this segment of the program did not know how
extensively it had been utilized. Hentschel also noted that the arrangement of office space within the outposts was such that no client was
afforded privacy in dealing with social workers or the medical staff.

In contrast to these deficiencies, Hentschel pointed out some
excesses of the program. The salaries of the personnel of the program seemed very high for a rural health program; in Alinsky's
terms, lieutenants were drawing generals' salaries.[48] The fringe
benefits the employees enjoyed were the most liberal set this Washington official knew of: seven-and-a-half-hour workdays; 10 legal
holidays; two 15-minute breaks; absences due to acts of God such
as snow, sleet, floods; an automatic 5 percent of the annual salary
given toward retirement, claimable upon leaving the program; work-
man's compensation; social security; 12 days annual leave; and 12
days sick leave.

Many of the defects of the program already were known to OEO
from previous evaluations. Hentschel, however, also brought to light
new criticisms, one of which, the conflict of interest of the physicians,
was to become a very important issue.

> The Board of Health . . . the delegate agency, is com-
> posed of the county judge, one surgeon, one dentist, one
> nurse, the wife of the state representative, two physi-
> cians and the county attorney. The physicians are re-
> ceiving fee for care of the program's consumers, while
> establishing policy for the program. This resulted in
> the rule passed by the board that no recipient can be
> served by a physician who does not practice in Floyd
> County.[49]

As has already been pointed out, this decision necessitated longer
trips for patients in outlying sections of Floyd County, such as Mud
Creek; it also meant that some poor persons were ineligible because
they preferred their Pikeville doctor. This decision also meant over-
flow crowds in the offices of the doctors in Prestonsburg who, if we
are to believe the description of need in the program proposal, were
already overworked. Hentschel observed, "Physicians in Prestonsburg were seeing up to one-hundred people per day," a situation that
had prompted the program's proposers to ask in their first budget
request: "Can that be good service?"

Appalachian Politics of Relief

The impetus to Hentschel's assignment to FCCHSP can be traced, almost directly, to the testimony of the Republican governor of Kentucky in 1969, Louie B. Nunn, before the House Committee on Education and Labor. This committee, chaired by Representative Carl Perkins—a Democrat who has represented Kentucky's Seventh District, which incorporates Floyd County, since 1948—heard Nunn make specific references to FCCHSP to illustrate alleged abuses of OEO programs in Kentucky.

> Here in Floyd County there is a health program. . . .
> There was $1,358,354 that was granted for the program.
> And do you know what went directly to the poor for medi-
> cal and dental care, according to the figures available to
> me? $382,250. This took approximately $1,000,000 to
> get $382,250 into the hands of the needy. . . . The point
> I want to make, it seems to me, sir, with all of the help,
> all of the poor people, that we have in Kentucky that we
> do not have to spend $1,000,000 to get them a mere
> $382,250 worth of medical care.[50]

The testimony of that morning session is remarkable for the exchange of charges, between Nunn and Perkins, of intimidation, violence, patronage, and partisanship. Heated exchanges between the governor and other committee members, as well as between the chairman and members of the committee, punctuated the meeting and vented the emotions of just about everyone there concerning the material at hand and the procedures of the hearing. Governor Nunn resented the fact that the bill about which he was testifying already had been reported out of committee in a hurriedly called early morning meeting that very day and some committee members sympathized with him. Nunn and Perkins—two astute politicians—knew full well that they were exposing the cornerstone of Appalachian electoral politics and more than likely all electoral politics; this may account for the heat generated by their exchange.

An aide to Governor Nunn, who helped prepare his testimony, explained OEO's role in partisan political terms.

> The political system [in Eastern Kentucky] is probably
> comparable to a fiefdom. . . . There's no solidity
> through the whole structure—one individual or one
> family controls. It's like a consortium of various chiefs
> and clans, they join together for their own benefit. This
> is reflected in the elected leadership that stays on and on.

For instance, the county judge there [Floyd County] he's a strong man, and I feel on his own; his strength lies in his ability to bring together a preponderance of political power. This is done through several means, not the least of which is the largesse of the Federal Government in terms of poverty programs, which, quite frankly, serve as a sop, as a palliative. This goes back to conceptualizing OEO as a New Deal, which is more in line with LBJ's experience when he was dealing with rural poverty in Texas. Mountain people see it as such: a type of chicken-in-every-pot program. Mountain politicians lean toward Johnson much more than they did Kennedy. They saw OEO come in as they had seen CCC and WPA. Jobs are handed out. Why the Floyd County health program, all the job applicants in 1968 (we had stacks of them) in sifting through them, nine out of ten of them were initialled by a person, I shan't name, but who is close kin to the county judge.

Perkins has never bought or advocated change factors of OEO. He doesn't see the need; he doesn't understand—you know—that change can be good. It's threatening to the base he continues to maintain his support from. He talks in terms of "taking care of my people." You would think, poor people—that's an incidental factor—because other people are capable of delivering the vote of poor people. That's what he depends on. Why the mother of woman who headed the CAP agency in Breathitt could deliver 2,500 Democratic votes at election time, like you lay your billfold on the table. So he saw he was threatened by it. He, being a good congressman, had annually delivered in some of his counties, $900 a year on a per capita basis.[51]

The implication that OEO had become a new New Deal had a special meaning in Kentucky politics. The relief of the New Deal not only made Democrats out of some Republicans—previously Republican, southeastern Kentucky since 1930 has been represented by a Democrat for all but one term—but also it created a political machine to make regular Democrats out of New Deal Democrats.[52] The catalyst in this latter transformation was the 1938 campaign for the Democratic nomination for the U.S. Senate between incumbent Alben Barkley and Governor A. B. "Happy" Chandler.[53] The machines created in this election maintained their strength, and in counties already Democratic before the New Deal, like Breathitt and Floyd, the Democratic organization was a formidable power.

Floyd County, for example, had been Democratic since the Civil War, but Democratic votes jumped to 70.3 percent for the elections from 1935 to 1944 compared with 58.5 percent of the vote in the elections of 1920 to 1932. Nearby Breathitt County experienced a similar increase in Democratic strength, 62.1 percent to 70.6 percent. Breathitt and Floyd counties became Democratic citadels within the New Deal tradition. The strength of the Democratic organization of Floyd County was demonstrated between 1944 and 1966 with 69.5 percent of the votes in general elections going to Democrats.[54]

The irony of this strength was that its base was the economic weakness of Floyd County and the dependence of its population upon relief programs of the government. Political machines traditionally have been linked to dependent groups, such as immigrants, and have dissipated when the population becomes less dependent, either by the development of other systems of relief or upward social mobility. There are few avenues of upward mobilization in mountain counties. Evidence of this is the large outmigration during the 1950s and 1960s.[55] These individuals that ordinarily would have formed a middle class did so only by leaving the area. Hence, the machines of these counties were unchallenged by an independent indigenous middle class. Further, a stagnant employment picture, creating greater demand for relief and outmigration, aided the political organization of the mountain counties as long as the relief arrangements could be controlled and exchanged for votes.[56] The extended families and close kinship ties often meant up to 20 or 30 votes for an important favor.

The import of Governor Nunn's remarks is clear; eastern Kentucky was receiving large sums of OEO money that, under the control of the Democratic organizations in some counties—like Floyd and Breathitt—were turned into the political currency of patronage. The dividends accrued to the poor, certainly, but also protected existing political strengths, especially those of Carl Perkins.

Congressman Perkins remarked that his coming campaign for re-election would be enhanced greatly by Nunn's technicians and their charts showing the disproportion of poverty funds to his district; "None of my people up there feel I am doing this type of job." Nunn retorted, "Your people know well what you are doing up here. They are Mainliners [employees of Operation Mainstream] now."[57] Perkins later charged Lynn Frazer, Kentucky's OEO director, with using OEO technical assistance money to gain affadavits from Operation Mainstream workers alleging political use of antipoverty funds.[58]

The relation of poverty programs to existing political organizations was not unique to eastern Kentucky and had been made plain by the experience of CDGM and the passage of the Green Amendment. Most often, however, the relation had been criticized by poor people who felt politicians were unduly interfering with their program[59] or by politicians who felt poor people had gone to excess. But here were two politicians exchanging charges that touched the heart of eastern Kentucky politics. One other differentiating factor of the political implications of poverty programs in this instance was the direct influence that Perkins had over OEO as chairman of the House Committee on Education and Labor.

This influence was not overlooked by the Kentucky governor, and although Perkins denied, strenuously, any interference with any OEO program or any influence peddling on behalf of his district, Nunn insisted:

> You don't have to [use influence] because you have every-one in OEO taking a hand for you. . . . Ask the investi-gator who went to Kentucky to do the investigation if he did not make this statement, "Everyone in Washington knows that Carl Perkins is the best friend that OEO had got and we are not going to kick our best friend in the teeth."[60]

Perkins acted in his defense by calling the three directors of the CAP programs that had been criticized in Nunn's testimony. This proved particularly unfortunate in the Floyd County case. Chairman Perkins ended up sheltering his old friend, Russell Hall, from members of the committee and leading him through questions that were not particularly difficult or penetrating. In some cases, the chairman actually provided answers to questions put to the witness.[61]

Despite, or because of, an apparent lack of preparation, informational gaps, and misinformation, the committee learned enough to be incredulous. One committee member was particularly impressed by the fact that the project director, Russell Hall, spent 20 percent of his time on the OEO program and the remainder of his time was spent on the public health program of two counties with one-tenth the budget. Statistics offered to the committee showed the enormous proportions that the referral portion of the program had reached. In the four-month period July-August 1969, 743 persons had been referred to private dentists; 1,775 had been admitted to hospitals; 8,190 had been referred to private physicians; and 4,443 prescriptions had been filled. Not one mention of the direct provision of medical care was made.[62]

Perkins' congressional position inevitably made him an important variable in the calculus of OEO and FCCHSP; for some people, Perkins' position explained the selection of Floyd County for a health program in the first place. An OHA staff member recalled the influence of Perkins at OEO: "Every problem in Floyd County eventually reached Perkins and when he called here, the building shook. . . . Eventually he saw the light and said, 'Just do what's right.'"

OHA Intervenes

It would appear that the light came to Perkins just about the time of Nunn's testimony. A Perkins aide verified that Perkins told OEO to "check 'em out," and the result was a site evaluation from December 2-5, 1969 by the University Research Corporation. The evaluation was prompted and financed by OEO and produced the kindest official evaluation the program was to receive. The problems of the program were attributed to its experimental nature and its uniqueness among OEO ventures. Some suggestions as to reorganization, new personnel, adjustment of salaries, rearrangements of personnel were made, but on the whole the report was very optimistic. The future appeared promising because the staff saw the potential of the program and seemed anxious to cooperate and work toward the program's promise.

This evaluation placated some and would be used later in defense of the program against renewed attacks. But more positive measures were needed despite the report and this need was widely recognized. It finally was expressed in the appointment of Hentschel in March 1970 as a technical assistant for reorganization.

Hentschel discovered conditions to be worse than OEO realized or than the incredulous House Committee on Education and Labor had been led to believe. An audit for the period from August 1, 1969 to July 31, 1970 showed that the program had underspent its budget of $1,364,990.25 by $1,320.27. It had overspent its allotment for patient care by $289,685.45. Simply put, $641,935.45 went to doctors, dentists, pharmacists, and hospitals for fees instead of the allotted $352,250. On the other hand, money had been saved on salaries of employees, especially those hired late in the year or not hired at all. In this category were a dentist, a dental hygienist, a dental assistant, several community aides, a speech therapist, a hospital referral aide, a transportation aide, and drivers. Money had been saved on other items as well. Of the given allotments, the following sums remained unspent: $5,592 of $7,000 for medical and health supplies; $5,072 of $8,000 for dental supplies; $29,003 of $53,200 for vehicles; $13,548 of $15,000 for corrective appliances and devices; $3,015 of $3,600 for postage; and exactly one-half of the $36,000 for rental of office space.[63] If the expenditures of a program speak of its priorities, then indications were that FCCHSP was moving relentlessly to a strictly referral system. This simply verified what the medical audit team had pointed out two years previously, "The design of the program is the strong desire on the part of all involved not to interfere with the existing patterns of medical practice."[64]

Hentschel's presence indicated that change was to be fostered at OEO's insistence. Even before Hentschel's arrival, however, there had been some indications of a felt need within the county for change within the program. The Board of Health—delegate of the program—desired independence from the Big Sandy CAP—the program's grantee—and discussed this at a joint meeting on February 24, 1970. The conflict revolved about the Big Sandy CAP's control of the funds of the program. The Floyd County board felt that control of the purse was control of the program and the threat of withholding funds was an intimidating factor akin to total control. They insisted that the Big Sandy CAP's only responsibility was to audit the program. Harry Eastburn countered that the responsibility of the Big Sandy CAP was to monitor the program. His concern had very valid aspects to it in that his agency was ultimately responsible for a program that was, it was becoming clear, a poorly administered one. Yet, he was reluctant to simply let it go and make the Floyd County group grantee. There was a matter of status at stake: without FCCHSP the Big Sandy CAP would lose nearly 25 percent of its size. The FCCHSP was the largest single program the Big Sandy CAP administered, and the future of the CAP agency was enhanced by continuing dependent relationships with agencies, not fostering independence. The continuation of poverty programs and the increase of other programs was always tenuous at best, and hence the future was best guaranteed by preserving the status quo in the face of a fickle future. One member of the Floyd County Board of Health pointed out other reasons for the CAP's continued control over the funds of the health program, which involved a conflict of interest: O. T. Dorton, president of the Citizens National Bank of Paintsville, was also financial officer of the Big Sandy CAP, and the OEO funds were kept in his bank in Paintsville.[65]

The confusion was compounded by OEO's position. Up until October 1969 there had been two health agencies within OEO. At that time the health concerns of OEO became the responsibility of the OHA. That office placed an emphasis on having separate corporations, apart from CAP agencies, run the health programs. Eastburn related to the Floyd County health program as just another program under his CAP agency, which in turn was under the regional office in Atlanta. But comprehensive health was no longer under CAP on the national level, it was a national emphasis program and had direct ties with the newly created Office of Health Affairs in Washington. Eastburn obviously did not welcome the intrusion of Washington officials in what appeared to him as essentially a local problem under the jurisdiction of the Atlanta regional office. Very important, also, the Washington-directed national emphasis status of OHA was significant of OEO's early criticism of existing institutional arrangements and advocacy for change, a criticism and advocacy that neither the Big Sandy CAP nor regionalization had ever demonstrated.

The meeting was divided over the question of separation, and action on the question was postponed. But Judge Henry Stumbo voiced the growing opinion for independence in words that would have haunted him a year later had they been recalled. "If the people of Floyd County can't run the program, they should not be entitled to the program."66

By July of 1970 the FCCHSP had spent over $3,000,000 in three years in becoming a referral program with few signs of becoming anything more. Now under pressure from the outside as well as unavoidable evidence of maladministration, change was inevitable for the program. OEO refused to refund the program for its fourth year, 1970-71, and thus made change necessary. As submitted the grant proposal was unacceptable and a list of remedial measures to be taken was returned to county officials. These recommendations included changes in the administration of the program, specifically a new Board of Directors. This board was to pass on new rules for the internal management of the program to be submitted by the new administration. Glen Hentschel was to act as representative of the OHA and was named interim full-time director of the program. Procurement procedures, job descriptions, and personnel policies were to be established. A new project director, medical director, and administrator were to be hired by the delegate agency, and final approval for these measures rested with the OHA.67

OEO was in a position now of fostering change according to its OHA guidelines or acquiescing to existing arrangements. This choice relates to the fundamental ambiguity of OEO. It chose here to seek its own preference in conflict with a local program and to use its control to develop a program in conformity with its wishes. In this particular case the result was not conformity. The cost of a health program in conformity to OHA regulation required changes unacceptable to some in Floyd County. This group was able to make its influence prevail in maintaining their values at great cost to the health program.

NOTES

1. Letter from T. P. Hipkins to John M. Frankel, Director of Health Division of Community Action Programs, March 9, 1967, p. 1.
2. Ibid., p. 3.
3. Interview with T. P. Hipkins, Lexington, Ky., March 14, 1972.
4. Ibid.
5. Ibid.
6. U.S. Department of Interior, Coal Mines Administration, A Medical Survey of the Bituminous Coal Industry (Washington, D.C.:

U.S. Government Printing Office, 1947), p. vii. [Hereinafter referred to as Boone Report.]

7. Harry M. Caudill, Night Comes to the Cumberlands: A Biography of a Depressed Area (Boston: Little, Brown and Co., 1962), p. 296.

8. Boone Report, pp. 191-93.

9. Ibid., p. 193.

10. Horace Hamilton, "Health and Health Services," in The Southern Appalachian Region: A Survey, edited by Thomas R. Ford (Lexington: University of Kentucky Press, 1962), p. 227.

11. Caudill, Night Comes to the Cumberlands, p. 293. While this is not tantamount to asserting health care as a right, it does make health care more than an individual concern and lays out social and economic responsibility for the health of some.

12. Ibid., pp. 298-99.

13. The demise of the fund, according to Caudill, was fostered by the excesses and fraudulent demands coming from miners and non-miners, especially in the early 1950s. Ibid., p. 300. But Caudill wrote before the abuse of union funds and mismanagement of the fund was well-known. For information on this aspect of UMW affairs, see Bill Peterson Coaltown Revisited: An Appalachian Notebook (Chicago: Henry Regnery, 1972), pt. 1. See also Thomas N. Bethell, Conspiracy in Coal (Huntington, W. Va.: Appalachian Movement Press, 1971).

14. Hipkins interview.

15. Floyd County Health Department Proposal Submitted for Program Year A, (Prestonsburg: 1967) p. 5H.

16. U.S. Department of Commerce, Bureau of the Census, 1970 Census of the Population: General Social and Economic Characteristics, Kentucky, vol. 1, pt. 19.

17. Proposal Submitted for Program Year A, pt. 2, p. 2.

18. Kentucky Department of Health, Vital Statistics, 1971. Floyd County's average disguises the great fluctuations in the infant mortality rate from 28.6 in 1971 to 14.9 in 1967.

19. Proposal Submitted for Program Year A, p. 5H.

20. Idem.

21. Ibid., p. 18F.

22. Figures provided by Kentucky Blue Cross and Blue Shield.

23. Office of Economic Opportunity Guideline: Healthright (Washington, D.C.: U.S. Government Printing Office, 1970), p. 8.

24. As was mentioned in the Introduction, statements taken from interviews in Floyd County will not be cited to preserve confidentiality. Statements concerning the program that are part of the public record will, of course, be cited.

25. "Quarterly Report Summary of Program Coordinator, (October-December 1969)" in FCCUSP, Proposal Submitted for Program Year D, (Prestonsburg, 1970).

26. John Vry, "The Floyd County Comprehensive Health Service: A Rural Health Program in Eastern Kentucky," unpublished paper, College of Medicine, University of Kentucky, 1969, p. 4.

27. Floyd County Health Department Proposal Submitted for Program Year B, (Prestonsburg: 1968), p. D-8.

28. Floyd County Health Department Proposal Submitted for Program Year C, (Prestonsburg: 1968), no page number.

29. Ibid., pp. B-1 and B-2.

30. Ibid., p. B-8.

31. Peter Schrag, "The School and Politics," in Appalachia's People, Problems, Alternatives, compiled by People's Appalachian Research Collective, vol. 1 (Morgantown, W. Va.: PARC, 1971), p. 376. Also reprinted in Appalachia in the Sixties: Decade of Reawakening, edited by David S. Walls and John B. Stephenson (Lexington: University of Kentucky Press, 1972), pp. 219-24.

32. Site Visit Appraisal of Floyd County Comprehensive Health Services Program, June 20-1, 1968 (Washington, D.C.: OHA, 1968), p. 2. [Hereinafter referred to as the Sparer Report.]

33. Ibid., p. 48.

34. Ibid., p. 1.

35. Ibid., p. 4.

36. Ibid., p. 59.

37. Ibid., p. 65.

38. Ibid,, p. 4.

39. Ibid., p. 17.

40. Memorandum to Jerry Sparer from Bonnie Britton, p. 5.

41. Ibid., p. 5.

42. Ibid., pp. 5-6.

43. Ernest Glen Hentschel, Exit Report from STAP Assignment with FCCHSP, mimeographed, p. 1. [Hereinafter referred to as the Hentschel Report.]

44. Crozier, in a very original way, describes the apparent dysfunctions of bureaucracy in terms of internal adaptation. Michel Crozier, The Bureaucratic Phenomenon (Chicago: University of Chicago Press, 1964), pp. 187-94.

45. Hentschel Report, p. 2.

46. Ibid., p. 2.

47. There was a type of precedent for this moral intervention by medical care; prior to the UMW Fund, miners were not permitted care for venereal disease under most prepayment plans. Such ailments were termed "misconduct infections." Boone Report, pp. 122 and 131.

48. Saul Alinsky, "The War on Poverty—Political Pornography, The Journal of Social Issues XXI, (January 1965) pp. 41-47.

49. Hentschel Report, p. 4.

50. U.S. Congress, House Committee on Education and Labor, Administration and Conduct of Antipoverty Programs, Hearings, 91st Cong., 1st sess., November 6 and 13, 1969, pp. 3-4. [Hereinafter referred to as Hearings, 1969.]

51. Harry Caudill has vividly portrayed the politics of relief in Senator from Slaughter County (Boston: Little, Brown, and Co., 1972).

52. Caudill, Night Comes to the Cumberlands, p. 212.

53. Malcolm E. Jewell and Everett W. Cunningham, Kentucky Politics (Lexington: University of Kentucky Press, 1968), pp. 6ff, also p. 195. See also Caudill, Night Comes to the Cumberlands, pp. 208ff.

54. Jewell and Cunningham, Kentucky Politics, pp. 194-95.

55. James S. Brown and George A. Hillary, "The Great Migration, 1940-60," in Ford, The Southern Appalachian Region, pp. 54-78.

56. See Tony Dunbar, Our Land Too (New York: Vintage Books, 1971), pp. 170-84, for the experience of Clay County, Kentucky in this regard. Concerning Mingo County, West Virginia, see Huey Perry, "They'll Cut Off Your Project": A Mingo County Chronicle (New York: Praeger Publishers, 1972); and K. W. Lee, "Mingo County," in People's Appalachian Research Collective, Appalachia's People, pp. 325-31.

57. Hearings 1969, pp. 24-25.

58. Ibid., p. 30.

59. Perry, "They'll Cut Off Your Project," pp. 106, 233, and 247. Kenneth B. Clark and Jeannette Hopkins, A Relevant War Against Poverty: A Study of Community Action Programs and Observable Social Change (New York: Harper & Row, 1968), p. 240.

60. Hearings, 1969, p. 30. See also John C. Donovan, The Politics of Poverty, 2d ed. (New York: Pegasus Press, 1967), p. 87, for OEO's reluctance to act to change HARYOU because of Adam Clayton Powell.

61. Hearings, 1969, pp. 287-303 and 388-97.

62. Hearings, 1969, p. 288. The critical reader may wisely doubt these statistics since the sheer logistics of transporting this many people during this time period would be incredible. It may well be that the figures related to the entire two year history of the program. They are included because Hall emphasized in his testimony that they were for a four-month period and because they give evidence of the volume of the program.

63. Audited Financial Statement and Other Financial Information August 1, 1969 to July 31, 1970. Lawton Ray Allen, CPA, Prestonsburg, Ky.

64. Sparer Report, p. 57.

65. Minutes of the Special Meeting of the Floyd County Board of Health and Representatives of the Big Sandy CAP and Washington OEO, February 24, 1970, p. 5.

66. Ibid., p. 7.

67. Letter to Harry Eastburn from Donald Pugliese, Chief, Program Operation Planning, July 30, 1970.

4

EKWRO AND THE ORGANIZED POOR

A New Beginning of Maximum Feasible Participation

The wheels of reorganization began turning very quickly after
OEO refused to fund the FCCHSP for its fourth program year. A
meeting concerned specifically with reorganization was held in Prestonsburg on August 13, 1970 and included members of the Board of
Health, the Big Sandy CAP, Lynn Frazer of the Kentucky OEO office,
and representatives from OHA. John Burton, assistant to Harry
Eastburn, director of the Big Sandy CAP, chaired the meeting.

There were indications at this meeting that the wheels of reorganization would move only along a path indicated by the already
acknowledged leaders of Floyd County. Both George Archer and
Joe T. Hyden offered vociferous opposition to the newly proposed
Board of Directors. Specifically they objected to a member of the
Big Sandy CAP being on the FCCHSP board; a member representing
the ARH, since the ARH McDowell hospital was only one of the three
in the county; and the number of consumers on the board. Eight
consumers, one elected from each outpost, it was felt were too many,
especially in the light of the CAP's own criteria of one-third target
group representation. They offered further objection to the absence
of either a doctor or a dentist on the proposed board.

Archer was a recognized community leader, three times elected
mayor of Prestonsburg, and very influential in the medical circles
of the area and the state. In the past Archer had been head of the
Floyd County Medical Society and enjoyed up until his death, on July
12, 1973, an informal role as dean of that association. In addition
to his achievements within the county, Archer had achieved statewide

prominence, having served one term as president of the Kentucky Medical Association and as a trustee of his alma mater, the University of Louisville. At the reorganization meeting, Archer made references to his "Washington connections" several times, seemingly an allusion to the link he had with Representative Perkins. On this August evening in 1970 he was protecting the interest of the group he was most closely associated with and let his influence be known. He pointed out to the members of the meeting that the success of any program hinged upon the cooperation of local medical practitioners. He warned that the services of these practitioners would not be provided, as far as he was concerned, unless changes were made in the proposed board of directors.[1]

Changes were made. The eight consumer representatives were maintained, as were the representative of the Big Sandy CAP, the county judge, a representative from the Department of Economic Security, and one from the Department of Child Welfare. In place of a representative from ARH, a representative of the hospitals of the county was placed on the board. Also, the school superintendent, previously excluded, was to be a member of the board, as well as several other representatives of community organizations including: the nursing society, the ministerial association, the dental association, the medical society, and organized labor. The board was expanded at its first meeting of August 20, 1970 to include a minority representative, a black, who CAP guidelines would insist retaining, even though the black population of Floyd County numbered 193 persons. Shortly after this meeting, the board was again modified to include a member of the Floyd County Pharmaceutical Association, formed on the evening of August 20, 1970. This member of the board replaced the Child Welfare representative, who never took a seat. Also at the meeting of August 20 the Eastern Kentucky Welfare Rights Organization (EKWRO) petitioned the board for a representative.

EKWRO's Views and Achievements

Most members of EKWRO are long-time residents of the county, predominantly from the Mud Creek section of the county. The size of that membership is a widely disputed figure. Critics of the group claim it represents a tiny minority of people of Floyd County and assess its number at 150 people, many of them supposedly Pike County residents. EKWRO's self-assessment is substantially different. In 1972 it claimed 400 or 500 dues-paying members and up to 1,500 to 2,000 supporters.

The dispute over its size does not diminish the fact that EKWRO's presence, in the short time of its existence, has been felt. Indeed, disputes over the size of EKWRO were always linked to its legitimacy to participate in the numerous controversies it was embroiled in. As its name implies, EKWRO is a self-help organization of welfare recipients and associates. The organization is premised on ideas very similar to Paine's political theory, as the constitution of EKWRO illustrates.

> Now and in days gone by . . . forms of aid have been used to control the people. First by giving aid not according to need, but for political purposes; second, by humiliating recipients so that they believe they deserve no rights. We want an adequate income that gives people that receive it the same rights, freedom and respect, that all Americans are entitled to.
>
> We believe people are poor because in this generation and in the generations past, they have been denied equal opportunity. In Floyd County and Eastern Kentucky, this happened when coal companies bought the land and mineral rights for as low as fifty cents an acre even though they knew the true value.
>
> They set up political institutions like coal camps, company stores and schools that would protect them and not the people. The result of this exists in the present day.
>
> The resources of our nation should be used to correct these injustices of the past and to give adequate income, education and <u>health</u> to Americans whose kin have died protecting this country and whose men have given their health and lives for the growth of the industrial might of this nation.[2]

With the beliefs that public relief is designed to manipulate the poor rather than serve them and that poverty has social and economic roots rather than being merely individual or cultural pathology, it should not be surprising that EKWRO's adversary role for the poor would put it in a series of confrontations with the agencies of public service, such as the schools, the hospitals, and local, state, and national governments regarding their dealings with the poor. The gains that EKWRO takes credit for include an advocacy program on behalf of poor people with the Welfare Department of Kentucky and a centralized water system replacing the system of individual wells that has had a very important influence on the health of the area. Two other achievements are recounted in detail below because they are indicative of EKWRO's ability to lobby, to mobilize other poor people, and to confront existing authorities and arrangements.

One of the biggest issues we ever tackled was the school lunch program. . . . Why we had two or three families that would be on school lunch programs right before elections and then they would be cut off. They made kids sit on the stage and study while other kids were eating in the lunch room. They smelled the food, you know, it'd get the kids discouraged about going to school at all. They just had millions of problems. . . .

Stuff like that went on and on until people finally decided to go down to town to see what could be done about it. When they went down, they found out that they didn't even have a school lunch program policy. So they asked for a policy to be written up and they just had hundreds of grievances. So they went back, about sixty people, to speak with Charles Clark [school superintendent]. He was standing there at the door with all of his people with ball bats and helmets and all that. He wouldn't talk to them. He just simply refused to talk. He wouldn't admit us or let us come in. He wouldn't do anything. It wound up in a fist fight and they arrested one of our people, worked him over. . . . We just had a long fight. We ended up having a school lunch program and one of the best school lunch policies in the state. . . . But it was a helluva fight.

Oh, I forgot, another thing we did. We had a terrible old rickety bridge that they had to let the children off the bus and the children would walk across the bridge and then the bus would come after them. As a matter of fact, during the summer they put up a sign saying that the bridge was restricted to cars and pickups. Then they finally said, "My gosh, school starts next week, we can't do that." So they forced the state highway department to take the sign down and made the children walk back and forth. We petitioned everybody on Mud Creek three times. We went to see the governor to get the money appropriated to build a bridge. Now we got a good concrete and steel bridge. That would never had happened if it wasn't for Mud Creek people and welfare rights groups. This big old bridge was up and there were holes in it and people were scared to death. A dog would walk across it and it would shake and you'd have to back off and let the other person on, it was ridiculous. We got every name on the Creek from Ligon on down on that petition. I don't know a single person that didn't sign it.[3]

EKWRO, in its four-year history, also has functioned as an alternative system of relief. It has sought to meet the immediate needs of some poor who are ineligible for relief programs or unable to wait for the bureaucratic process to deal with them. It also has functioned to make agencies and government more responsive to the poor in terms of relief programs and black lung compensation.* EKWRO members feel they have succeeded even if they have not received sufficient credit. "The poor people in this part of the country is getting out and doing the politician's job."

EKWRO also has acted in a manner similar to a labor union, creating a bond among some poor who recognize common ties and grievances and articulating their grievances face to face with authorities who are at once viewed as the source of their problems and their remedies. EKWRO leaders and rank and file recognize their resemblance to a labor union and the necessity of organizing their own numbers to secure benefits, their rights, and even their names.

> When I was working, I was a strong union man because I know the company; they'd fuck you over if they got the chance. People they've got to stick up for what's theirs, if they don't they'll never get a thing. When you're in compensation you can be a "thing," or an "it," or a "him." But when you're working and paying taxes you're "sir" or "mister."
>
> The only way people can have a voice, the only way EKWRO has ever had a voice, is being together, being organized being able to bargain with different agencies. They were unhappy with comp health, school lunches — they bargained. In the beginning they struggled just like the unions did to get together. I think that's where we stand now.[4]

EKWRO is recognized within and outside of the county as unique in the usual distribution of power and influence within the county.

---

*The black lung compensation program is designed to provide some financial security for coal miners disabled by pneumoconiosis or, in case of death, for their widows and children. The program has been criticized by EKWRO and others for its reliance on x-rays as a testing method and for the delays often encountered in processing claims. Criticism is also leveled at the role played by professional attorneys in the claims process and the exhorbitant fees charged by these people. EKWRO has been part of the attempt to provide lay advocates, instead of attorneys, for black lung victims.

Perhaps more than unique, EKWRO's philosophy and militancy in tactics has made it an uninvited factor in the poverty industry of the county and also unwanted by those customarily in charge. As one state official described it,

> They're some well-meaning people in EKWRO and some revolutionaries. I don't use that word in the same connotation as Mr. Hoover, the late Mr. Hoover, might have. But there ain't any other damn way to lay it out, except in terms of the present political and social structure, they're revolutionary as hell.

The radical nature of the efforts of EKWRO stems from the contrast of its demands and tactics with the taken-for-granted values and attitudes of those in power. This is made clear by a professional once connected with the program.

> It [FCCHSP] really wasn't a very good program, and there was little they [EKWRO] could do that was wrong in trying to change it. They may have gone too hard and too fast, but who is to say. All they wanted was equality and recognition by the rest of the county—that's not so radical. It is for the establishment that is used to controlling them.[5]

EKWRO offered a new interpretation of the poverty of the area as well as new methods for dealing with poverty and the poor.

> I think the outstanding cause of poverty in Floyd County is that it is controlled by a few people. Those people say they want industry to come in and that they want to see poor people struggle out of poverty and all that. They don't want that. They oppose everything from a wet vote to industry coming in. They encourage people to up the prices on their land when industry tries coming in or they have always been for the company. I think it's just a few people keeping the majority down. They want to keep the people under control so that they can always make sure that you vote right. If people had different jobs and incomes, there might be different mayors and officials and all that. I think it is just the power structure keeping the people down. You see there are very few people benefitting from the money and they keep that to keep the power and to keep the other people down. You see they don't want people out of poverty because then you wouldn't be obligated to them.[6]

The Organized Poor and Politics as Usual

The concept of an organized independent group of poor people ran counter to the essence of Floyd County—and perhaps Appalachian—politics, which evidenced many of the classic characteristics of the political machine.[7] The vote-getting ability of Floyd County Democrats is formidable and is one source of county officials' strength in dealing with elected state and national officials. The 1972 results show McGovern carried only one county outside of the Seventh District. Floyd County, part of the Seventh District, gave him—a relatively unpopular candidate—55.7 percent of the vote and the largest plurality of any county in Kentucky—1,515. Likewise, the Democratic candidate for the U.S. Senate received his third largest plurality, 4,596 votes, from Floyd County; this was 13.5 percent of his statewide margin of victory. He garnered 68.1 percent of the vote of Floyd County, while his statewide total was only 51.1 percent.

The ability to produce votes in these proportions depends on patronage, high rates of unemployment, and extended families. Because jobs are scarce, patronage jobs are still lucrative, and the holder of such a job can induce a large number of kin to express their gratitude at election time. High rates of unemployment and poverty also make welfare benefits a necessity and place many people in a position of dependence on county government as the real or supposed source of relief benefits.

This dependence can be transformed into votes, but what must be made clear is that not all Appalachian "machines" use their position for personal aggrandizement or fortune. Judge Henry Stumbo of Floyd County is a man of modest means despite over 20 years in office, and like "bosses" in other areas he is more a power broker than a power himself. Another point to be made clear is that machines often functioned as the sole agency of relief. As Peter Schrag points out, the Turner machine of Breathitt County and others similar to it have been benevolent bosses, without whom things might have fallen apart.

> At a time when Appalachia was out of the national consciousness and the mountaineer was a figure for mythology and amusement, the Turners did what they could for their people. The quid pro quo was patronage and power.[8]

EKWRO represented to the machine of Floyd County what the middle class emerging from second generation immigrant families once represented to urban machines, a threat to their base of power—a dependent and unorganized poor population. Especially if they could gain control of poverty programs organized groups of poor would rob

93

the political machines of a portion of their strength—relief and service for the poor—while gaining it for themselves. Further, just the capacity to organize themselves represented the potential threat of their creating an alternative set of institutions, whether they be grocery stores or health services, and establishing alternative practices such as higher wages, cooperatives, or salaried physicians. This was clearly seen in Breathitt County, where OEO was and is guided by the Turner family. In Floyd County, the Big Sandy CAP has by and large played a supportive role to existing arrangements. The VISTA volunteers, the most disruptive element of the Big Sandy CAP, were introduced only briefly in Floyd and never into the surrounding member counties of the Big Sandy CAP.

Some of the poor recognized the potential of their organizing and controlling the poverty programs. Huey Perry, CAP director of Mingo County, West Virginia, explained the implications of organization and control by poor people for his county.

> Now the poor could organize for the purpose of destroying the Noah Floyd [state senator] political machine and attempt to replace it with a county government that would be responsive to their needs. . . . The strategy was to direct the energies of the poor away from development and implementation of federal programs, which normally treated only the symptoms of poverty, toward the building of a political base from which the poor could attack poverty itself.[9]

The power of such groups as EKWRO was limited, however, since it was not completely separated from the political arrangements it opposed. What power such groups had came from the rhetoric and ideology of OEO and the mandate for "maximum feasible participation." But this dose of traditional democratic participation ran contrary to party structure and the mechanics of electoral politics. The CDGM had illustrated this, and the Mingo County poverty program is a chronicle of reluctant bureaucratic cooperation for a food cooperative, threatened suspension of funds for politically embarrassing demonstrations, political maneuvering at the congressional level for control of the local poverty agency, and an FBI investigation.[10] Awareness of its fundamental limitation came gradually; in the meantime EKWRO members proceeded as if with congressional approval and a belief in what they considered and were told were fundamental American values.

EKWRO's political participation created further friction. An important characteristic of machine politics is its personal nature,[11] a characteristic dominant in Appalachian politics.

Relationships between elected officials and the people
were expected to be personalistic and friendly, like relationships within the family, rather than impersonal, objec-
tive and specific to an issue. Favoritism of a govern-
mental employee in an official capacity toward his own
family at the expense of others was understood as a loyalty
more or less to be expected and, hence, tolerated as a
fact of life in the mountains.[12]

Politics in the Appalachian counties remain an informal and primary
relationship and are among the least affected social relationships of
the changing times.[13] When charged with nepotism for hiring his
nephew for the FCCHSP, Judge Stumbo replied that he only regretted
not having more kin to give jobs to.[14] EKWRO's politics stood in
sharp contrast to this informal, personal political style vis-à-vis
the county judge and relief agencies. Its emphasis was on the accountability of county officials, rather than trust, and the achievement of
the rights of poor people, rather than the favor of those in power.

EKWRO, a New Kind of Poor

EKWRO's style of organizing and mobilizing poor for the poor's
own benefit is not altogether unfamiliar in a region that prides itself
on self-reliance and that can recall the struggle for unionization of
the coal mines. But EKWRO's style contradicts what many Floyd
County residents think about politics, especially the more powerful,
just as it contradicts their thoughts about poor people. The culture
of poverty as prescribed by the nonpoor not only specifies the limits
of income and standards of living but also which characteristics the
poor are expected to demonstrate. The chief element of the culture
of poverty is acquiescence, according to Murray Edelman.[15]
But acquiescence is not a characteristic of EKWRO; consequently,
EKWRO is not viewed as representative of the poor, as we shall see
more fully later. The contrast of EKWRO's militancy with the subcultural values ascribed to Appalachian poor explains in part EKWRO's
difficulty in achieving a wider base of support. EKWRO shared with
these other poor people the stigma of being poor but differed in their
behavioral adaptation to this stigma. Erving Goffman suggests there
are two modes of dealing with a stigma such as poverty: the first
is to accept the norms others use to define you and regard others,
not yourself, as the category relevant to realizing and practicing that
norm; the second is to alienate one's self from the community that
upholds the norm or not to develop any attachment to it in the first
place.[16]

The definition of poverty and the strategems for antipoverty presumed we could fight poverty and maintain our beliefs as well; but not all poor people shared this assumption, and acquiescence gave way to articulate alienation such as in EKWRO's case. OEO had experienced this before, such as Shriver's embarrassment before the convention of poor people in April 1966;[17] the discovery of dissatisfaction was always startling, especially in light of the consensus of attitudes toward poverty and the acquiescence of the poor. Pointing out OEO's experience, Clark and Hopkins note,

> The poor as aggressors or as rude initiators of action, unresponsive to benevolent control, ungrateful and distrusting, and even violent, are less appealing to indulgent political leadership than the humble and apathetic poor.[18]

In addition to this, EKWRO was the sort of passionate movement that Kennedy had assured his Yale audience was not necessary to the solution of administrative and technical problems.

EKWRO's departure from the traditional and established views can be assessed by contrasting the interpretation of poverty offered by a professional of Floyd County, who also is a member of the FCCHSP Board of Directors.

> This has been a mining area since the early 1900's and coal mining is—it's not a very dependable source of economy. It's seasonal. There have been long strikes. Even during the hey-days of the coal business here in Floyd County, there were seasons. The best paid men in the valley, coal miners, were laid off for long periods of time. And of course up to the last three or four years the coal industry was just about wiped out. There is a lack of diversified industry here, you're either a miner or a oil or gas worker, or in the service agencies, banks, merchandise outlets. And when the timber is gone and the oil and gas supply is depleted and the demand for coal is gone, you're bound to have poverty. And I think it is significant in this connection that the uncertainty of employment with what industry we did have has led to a horrible outmigration. For instance, Floyd County between the 1960 census and the 1970 census lost 12,000 people going to areas where they could find reasonable dependable employment—Ohio, Michigan, Indiana for factory work.

The causes of poverty appear as "out there," beyond the control of men. There is no mention of the responsibility for this poverty, as in EKWRO's assessment, and the only remedy mentioned is the unacceptable but inevitable outmigration. Another professional in Floyd County, and board member of the FCCHSP, explicitly individuated the causes of poverty: "Laziness, they don't have the damn guts to get up and make a living." From this viewpoint EKWRO appeared as "professional, professional—how shall I say it?—at the art of receiving any funds that's on a give-away program."

Leaders of EKWRO have had to deal with pejorative views of their organization and its activity. They explain the pejorative view as a defense mechanism.

> You notice that when they call a person professional poor that they're talking about people who know their rights and who are capable of dealing with them on their level. They call us folks professional poor because we're able to stand up and ask for our rights. Any time you question the power structure who are controlling the people you get called some kind of name. You know they go to Washington and they see some federal money and they put up the prettiest story in the world. And they get a bunch of federal money in their pocket, the power structure does, but the people, the people, half the people never hear of it. They never hear of these programs.[19]

EKWRO's role in the FCCHSP controversy should be placed in this context of preceding actions and consequent attitudes. Its role was colored by the perceptions of those it had already tangled with, some of whom were already on the newly organized board of which EKWRO was critical.

EKWRO members complained that the election of the Mud Creek representative had been planned by the administrators of the FCCHSP.[20] The poor people were not consulted about the procedure for the election and were not even admitted to the original site of the election because of an injunction—stemming from an altercation with the school superintendent—against some EKWRO members going on any school premises for any purpose. The health program administrators agreed to temporarily suspend the court injunction for the election, but EKWRO insisted that they did not have this power. The fact that program officials believed that they did have power to suspend a court injunction indicated to EKWRO the interrelatedness of the health program's administrators and the people EKWRO had previously confronted. The site of the election was changed, and Helen Wells, program coordinator and de facto chief administrator of the program, conducted the election.

EKWRO members who were there felt that Wells "was clearly not sympathetic to Mud Creek residents." Nominations were accepted hurriedly and without sufficient explanation of the procedure that stipulated that a five-member board was to be elected for the outpost and that one member of this board would be elected to represent the outpost on the Board of Directors of FCCHSP. Many persons did not understand that there would be five separate elections for each position and that a person could be nominated only for one position. Thus, several EKWRO members were nominated for the same position on the board. Wells refused to cancel the nominations after the misunderstanding was brought to her attention.

Several EKWRO members sought to decline the nomination and eliminate competition among themselves but were overruled; only one EKWRO member was successful in withdrawing his name from only half the ballots. As it turned out, votes for him were not counted at all. When another member of EKWRO was nominated for a three-year term, it was determined that she was eligible for only a one- or two-year term, and her name was placed on the ballot for a one-year position that had three Mud Creek residents—all opposed to the present program's administration—already running. Meanwhile, on another ballot for a similar one-year position, Oliver Hall, "long the leader of political opposition to Mud Creek poor people," was unopposed by any of member EKWRO.

EKWRO also complained that transportation aides who brought poor people to the meeting passed out papers with slates of candidates that program administrators wanted to see elected. Nelson Mainstream men, it further was alleged, were told by their boss, Oliver Hall, that they had to be at the meeting; and it was implied that they had to vote for the approved slate of candidates. The voting was not secret, which led to intimidation, and the ballots of the illiterate were checked off in violation of their preference and in favor of the people running the meeting and their candidates. Two administrators of the Nelson Mainstream programs were elected to the outpost's board, and another member of the "slate" of approved candidates was elected representative to the FCCHSP Board of Directors.

When EKWRO sought to explain the election irregularities and to present substantiating affidavits to the Board of Health—then still the directors of FCCHSP—its members were not admitted into the meeting. A grievance committee was set up by the board to hear EKWRO's charges only after the election already had been declared valid. On August 5, 1970 some 200 Mud Creek residents and EKWRO members met and elected Eula Hall to represent them on the board of directors of the FCCHSP, which was contrary to the results of the former election.

It is important not to overestimate the strength of EKWRO. It is one group from one area of Floyd County where one of the eight outposts of the health program was located. Its active membership was no more than several hundred people mostly located in the Mud Creek area, which had a total population of approximately 6,000. But it is important, on the other hand, not to underestimate EKWRO. At the time it was the only group of its kind in Floyd County and perhaps the most active group of its kind in eastern Kentucky. It had wide sympathy among nonmembers in the Mud Creek section of the county and access to legal and technical assistance from resident professionals of the county.

When the petition to give EKWRO a seat on the new Board of Directors of the FCCHSP was made to the new board on August 20, 1970, a motion to deny the petition was made by Charles Clark, school superintendent, seconded by the county judge, and passed.

> The general consensus of the group was that the county had been properly represented to the board and citizens from Mud Creek section were represented. It was believed that all present act in the interest of all sections of the county and the representation of these groups was not necessary.

Similar reasoning was offered when a motion to seat a black representative was made. But it was pointed out that CAP guidelines would be violated, and approval of the program jeopardized, without a black representative. A black representative was shortly thereafter appointed.

The decision by the board to deny EKWRO a seat confirmed EKWRO's fear that the newly reorganized program, like its predecessor, would be run for the poor by those who supposedly knew their interests best.

ARNOLD SCHECTER AND THE OUTSIDERS

Proposals for Change

A budget to finance a program very similar to what had preceded the reorganization of the board was drawn up and approved by the finance committee of the newly organized board. This budget was brought before the full board at their October 15 meeting, at which time the board also was introduced to Arnold Schecter, the recently hired, full-time project director. He informed the board that OHA had assured him of a 60-day extension of the 90-day period, already elapsed, so that he could reorganize and prepare a budget. After some discussion a motion was made, seconded, and passed to accept the 60-day extension to give the new project director the time to submit new ideas and work up a budget for a new program.

Schecter had ideas for a far more comprehensive program than the proposed budget described. Floyd County seemed an "ideal laboratory" to try some ideas he had concerning health care delivery. More than a laboratory for new techniques, Schecter saw the opportunity to bring such proven techniques of emergency care to Floyd County as helicopter evacuation, which Schecter had had experience with during his days as an army flight surgeon. Helicopters also would facilitate moving key people around within the county, or a multicounty area. Given the shortage of trained medical personnel, the ability to move available professionals around quickly would increase their effectiveness in reaching people. In addition to moving personnel around, Schecter proposed to deal with the shortage of manpower by the use of nurse practitioners, paramedics, and even closed circuit television.

His ideas received a cool reception within a program beset by internal disarray and external criticism. While Schecter was trying to win support for ideas far more innovative than the program had ever experienced, the program was existing on time borrowed from OHA and was threatened with collapse because of past failures. Nonetheless, Schecter's suggestions forced a far-reaching examination of the program by providing alternatives to old practices.

Schecter was selected as project director in August 1970; when he arrived on October 11, 1970, he found that the program's offices had been moved from Prestonsburg to Wheelwright at the southern end of the county. Prior to the reorganization, the Board of Health had provided over $8,000 of in-kind support annually to FCCHSP by supplying the program office space within the Health Department Building. But now the fiscal court was supplying $13,650 of in-kind support for office space for the health program in Wheelwright.

Wheelwright was a model coal town dating from 1930 and originally owned by Inland Steel Coal Company. By 1970 its population was seriously depleted due to the decline in mining, and the town, far removed from other populated sections of the county, fell into disarray. The fiscal court provided Mountain Investments, Inc., the realtor in charge of the town, with much-needed revenue, and it provided the town with additional reason for being, that is, it became headquarters for the county's comprehensive health program. This arrangement, while it had its benefits, was not satisfactory to Schecter.

The location was unbelievably remote, unbelievably remote. It was impossible, even though I worked a sixteen
hour day routinely, seven days a week, to communicate
with the rest of the damn county to say nothing of the Big
Sandy CAP. . . . Judge Stumbo made an interesting comment when I went to speak to him. He said, "Those people
in Wheelwright helped elect me in the last election and I
promised them we would move there." So we were making
the town, really, for Mountain Investments.[21]

Despite this disadvantage of distance, Schecter moved quickly
to try and implement his program. An alternative budget of $2.9
million was drawn up and circulated among board members. This
budget contained allocations for closed circuit television in one outpost, for a helicopter evacuation service, and for the salaries of nine
new physicians. In addition to the physicians, the budget provided
for the employment of medical student externs, nurse practitioners,
lawyers, a nurse for family planning, technical assistants, a pharmacist, and an increase in the nursing staff as well as two additional
physician's assistants.
    Schecter also almost immediately began recruiting doctors for
the program, as a prerequisite for any improvement in the quality
of care. In addition, he felt that only by recruiting people from the
outside who were attracted to the program that he envisioned could
morale among physicians and program staff be kept high enough to
both do the job and overcome whatever local opposition might develop.
The recruitment ads that Schecter used stressed the innovative aspects
of the program and appeared in publications from Chicago to New
England. Despite the difficulty in recruiting for a rural area as remote as Floyd County, Schecter's efforts reaped 30 responses, 10
of which he considered good in that the respondents were both qualified
and available.
    However, it must be recalled that Schecter was proceeding
along these innovative paths while the rest of his program lagged
behind in such fundamentals as the financing of the program-even
as previously conceived-and getting a budget together before the end
of the second period of grace from OHA. Schecter now acknowledges
that his strategy might have been wrong. Having little experience in
working with community groups, Schecter was presuming that he could
win acceptance for his ideas after they had been established.
    Poverty in Floyd County had the same tabula rasa appearance
to Schecter as American poverty did to Shriver and the OEO planners
during the frantic days of preparation in 1964. Further, Schecter
shared the new class faith in administered solutions and its view of
problems as "technical." Schecter's clean sweep approach extended

to ridding the program of staff with whom he was dissatisfied. He was convinced that many of the staff were doing far less than their salaries would warrant and was dismayed by the incompetence of some important staff members and the appearance of patronage in their appointment; he worked his staff very hard and as a consequence received several welcomed resignations.

Schecter was advised to slow down, to not try to do the whole thing at once. Friends pointed out that it made little sense to recruit doctors for clinics not yet constructed. Even members associated with EKWRO feel in retrospect that Schecter was trying to achieve too much too soon. Those among the elites who would later oppose Schecter were put off by his manner early, especially by the scale and speed of his efforts. One board member bitterly opposed to Schecter in the end recounted,

> Because I was anxious to have the program succeed, be-
> cause I saw its potential, I had made it a point to give the
> benefit of my experience and my knowledge of social prob-
> lems and so forth, here in Floyd County to any person who
> was attached to the Comprehensive Health Program and I
> made it a point to speak to the last director [Schecter].
> Perhaps it would serve his service and the program to an
> advantage if he didn't try to move too fast. I suggested
> that if I were going from Eastern Kentucky to Chicago to
> get involved in a special program that affected people
> there, I would spend some time visiting all the people in
> the community, in the area to be served, to become famil-
> iar with what's gone before with a view towards making
> my efforts more meaningful and more successful. Now,
> he didn't listen to me. In six weeks he had completely
> alienated the fiscal court of Floyd County against my
> advice; and in another three weeks he had completely
> alienated the medical association, the local Floyd County
> Medical Association. At this point the two most powerful
> groups in Floyd County were opposed to him and his ideas.

Schecter was not unaware of his growing opposition, but he maintained his confidence because he felt he had the backing of OHA and that they had real power. This was an easy mistake to make, since it was part of the early OEO ambiguity that to effect change on the local level traditional levels of authority and inadequate institu-tional arrangements might be by-passed and challenged. This was changed of course by the Green Amendment and probably was never true in the practice of OEO, especially in the Big Sandy area. The confusion was compounded by the reorganization within OEO and the direct links between Schecter and OHA. The direct communication he enjoyed with OHA and the encouragement he received for his ideas—surplus helicopters were located for his medical evacuation program—led him to assume that responsibility for the program rested with him and that OHA had the power to enforce and implement the policies it was encouraging him to introduce.

It took Schecter some time and bitter experience to realize that OEO would not or could not back him up, and without this support he soon became the archetypical unwelcome outsider in the eyes of the local authorities.

Change and Threatening and Beneficient Outsiders

The county and its officials had had experience with outsiders like Schecter throughout the antipoverty decade of the 1960s. In that decade, spurred by the voluntarism encouraged by the Kennedy image of participation in government and national service, many people had come to Floyd County in search of poverty and meaningful involvement to eradicate it.

The activities of these antipoverty groups were not entirely welcome within the county. The AV's, for example, made attempts at community organization in the Mud Creek section in the early 1960s and helped form Community Action Council 979, named after the main highway running along Mud Creek. When this local council asked the Big Sandy CAP for VISTA volunteers to work within the Mud Creek section, five volunteers were sent on the condition that they were not to work or have contact with the AV's and were not to engage in community organization efforts. After the AV's were defunded and the VISTA program was phased out of the Big Sandy CAP,[22] their efforts left an attitude and an organization that officials still resent. According to one county official:

> Their intentions may have been good, but the young people were leading without knowing the full story. They found some people who were poverty stricken and they started the old idea that simply because you're an American—an American citizen—you're entitled to all the fruits of American society. They forgot to mention that you should put an effort forward on your own. It was as if they were saying to the poor, "There are fifty dollar bills growing on each tree if you know just exactly how to get them off. Pie in the sky!—You're entitled to it because you're an American without any effort on you part.
> It appears they explained the lack of these things as the fault of those people in Prestonsburg, the establishment,

who were denying them these things. The school system
and the county officials were in cahoots to keep these people ignorant and illiterate so they would be more amenable
to manipulation.

These young organizers quickly were labeled "outsiders," a term
that designates more than a relationship of geography. The significant
meaning of the term is in the conformity of a person's thought and
action to the expectations of those with whom the person is dealing.
A physician at McDowell put it this way:

> Outsiders are those who have no ties, no plans, or inten-
> tions to stay in this area. They go around telling people
> what's wrong. I was an outsider I guess coming from
> Knott County but now I'm an insider. It depends on the
> context you're in. A person from New York is not an
> outsider to EKWRO. It depends who you're with and
> talking to and what you're talking about.

Outsiders are sometimes distinct and stand out in sharp relief
to others whose names, faces, behavior, dress, and beliefs have been
assimilated within Floyd County for as long as any one can recall.
The outsider also is resented sometimes for assuming that difference
is a measure of superiority or for his/her reasons for coming to
Floyd County.

> They come down here from New Jersey, Minnesota, from
> New York, from Boston, and they look around and they say,
> "Wooooeee! Here is poverty." They are as elated as Co-
> lumbus must have been.

The stigma of outsider most often is applied with greatest ardor
to those not in conformity with the world view or cultural premises
of the people who stand to garner the most benefits without change
or who have most to lose from change outside their control. Thus,
a distinction is made among those coming from outside of the county.
Some are seen as having a chip on their shoulder for the "establishment" when they arrive in the county. One member of the clergy in
Floyd County lamented the tremendous force for good that was lost
to the people of eastern Kentucky because many outsiders did not
join efforts or share concern with the establishment. Other elite
members complained frequently of outsiders who come in and survey
and study the people, "measuring the size of their heads, but who would
benefit the area much more if they were to leave one new outhouse
behind them as a record of their efforts."

On the other hand, there is a category of beneficient outsiders, such as the federal funds financing the cost of the hospital under construction in the northern portion of Floyd County. Again, two professionals, members of the FCCHSP Board of Directors and opponents of the threatening or meddling outsider, are deeply endebted to Alice Lloyd, a woman from Boston, who established a school of higher education in Knott County. These two men are self-made men in the pattern of the American myth, yet their success is strongly linked to the intervention of Lloyd, who rewarded and directed their aggressiveness. They are very conscious of her influence and have a far different view of her as an outsider.

> Now Ms. Lloyd, she was from Boston and she had a very
> difficult time being accepted. But she had the patience
> of Job, and the intelligence of Einstein, and a philosophy
> that would rival that of Plato. If there is a God, she was it.

It is not very difficult to recognize the basis of the distinction: those outsiders who do not challenge the existing relations of authority and power or who contribute to the upward mobility of present elites are beneficient outsiders. But threatening outsiders are far different. "In my own mind, I would say he is a person who has entirely different ideas from what we have."

> Much of this "anti"-publicity came about by "outsiders,"
> VISTAs, Appalachian Volunteers, the young lawyers who
> were attached to those organizations, using local people
> to mouth their sentiments. Please believe me, what has
> happened in Floyd County in the last forty or fifty years
> is absolutely, positively unbelievable. The progress has
> been more striking educationally, politically—positively
> unbelievable. But in order to understand and appreciate
> that you would have to know where we were twenty-five
> or thirty years ago and these young dreamers, do-gooders
> if you will, have no idea where we were thirty years ago.
> So they, by just one swell [sic] swoop, indict people and
> the local establishment. They are the people who are
> holding the poor people of Floyd County under their
> thumbs for the purpose of using them.

Some middle-class citizens associated with the project did not distinguish categorically among outsiders and used definitions that encompassed both the role of those outsiders such as Alice Lloyd and the later OEO lawyers.

> Outsiders are people who are brought in from another
> area to work with our people and to teach us how the
> rest of the world is. They offer a new perspective and
> won't tolerate what others have become accustomed to.
> The poor people trust them, it is the middle class and
> the politicians who resent them.

What must be obvious by now is that an outsider, a threatening outsider, is not just a person from another geographic location but a
person who does not accept or approve existing social and political
relationships or mores and sees them as disadvantageous to lower-
income groups and advantageous to others. It is possible to be an
outsider in Prestonsburg if you are from Martin, which is in Floyd
County but 14 miles away. Distinctions frequently are made among
the people of the county on the basis of the proximity of a person to
informally constructed group standards. As we saw previously, the
Big Sandy CAP was viewed as an outsider when Floyd County officials
were anxious to control their own health program. There was some
basis for this charge of outsider since the Big Sandy CAP was headquartered in Paintsville, the county seat of Johnson County, which is
as Republican as Floyd is Democratic. The Big Sandy CAP became
less of an outsider when Judge Stumbo became chairman of that group.
But the rift was completely settled, as we shall see later, when the
FCCHSP and the Big Sandy CAP allied forces against Schecter and
EKWRO, and the threat they posed to both of them was larger than
any threat they posed to each other.

Without a doubt the single greatest determining characteristic
of an outsider is the relation to the existing structures of power and
prestige and the procedures followed to instigate change.

> This term in that context [among supporters of EKWRO],
> [means] that these people come in and try to institute
> change, which is not bad, I'm not against change. How-
> ever, they probably don't do it through channels as much
> as they do through publicity and things like that. Of course,
> we're supposed to be—not me I guess, I'm over this—the
> generation now is supposed to be "change now," you know.
> Instead of waiting for other people or "the establishment"
> to do it. But still, maybe I'm old fashioned or something—
> grey hair I guess—but still I feel even if our country may
> not be just right or doing the right thing but still if we
> don't go through these channels we're in trouble. . . . You
> have an uncoordinated, incoherent way of doing things and
> if it keeps going and going, you just have confusion on
> everyone's part.

106

Again, it should be noted that change through channels implies change with benefit, and without threat, to the status quo just as surely as change initiated from above does.[23]

The premise that the relationship of a person to the establishment is determinant of an outsider or an insider is recognized in the rebuttal offered by EKWRO leaders to the charge that their organization has been the tool of outsiders.

> An outsider is usually something like when you tackle a program like Charles Clark, the school superintendent, you get tagged an outsider for being outside the area. He does that to keep from talking on the real issue. He runs up outsiders, communists, and all this kind of stuff. Another reason they do that is publicity, they set people up against an organization because of summer volunteers, or doctors, or anything they term outsiders. An outsider, as they see it, is anyone not from Floyd County or the head of Big Mud. You can be an outsider if you go away to college and in two or three years you get a Master's Degree. If you're on their side then you're an insider. Harry Eastburn is from Alabama. He's never been called an outsider because he goes along with the clique—see.
>
> We've got boys from Louisville who are called outsiders—right from this state here! Anyone who is opposed to them is an outsider, an outside agitator.[24]

The Margin of Feasible Change

An initial visit with Perkins on Schecter's eighth day of work established the honeymoon period of his brief period of tenure when he wielded his greatest influence and almost achieved the separation of the FCCHSP from the Big Sandy CAP. The stormy history of the relations of these two agencies grew intense after Schecter's arrival and reached hurricane proportions at a November 17 meeting. The Big Sandy CAP rejected the proposed 90-day budget for the FCCHSP, which meant that the FCCHSP could not pay any bills and would have to halt hiring for the program. It was this kind of influence and intimidation that the Floyd County people had feared and resented. They reacted swiftly. Judge Stumbo, who was vice-chairman of the FCCHSP and chairman of the Big Sandy CAP, made a motion to reques OEO that the FCCHSP become the grantee of the program. He later denied making the motion and had it stricken from the record; but participants at the meeting recall it, and it was seconded and passed unanimously. Also at the same meeting a motion to transfer all

107

FCCHSP funds from the Paintsville Bank to a Floyd County bank was passed.

In a rush of euphoria the board also authorized Schecter to investigate the possibility of relocating the central offices elsewhere in the county. Further—what had been and would soon become again the major impediment to devising a new program—the recruitment of doctors to staff outposts was agreed upon at this meeting. Though heavily qualified—only one clinic was to be established and the consumer's right to freedom of choice of physician was to be carefully guarded—the motion was nonetheless a significant break from the past. These actions were reaffirmed at a meeting on November 20, 1970 but never acted upon.

In a showdown meeting between FCCHSP and the Big Sandy CAP, which was attended by large numbers of EKWRO members and Floyd County residents, a conflict was averted when Judge Stumbo suggested postponing the request for disaffiliation from the Big Sandy CAP because it had not been on the agenda and would therefore be out of order. He also felt that it was bad strategy to plead for the Big Sandy CAP's cooperation in disaffiliation.[25] The moment of confrontation passed and circumstances would never be so favorable for Schecter again. The honeymoon ended shortly thereafter.

The budget remained the thorniest problem of the board. The expansion of outposts to include medical service and physicians; the installation of closed circuit television at one outpost; and helicopter-ambulance service—all inflated Schecter's budget to nearly double the size of other previous budgets and made the board increasingly apprehensive of the wisdom of Schecter's approach. Schecter could have gone to OHA with a request for funds to begin innovations as well as carry on the former program, or he could have approached OHA with a total program of innovations with the hope that part of the program would be granted and the remainder achieved a bit at a time. Schecter chose the second strategy, but many board members did not recognize the tactics of his budget requests. One consumer member of the board complained about never being able to figure out Schecter's plans. While she agreed that there was a need for more doctors, she thought Schecter's way was too exorbitant: "Everybody knows that with that much money, the poor would get no medicine at all. He had some wonderful ideas, but you couldn't get him down."

It is important to note that opposition to Schecter was not necessarily opposition to his ideas. The same consumer member that complained that Schecter's concern for the poor was not always evident and that he seemed to be pulling "agin'em" (physicians) also maintained that "staffed outposts with doctors, that would be nice and might bring medicine down [in cost]." Another consumer board member was given the opportunity to compare the Floyd County program with another comprehensive health program when he and several other board members visited Park Duvalle in Louisville on a trip organized by Schecter.

> Now I ain't got much education, but I got sense and any man with eyes could see the minute he walked through that door that you could get anything you needed. You could even get a tooth pulled passing through. They had everything but a place to go to bed and I'm sure that they had a room to put you in case of an emergency. They was more modern than anything we have; not now, with that new hospital in Pikeville and the new one up by Prestonsburg. They had an ambulance right there to take you to the hospital. I got back here and looked around and I thought it was pitiful. We got as many poor here as there in Louisville and bushels of money baled up like hay and we got nothing. We could have had a medical center where poor persons and people who could pay could get everything they needed. We could staff them with students, they have to spend a year before they become doctors and buddy, the poor people would flock to them. Good health care, it don't matter from where, people will flock to it. Why those students they know as much as them doctors that's practicing 20 years.

Staffed outposts, new doctors, and the direct provision of medical services—these were the elements that incurred Schecter's most bitter and devastating opposition from the Floyd County Medical Society; they were also the measures necessary for a comprehensive health program in OHA's terms.

THE DOCTORS AND COMPREHENSIVE
HEALTH CARE

Prevalent Values and Objections to Change

The doctors of Floyd County, frequently divided by allegiance to competitive hospitals and professional envies over competence and income, had a mechanism of unity in the Floyd County Medical Society. This association, infrequently called into session, was used to mobilize and focus the opposition of the doctors of the county who had coalesced quite firmly against Schecter. As a measure of internal unity, a doctor from the McDowell hospital, William Pratt, was elected

109

president of the medical society in mid-1971, indicating that the rift between the doctors in Prestonsburg and elsewhere in the county with those in McDowell was over. More important than past differences was the present threat of a medical program within the county directed by outsiders. An expanded comprehensive health program to include nine physicians, two nurse practitioners, two dentists, a pharmacist, and other allied health care professionals, as well as expanded facilities for the direct provision of medical care to the program's participants, meant considerable change in the medical organization of the county.

The doctors of the county opposed this expansion for several reasons. First, it seemed to them needless duplication; efficiency was the hallmark of good administration, and good administration was what was required for the county's health problems. A new hospital was under construction and would better provide much-needed facilities in greater abundance. To promote a separate program would mean diminishing the importance of the new facility as well as the already existing facilities and services. To avoid duplication, area planning of health needs had been under way for some time and a definite trend of centralization and specialization had been established. Hospitals throughout the area were equipped to handle one of the areas needs: at Williamson, there was a center for cardiac cases; at Pikeville, a center for cancer; and at Prestonsburg, a center for black lung with a $500,000 unit reportedly ready for operation in August 1972.

Another pressing concern was the threat an expanded comprehensive health program posed to existing facilities. One physician maintained that the entire McDowell hospital could be financially jeopardized if its clinic lost one-third of the outpatient use of its pharmacy and X-ray facility. Likewise, the seven pharmacies of the county seemed sufficient without creating a new one. What was especially alarming about the competition was its source, federal government money. This seemed tantamount to socialized medicine and the medical society treated it as such. The hallmark of much of medicine in the United States and especially Floyd County has been free enterprise; and medicine is easily one of the last and most profitable bastions of the private entrepreneur.[26] One board member, a dentist, expressed himself vehemently in terms of liberal belief in proportionate, not redistributive, taxation and individual effort.

> Do you think I want them coming in here and setting up
> clinics with OEO money, my money!! Why that's just
> setting up competition with my own money, my tax money.
> Why I own part of that pharmacy in town here and I would
> be crazy to set up competition with my private money by

110

my tax money. Setting up pharmacies with tax money, why, that's just socialism and it's dreamers like Schecter, and other fellows that come here, and you, that think that the government should pay for it all. They forget about freedom of choice. If dentists and pharmacists and doctors want to practice, let them get out and hustle like us.*

Schecter's proposal was further criticized because of the staff and personnel it would employ. Paramedical personnel already had been introduced into the county both in dentistry and surgery. Indeed, neighboring Knott County has had the equivalent of nursing practitioners for as long as the Frontier Nursing Society has been in existence — since 1925—yet the attitude expressed by the medical society's president was one of caution.

If by paraprofessional help you mean someone I tell to go out and take a blood pressure, yes, we can use them. But if by paramedical you mean someone I tell to go out and take a blood pressure and increase the dosage of medicine if it is up, no, that's too much responsibility. The same with nurse practitioners, it's too much responsibility. We're a very conservative group. We won't necessarily fight it if it comes, but we're not for it now. Most doctors feel that way.

This attitude of the medical society was contrary to OHA guidelines, which specifically called for the use of paramedical and paraprofessional personnel and the training and employment of the poor in these roles.[27]

There was also a consensus that the physicians recruited for Schecter's program would be the "rejects" who could not make it anywhere else in the county. Part of this belief is based on the difficulties the medical society has encountered in staffing the new hospital. In some cases they had brought in 10 people to fill just one post; in other cases, 20. If positions in a modern hospital located in a populated area were going unclaimed, who, it was asked, would live back in these hollers with outdoor privies, no sidewalks, no water, and no sewerage? Even more pointed was this question: who would do these things if he/she could earn substantially more money in an urban environment? Recruiting doctors requires schools, playgrounds,

---

*It should be recalled that when in firm control of the program, the medical society had limited recipients to attending Floyd County physicians.

and other amenities and living conditions for the doctor's family. Doctors who would come at salaries lower than those available elsewhere and suffer these inconveniences would have to be inferior, incapable of meeting the competition of the marketplace on their own.

In addition, these new physicians would add to an already serious problem of the county.

> These people they would bring into the county would stay just long enough to discourage the young doctors who are coming out of school and want to come back to this county. They would go elsewhere. It's just what we've been doing all along—sending our people elsewhere.[28]

Joe T. Hyden, a dentist in Floyd County and a board member, also was connected with a scholarship program for rural youth interested in health professions and voiced objections similar to these.

> We felt that we had many, many, many people, highly qualified, to take over these jobs, local people and who could qualify under the poverty program. We felt that a local person would know the situation and especially if he had the education and would be better prepared to handle it than someone from New York or New Jersey. I was on his [Schecter's] side, I was trying to help him; before I knew it, he had turned against all the doctors and dentists and professional people. It's as simple as this: they wanted to come in, they wanted the doctors to locate in Mud Creek country. We knew doctors didn't want to locate there. . . . I believe, I don't know, we got in the twenties some place, physicians in this county, we only got about 35,000 people. We got a much better ratio than a lot of other places so why bring them in here. Then secondly, hell, I can count now about thirty-two boys and girls in med school coming out and so far as I know everyone of them is going to locate in Floyd County. We were fighting this thing, in other words, before Schecter and those people had ever heard of it. That's been our life.[29]

The health professionals of the county had some corroborating authority for their position. Certainly, outmigration and a talent drain were undeniable realities. Further, even the Boone Report listed fee for service and freedom of physician selection as two safeguards for promoting competition and the quality of care.[30] Also, OHA requirements seemed directly contradictory to ongoing efforts of medical reorganization in the Appalachian area.[31]

Yet, some of the opposition to Schecter and his ideas was much more scurrilous and reminiscent of the Boone Report's criticism of the physicians of two decades earlier for their "attempts" toward monopolistic control of medical practice.[32] One county resident recalled one meeting when Schecter was subject to a verbal attack.

> The whole experience really made me sick of the establishment, and I'm a politician. I enjoyed phoning others and gathering votes and trading votes before each meeting. But politics to me is not meant to run a person down. The doctors couldn't understand why Schecter would come to Floyd County for $30,000 when he could make a lot more, say $150,000. Because of that he must be a communist. The medical society held a secret meeting and invited five board members to influence them. They subjected Schecter to a very vicious attack. They accused him of being of fake, of not being licensed and of being a quack. When someone asked, "Won't you at least give him a chance?" One member stood up and said, "Hell, no! We won't give him a chance." When he said it, he jerked his hand in such a way that his wedding ring flew off his finger and rolled to the opposite side of the room.

Schecter was asked at this meeting to defend several points, among them were the proposed nurse practitioners and the authorization for his advertisements for doctors. Especially pertinent to the investigators, it would seem, was the nature of his certification; they had discovered that Schecter had once taken and failed the Illinois State Examination. In his defense Schecter explained that the examination was one that many failed and that he took it without preparation, having been engaged in research and away from practice for a long while. A case was built that Schecter actually had been licensed in Kentucky by reciprocity and had never passed the Kentucky State Examination, an allegation that was false but received wide circulation and some credence.

Such personal attacks are evidence of the depth of the issues involved. Schecter's proposal ultimately raised the question of the nature of medical service. If it was a right, then it was best protected and achieved by the people to whom it belonged; if it was a service or a commodity to gain for a fee, then it was understandable that it be controlled by the providers. Charity implies the latter situation and depends on the generosity of the giver rather than the rights of the recipient. But OEO's healthright programs were premised on health care as a right, a view not widely shared by the medical society. Perhaps the view of the doctors was best portrayed by a minister of the county.

I believe that every person ought to be provided for with health care. I'm a little hesitant about the word right, for this implies imposing yourself on someone else. I do feel that for those who are unable to pay, our government ought to provide for them. I think we have a moral responsibility to see to it that they are provided for properly.

Schecter did not represent an alternative conception of health care in Floyd County as much as he represented a tacit criticism of the physicians' moral responsibility and the insufficiency of the system that they had established, as well as the changes in facilities and personnel for which they had made provisions. EKWRO, on the other hand, was a very explicit criticism of the medical society's unwillingness to allow poor people a health program legally—by federal regulations—and morally—by reason of their right to health care—their own.

The Medical Society Intervenes

The medical society found its spokesman to counter Schecter in J. D. Adams. Adams fit the classic mold of the eastern Kentucky physician: he was from Floyd County; after attending the University of Louisville Medical School, he had spent little time returning to Floyd County and seemed heir apparent to Archer in influence. He shared hospital and clinic facilities with Archer, became one-third owner of the nursing home in Prestonsburg, was allegedly part-owner of Minix Drug Store (by family ties), and entered electoral politics in November 1970 when he was elected to the school committee. The medical society in December 1970 chose Adams to be a representative to the new FCCHSP board. This election took place after the society's meeting with Schecter and just prior to the FCCHSP's board's final action on the budget and the proposals Schecter was making. These items were on the agenda of the very first FCCHSP board meeting Adams attended in January 1971; however, the first order of business concerned his own eligibility. When the board was reorganized it was assumed that members would serve one-year terms.[33] But in fact, since the board's reorganization, other board members had resigned and been replaced. The one difficulty was that Cook, former medical society representative, had not resigned; hence, Adam's replacement of Cook was challenged by Schecter.

Judge Stumbo made a motion to amend the by-laws to read that any association could designate its representative at any time. It was pointed out that the by-laws prohibit such an amendment unless it is at a meeting called specifically to discuss the proposed amendment.

A recess was called to work out this parliamentary bind. An attempt was made to telephone Cook for his resignation, but he was in surgery when the call came through. When the meeting reconvened a number of parliamentary motions came in quick succession. It was moved, seconded, and approved that Article X of the Articles of Incorporation be changed to read,

The by-laws may be adopted or amended by the majority of the members of the corporation.

Deleted was the phrase, "if so provided in the by-laws by the directors of the corporation." This in effect negated the provision of Article Thirteen of the by-laws, which required a special meeting for changing any Article of Incorporation. It also obviously violated this same article. The judge then moved, and seconded, his original motion of amendment concerning an association's right to designate its representative at any time. The motion was no longer illegal because of the vote just taken. The motion carried. Judge Stumbo moved the coup de grace to seat Adams. It was seconded and carried.

The meeting went on to consider the recommendation of the finance committee that was to review Part A of the new budget. Part A was substantially the budget approved before Schecter arrived in October, and would have provided for a program very much like the one that had existed. Part A was reported out favorably to the full board and passed. Part B of the budget was the section composed of the innovations Schecter proposed. This was not approved but was referred to the planning committee for further study and recommendation. The planning committee was composed of two consumers, one of whom was allegedly being treated free of charge by Archer; a pharmacist from Minix Drug Store; and the administrator of the nursing home, Mountain Manor, a third of which J. D. Adams owned. The chairman of the planning committee was Adams.

This decision regarding the budget was not final, however, since the finance committee of the grantee agency, the Big Sandy CAP, also would have to approve it. The finance committees of both agencies worked on Part A and fashioned it into acceptable form, and on January 18, 1971 the budget was brought up for a vote. One consumer objected that she had not had time to examine the budget or the changes made and that it was being "pushed on them too quickly." Schecter also objected to the proposed budget. Already gone were the innovations he had hoped to bring about and the increased staff he had hoped to recruit; but, more important, former abuses were reappearing. The salary of the assistant project director, Helen Wells, was changed from $8,000 to $12,600; positions for health educators and dentists were omitted; and the Big Sandy CAP was to have final say in all hiring practices. The FCCHSP board regressed one step further and changed references to the provision of health care to "referral." A motion to vote on the compromise budget by secret ballot was made and defeated in an open vote, 12 to 5 (all consumers or their representatives). The budget was approved 12 to 4. Criticism was voiced again regarding the lack of time to consider the budget. The meeting ended in the ensuing confusion without a motion to adjourn and with the belief on the part of some members that the program could now be funded. They were partially correct.

NOTES

1. Minutes of the Floyd County Comprehensive Health Program, August 13, 1970, p. 2.
2. The Hawkeye, newsletter published by EKWRO, September 9, 1971, p. 4.
3. The lack of guidelines for school lunch programs and the political purposes to which the program was put without guidelines has been documented in another study, see Bill Peterson, Coaltown Revisited: An Appalachian Notebook (Chicago: Henry Regnery Co., 1972), pp. 183-86.
4. EKWRO's self-perception as a labor union was consistent with part of the ambiguous nature of CAP's. In fact, Jack Conway, first director of CAP within OEO, was on loan from the AFL-CIO and brought with him a concept of maximum feasible participation as community action; John C. Donovan, Politics of Poverty, 2d ed., (New York: Pegasus Press, 1967), pp. 165-67.
5. This observation bears close resemblance to Schrag's description of an Appalachian county's world view and its consequence.

> The middle-class burghers of the county seats—small businessmen, coal operators, lawyers—who often congratulate themselves on their generosity, behave with the wisdom of a lumpen proletariat when it comes to the genuine problems of the community. Dependent themselves on the existing structure, they often tend to deny the existence of chronic unemployment, of regional decay and of home-grown corruption. Like those of the federal government, their charitable acts leave the essential structure untouched; rather, they serve simply to keep the waste and the misery from becoming too unconscionable. The effect, if not the intent, is to keep the natives sufficiently dependent in order to prevent any fundamental change from taking place.

Peter Schrag, "The School and Politics," in Appalachia's People, Problems, Alternatives, compiled by People's Appalachian Research collective, vol. 1 (Morgantown, W. Va.: PARC, 1971), p. 378.

6. On this point see also Dunbar, Our Land Too (New York: Vintage Books, 1971), pp. 176 and 184-85.

7. For an oft-cited discussion of the political machine, see Robert K. Merton, Social Theory and Social Structure, enlarged ed. (New York: The Free Press, 1968), pp. 126-37.

8. Peter Schrag, "Appalachia: Again the Forgotten Land," in Appalachia's People, p. 383. For a fictionalized account of the Appalachian politics of relief see Harry Caudill, Senator From Slaughter County (Boston: Little, Brown, and Co., 1972). For more on the "machine" characteristics of Appalachian politics see Malcolm E. Jewell and Everett W. Cunningham, Kentucky Politics, (Lexington: University of Kentucky Press, 1968), pp. 169-70; Theodore H. White, The Making of a President: 1960 (New York: Atheneum Publishing Company, 1961), pp. 97-100; and Dunbar, Our Land Too, pp. 171-72. Voting irregularity was also part of the ability of machines to turn out large votes. In 1969 the Floyd County Times estimated the number of registered voters to be 29,000 while the 1970 census reported the population 18 years and older to be 22,569. This gives us a percentage of registered voters of 128.5 percent of the eligible population. Conditions such as these undoubtedly influenced the grand jury in its 1961 opinion, "that a state of lawlessness exists in Floyd County, particularly in connection with absentee voting law violation and vote buying." Floyd County Times, May 18, 1961, p. 1.

9. Hugh Perry, "They'll Cut Off Your Project": A Mingo County Chronicle (New York: Praeger Publishers, 1972), pp. 134-35.

10. Ibid., passim.

11. Merton, Social Theory and Social Structure, p. 128. "The machine welds its links with ordinary men and women by elaborate networks of personal relations. Politics is transformed into personal ties."

12. Harry K. Schwarzweller, James S. Brown and J. J. Mangalam, Mountain Families in Transition: A Case Study of Appalachian Migration (University Park: Pennsylvania State University Press, 1971), p. 59.

13. John B. Stephenson, Shiloh: A Mountain Community (Lexington: University of Kentucky Press, 1968), p. 40. See also Dunbar, Our Land Too, p. 177.

14. Judith Randall, "Poor Rap OEO Health Project: Perkins Hit," Washington Evening Star, May 4, 1971.

15. Murray Edelman, Politics as Symbolic Action: Mass Arousal and Quiescence (Chicago: Markham Publishing Co., 1971), pp. 55-56. This quiescence often is attributed to the culture of poverty

in the form of a characteristic without a dialectical relationship to pervasive American culture. In other words, Appalachian poor often are considered a subculture because of unique cultural traits rather than a cultural and political by-product of the very values they are said to be without. The dialectical relationship between the cultural adaptations of the poor and pervasive cultural values also may be found in an examination of the work of Paulo Freire, Cultural Action for Freedom (Cambridge, Mass.: Harvard Educational Review, 1970), and Pedagogy of the Oppressed (New York: Herder and Herder, 1970).

Stephenson presents a far less dialectical account of the quiescence of the poor, which takes little note of the function of such concepts as "contentment," "individualism," and "familism" for maintaining an individualistic view of the causes of poverty and its remedies. Compare Stephenson, Shiloh, pp. 92-112. Also see Jack Weller, Yesterday's People: Life in Contemporary Appalachia (Lexington: University of Kentucky Press, 1965), pp. 28-40. The explicitly pejorative nature of many "one-dimensional" analyses of Appalachian poverty is explained in James Branscome, Annihilating the Hillbilly: The Appalachians' Struggle with America's Institutions (Huntington, W.Va.: Appalachian Movement Press, 1971).

16. Erving Goffman, Stigma: Notes on the Management of Spoiled Identity (Englewood Cliffs, N.J.: Prentice-Hall, 1963), p. 129.

17. Kenneth B. Clark and Jeannette Hopkins, A Relevant War Against Poverty: A Study of Community Action Programs and Observable Social Change (New York: Harper & Row, 1968), pp. 195-96.

18. Ibid., p. v.

19. In no respect are the groups of organized poor quite as similar to the labor movement as in the response both received in eastern Kentucky. The charge of "communist" was hurled at both, and although no troops were called out in the 1960s Governor Nunn sent the Kentucky Un-American Activities Committee to investigate antipoverty activities in the southeastern Kentucky area. See Harry M. Caudill, Night Comes to the Cumberlands: A Biography of a Depressed Area (Boston: Little, Brown and Co., 1962), pp. 197-99, for the red-baiting of early UMW activities. See also Peterson, Coaltown Revisited, pp. 142-47; Gene L. Mason, "Stripping Kentucky: The Subversive Poor," The Nation 207 (December 30, 1968): 721-24, for the experience of Appalachina Volunteers in Pike County. Perry, "They'll Cut Off Your Project," p. 45, recounts the reaction of one Mingo County official to a committee of poor people established to supervise election practices in the county. "They are dirty, nasty: they won't shave. As far as I am concerned, the majority of them are communist inspired."

20. Letter from EKWRO to Steven Joseph, Director of OHA, August 18, 1970. EKWRO sent sworn affadavits substantiating their allegations along with their letter.

21. Interview with Arnold Schecter, Louisville, Ky., July 11, 1972.

22. For a more complete account of the AV's and especially the controversy they incurred in Pike County, see Mason, "The Subversive Poor."

23. Contrasted with this "official" view of outsiders, Dunbar cites a longtime community worker who feels that "outside organizers have maintained a fine record of discouraging militancy among poor people." Our Land Too, pp. 164-66.

24. Saul Alinsky points out a certain validity to charges of outside agitation, since "the power establishment" of an area generally crushes would-be social changes of the area. Alinsky, Reveille for Radicals (New York: Vintage Books, 1969), p. 219.

25. Minutes of Special Meeting of the FCCHSP, November 23, 1970, Paintsville, Ky.

26. A critique of the profit making nature of the American health industry may be found in Health Policy Advisory Center, The American Health Empire: A Report from the Health Policy Advisory Center (New York: Vintage Books, 1971).

27. Office of Economic Opportunity, Guideline: Healthright Programs (Washington, D.C.: U.S. Government Printing Office, 1970), pp. 7-8.

28. George Archer in Floyd County Times, January 21, 1971, p. 1.

29. Interview with Joe T. Hyden, Martin, Ky., May 19, 1972.

30. Boone Report, p. 133.

31. ARC's health program, for example, which does not include Floyd County, does not emphasize consumer participation nor modification of the existing delivery system. "The Appalachian Health Program: A Progress Report," in ARC Appalachia's People, pp. 142-47.

32. Boone Report, p. 133.

33. Wendy Wheat, program analyst from OHA, would give the opinion that Adams' election was premature since OHA had presumed the 90-day period for reorganization was long enough to elect a board of directors, each of whom would serve one year. Letter of January 12, 1971 to William Cook.

THE POWERS ALIGN

Elite Unity and Action

OHA approved the budget of FCCHSP at a meeting in Washington on January 22, 1971; in addition, William Bicknell, acting director of OHA, indicated that some of Arnold Schecter's innovations should also be implemented. Specifically this meant recruiting additional physicians, dentists, and pharmacists and establishing a pharmacy and X-ray lab. The program was to move toward comprehensive health centers where outpatient medical and dental needs could be met under one roof.

The Washington meeting determined the opponents of Schecter to take control of the program. Schecter, they charged, initiated discussions of Proposal B at the Washington meeting despite the board's decision to refer that proposal to the planning committee. More important, Schecter's direction of the program kept open the possibility that the FCCHSP would bring about extensive change. To forestall these changes several members of the FCCHSP Executive Committee met in a special morning session on January 28. Schecter was dismissed, effective immediately, and the Big Sandy CAP was asked to supply a staff member as a temporary acting project director. The one consumer present at this meeting, Frank Daniels, cast the only dissenting vote; two other members of the executive committee, including Schecter, were not notified of the meeting.

Implementation of the decisions of the board seldom had been swift in the past. Decisions to staff outposts with doctors, to transfer funds from Johnson County banks to those in Floyd County, and to sever relations with the Big Sandy CAP had not moved toward

achievement in nearly two months. But it was different this time.
A telegram was sent to Arnold Schecter informing him of his dismissal that same day, and a hand-delivered notice informed the Big Sandy CAP of the committee's action. Eastburn immediately replied in another hand-delivered notice, which informed the committee that the Big Sandy CAP was "more than happy to aid you in your time of difficulty"[1] and that John Burton of the Big Sandy CAP was named temporary acting project director.

In a single morning, decades of political alignments were reversed by the accord reached between the Floyd County and Johnson County leaders. The officials of FCCHSP were asking to be dependent upon a program viewed as dominated by Johnson County officials. The county judge, Henry Stumbo, vice-chairman of FCCHSP, had stated less than a year earlier, "If Floyd County can't run their own program, they don't deserve it." Now he was chairman of the Big Sandy CAP and control of FCCHSP was endangered. One board member recalled:

> From August to January the Judge slept through the
> meetings. He just went along with everything that came
> along. You know, there was no dissenting vote in all that
> time, August to January. And he would keep saying, "Skip
> the details, let's get some action." Sometimes he would
> ask what happened to such and such a motion and it would
> be explained to him, "Judge, we passed that five minutes
> ago." But when the power structure spoke, he had to act.
> The judge has little money. He is a man of modest means,
> unlike other people within the establishment. But he does
> have the power of thirty-seven years. He didn't want out-
> siders coming in and getting jobs.

The evening of the day of the executive committee's action the FCCHSP board held a meeting that was limited strictly to the agenda matter: the approval of a grantee-delegate agreement between the FCCHSP and the Big Sandy CAP. Despite Schecter's objection that the contract gave the Big Sandy CAP control over policy and personnel and despite the board's opposition to this contract for nearly a year, the contract was approved. The meeting was adjourned after the contract was approved without discussion of the executive committee's action, but the events put in motion by that action continued. On January 29, John Burton requested a meeting with the executive committees of FCCHSP and the Big Sandy CAP in Prestonsburg. The tone of this meeting, unlike the stormy nature of previous meetings, was one of cooperation and deliberation. Burton asked the committee what they wished of him and later promised to bring all questions to the board before making final decisions. Predictably, both executive committees approved Burton's appointment. The first action of the newly instated temporary acting project director was to ask the FCCHSP executive committee to rescind the forced letter of resignation from Helen Wells, effective January 31, 1971, that had been twice accepted by Schecter. The motion was made to act favorably on this request by J. D. Adams and seconded by Charles Clark; it carried 4 to 0. It was necessary for the Big Sandy CAP to act on the motion as well since they now had control of personnel matters, and without surprise they concurred unanimously. These remarkable days of reconciliation bore out an observation of earlier OEO programs that had represented a threat to the elites' values and privilege: namely, that elite opposition to such programs was nonpartisan.[2]

Opposition to Elites

From this point on, the FCCHSP had a schizoid nature. The Personnel and Grievance Committee, responsible for hiring and firing, had five members, three of whom were among four recognizable dissidents who had voted for secret ballots, against the budget that had no innovations, and against the contract with the Big Sandy CAP. Thus, this committee's majority reflected views far different from the rest of the board. When they met on February 5, 1971, they determined the action of the executive committee to be invalid and reinstated Schecter. The committee went on to request investigations of the program by Congress, OEO, and the governor's office "because we feel this program is very much needed here in Floyd County but we think the program is not really being run by and for the people it is supposed to serve."

In addition to this opposition within the board, a coalition of Schecter, his supporters on the staff and on the board, and EKWRO emerged shortly after Schecter's dismissal. The members of this coalition only partially overcame previous and ongoing differences of opinion in order to work together. Schecter saw the conflict as involving OHA and Perkins and revolving about their failure to carry out the stated policies of the program; EKWRO, on the other hand, emphasized the criticism of in-county arrangements of medical and political power and saw OHA and Perkins as a reflection of these arrangements.

The board meeting of February 8, 1971 was one of several angry debates and was held despite a snow storm that literally paralyzed the area. The meeting, which took place in Johnson County, confirmed both actions of the executive committee—namely, Schecter's dismissal and Burton's appointment—and overruled the Personnel and

122

Grievance Committee. The full board also considered reinstating three persons previously connected with the program who had resigned under pressure from Schecter. The board during the next several months acted on this motion and reinstated Helen Wells, Paul Wells, and Earl Compton. Both men were reinstated with full back pay, even though during that time the program was moribund, awaiting the arrival of new funds, and despite the new budget, which made allocations neither for their positions nor their salaries. The action to reinstate Compton was taken after the personnel committee, minus one dissenter, was deadlocked 2 to 2. When it was learned that the board intended to reinstate Compton, seven of the eight outpost nurses, as well as the medical director, Robert Titzler, threatened to resign. They considered Compton unqualified for his position and were prepared to inform the board as much, though they were never asked. This procedure furthered their belief that the board gave no attention to the opinion of the professionals within the program.

A tremendous amount of time was taken up with matters of reorganization, budgets, and job descriptions, which required board members to attend two or three meetings a week. What must be emphasized is that at this time the program was moribund. No services or referrals were being made since the program had no funds. Finally, on April 5, 1971 the board received the welcome news that a statement of grant had come from OHA and that $984,740 would be available to fund the program until July 1971, retroactive to December 1970. However, this was not the only news that had come from OEO. A letter of March 18 from Frank Carlucci, director of OEO, included a memo from Thomas E. Bryant of OHA that detailed serious deficiencies of the program. Carlucci requested that a list of corrective measures, already taken or planned, be submitted by April 15 if the program was to be continued.

THE STRUGGLE TO DEFINE

Proposed Meanings of "Comprehensive"

Bryant's memo raised the perennial problem of the nature of comprehensive health care. After three years, the FCCHSP was still disappointingly far removed from a comprehensive health program specified by OHA regulations.

> The project has failed to develop a health-care program
> which emphasizes comprehensive, family-oriented health
> care for the low income residents of Floyd County. The

project continues to utilize as its basic mode of operation a system in which patients are referred in a haphazard fashion to private physicians and dentists. This type of operation has substantially made it impossible to achieve the goals of the OEO grant which involves the care and treatment of entire families in a situation which insures both continuity of care as well as an attempt to deal with basic health and environmental problems in the area.[3]

The doctors of the county were willing to alter the form of their participation in the program somewhat. The physicians at the McDowell hospital, for example, volunteered to go out to the outposts for inservice education, but they did not volunteer for outpatient care at the outposts since, in their estimation, those outposts did not have the facilities for adequate service. At a meeting on February 10 in Paintsville, J. D. Adams outlined the physicians' new position: doctors would visit the outposts and give lessons and lectures on health care; a scholarship fund had been suggested to prepare paramedical personnel in the local community college; further plans were in preparation and both the doctors and the pharmacists had been encouraged to make their contributions for modifications and improvements. But the physicians' position remained unchanged on at least one point, "As for setting up satellite clinics, complete with x-ray facilities, specialists and everything else, I think you are in direct competition with existing institutions when you do that."[4] However substantial these changes may have seemed to the physicians who proposed them, they were still far distant from the OHA definition of a comprehensive health program.

The meeting exploded as several pointed questions revealed the contradiction of OEO's clearly stated nature of a comprehensive health program with the physician-dominated view of the FCCHSP. The uproar also elicited the crowning irony of this meeting, which had been called with the intent to reorganize the Floyd County program and to examine ways to get consumer participation: it was decided to go into closed session. This decision prompted one EKWRO member to shout, "When the rich men speak, the poor have to sit down. When the poor people talk, the rich men adjourn their meeting."[5]

Opponents of the present program, including EKWRO, were fairly certain as to what comprehensive health was and was not.

It should be a program that provides all medical care for the poor. The poor who can't afford insurance and all that. Instead the one we had was a taxi service. You should have an ambulance service, your own pharmacist

. . . your doctor should be out here in the community where people could get to him, you should have R.N.'s and people on call twenty-four hours a day. You know comprehensive health should be what it says, comprehensive. It should be with people and not in the county seat and the doctors should be concerned with people, not money. There should be doctors like pediatricians for sick kids. You know poor people have high rates of sick kids. The main problem was, actually, the people weren't getting no benefit. I'll tell you, the politicians of the county and the doctors of the county were the ones getting all the benefit out of the thing.

EKWRO had offered OHA alternative proposals for a health program, as well as criticisms of the present one. The first proposal was submitted on July 1970 shortly after the election of the Mud Creek representative to the new FCCHSP board, which left EKWRO members dissatisfied. This proposal called for an independent Mud Creek outpost and explicitly addressed the connection between health care, power, and effective change.

The FCCHSP illustrates what easily happens when programs to provide valuable medical service to poor people are not controlled by the poor people themselves. Comprehensive health program does not approach its potential to provide valuable medical service to poor people, and it serves to strengthen the control that a few people in Floyd County have over the majority of county residents. NOW WE WILL CONTROL OUR OWN PROGRAM.[6]

A board of directors for this outpost was suggested, with members of EKWRO, the Community Action Council 979, and elected representatives from among Mud Creek residents participating in the program. Local control was seen as a necessity, since any good health program would emphasize preventive medicine—which entails environmental, occupational, and social change. Rather than separate entities, without purpose and direction other than their own, these changes were viewed as requiring integration into the overall aspirations of the community in order to be effective. Such integration was impossible without local control. Likewise, because it entailed social change, preventive medicine would be ineffective as long as it was not carried out by the people who were themselves the patients. Local control, it was argued, was a right as well as a necessity for a successful local health program—an argument resembling one of the early understandings of "maximum feasible participation."

The EKWRO program envisioned the direct provision of services and the hiring of MD's, RN's, at least one dentist, and local residents —within OEO poverty guidelines—as staff for the Mud Greek outpost. All personnel were to be hired on a salary basis, not fee for service, and medical assistance would be available around the clock. Services, which were to be provided under one roof, were to be free to the patient, and payment was to come from various third-party arrangements—with OEO funds as a last dollar source of payment. Health education and transportation also played important parts in the proposal.

While EKWRO offered alternatives to match the OHA guidelines, officials associated with the FCCHSP offered criticism of these guidelines as a rationale for their opposition.

> No bureaucrat of the federal government can determine
> what needs to be done in every section of the country.
> They just can't sit on their pedestal and set guidelines
> for every neighborhood and ghetto.

Bureaucratic intervention by OEO was particularly ill-advised because it seemed that OEO at heart was "a black man's program" designed to aid cities and urban areas with their problems but almost completely out of place in a rural setting.

> Most of the programs seemed to be conceived with a lack
> of understanding of the people they are trying to help.
> Now whether these ideas germinate in Washington by
> fuzzy-headed philosophers without knowledge of the
> rural nature of people they're trying to help, I don't know.
> I don't know who's had any input into these federally con-
> ceived financed programs. We had no input here in Floyd
> County. I don't know a single solitary soul here who's
> been asked for advice.

The opposition to OEO's intrusion into the FCCHSP had another side to it. That is, if professionals complained that OEO was unfamiliar with Floyd County, it was necessarily implied that they were familiar with the county and its needs and, moreover, had been meeting those needs for a lengthy period of time. The record of charitable care provided by the physicians and dentists of the county was offered as evidence of this accomplishment.

> We were fighting this thing before Schecter and those peo-
> ple ever heard of it. That's been our life and we've car-
> ried these people and still carry them that are not on these
> different programs or anything else.

126

Until the very end of the program, J. D. Adams offered his 10 years of practice and charity as an indication that some of the criticisms had been unfair, as well as an indication of his own concern. It also indicated that he and other doctors could and should be trusted to direct the program.[7] But to justify control of a health program by past charity was to ignore a central point: medical care was not merely the need of the poor, but their right. This was the working premise of OHA and the conviction of EKWRO. Health care may appear as charity only if it is viewed as a commodity of the provider to be exchanged for a value; but justice also was involved. According to OEO regulations the poor of Floyd County had a right to a comprehensive health program. Any program short of that goal, a goal that would include all of Adams' suggested changes plus the direct provision of service, was a denial of the poor's right.

Moreover, the charity of some medical providers was that of noblesse oblige with a corresponding attitude of "blaming the victim."

> No one has told them [the poor] there's something better. There's just no desire to raise themselves up above their present level. They see their daddy and they figure to be like him. There is a loss of pride of ownership, too. The Constitution says that we have the right to pursue happiness, not to have it. With rights go responsibilities to fellow man. Some people think they have a right to a lot of things they don't have a right to.
>
> You take some of these families four, six, ten kids. They can only hope two will make anything out of themselves. The poverty program could have been far more successful and cost less money if they had adopted just one measure: ten thousand dollars per sterilization. I would say the number of vasectomies increased one hundred per cent in the past $1\frac{1}{2}$ years but the number involved is still very low. There is just pride involved. For some a vasectomy means you're not a man. I don't know why.

A physician concurred, "Most physicians are for sterilization, but not the people."

The argument of the elites for control of FCCHSP also was based upon their demonstrated capacity to improve things.

> You take industry, they're getting it in here. Who's getting it here? EKWRO's never done a damn thing. Perkins' never done a damn thing to get it in here, to speak of. It's been fellows like—the go-gettingest man in Eastern Kentucky and Floyd County in particular right now is

Dr. George Archer. . . . He's got a head full of stuff and can
present it far better than I can. He's been in it, he's really
done things. We wouldn't have the hospital going in down
the river if it weren't for him. We wouldn't have the courthouse, were it not for him. They wouldn't have the big park-
ing lot next to the bank, were it not for him. Oh, he gets
fierce when he gets into it about that bunch on Mud Creek.
But he's a fighter. Little Adams is too. [8]

Control of the FCCHSP struck at the heart of the ambiguity
of OEO's "maximum feasible participation" and raised the basic
question of an antipoverty strategy: was it to be within or outside
present institutional arrangements. Helen Wells raised the essence
of the question during a last attempt to maintain elite control of
FCCHSP.

I would like to say that I started working with the CAP
program in 1965 . . . as I understand the War on Poverty, it is to take the poor people and the disadvantaged
out of their plight and into the mainstream of American
society. We in our community took the approach of working with the total community . . . trying to change things
as we could to try to help the poor people, rather than to
try to please the Big Mud faction and create complete
chaos. . . . As I understand OEO, it's to be programs
planned by the people on the local level and not by Harvard
loafers and graduates from up-East somewhere, but by our
people, what they say they need and how they say they want
those needs met. What we would like to see done, our
people, the majority, not the minority. America still rules
with the majority. It still goes with the majority and the
majority of our people are saying one thing and a small
minority are saying another. You could take an election,
ballot box vote, and I would bet my life on it, that the
votes for our program would be a majority.[9]

Arthur Pope, member of the Big Sandy CAP, offered a clear
and concise defense of the program dealing with reasons for maintaining the program under the auspices of the "establishment," even
if that was unsatisfactory to OHA.

To begin with, I didn't know too much about the comprehensive health program. But I understood OEO to be an
organization seeking to bring the mainstream of services
to the poor, the poor people in this country. To cause

them to be a part of it and thereby to elevate their potential, education and so forth. . . .   Then I went back and listened to the proposals put up by this minority of people down there . . . and I said this program causes segregation of the poor from even the middle-class. It puts them out in their own hollers and it puts them back to their own doctor who will just see them and they won't see no one else and they don't want to become part of anything except their own little world. Then they'll become part of cells or pressure groups seeking power. Power to destroy the establishment. In their own community without concourse to the outside . . . they become just a cell to be wielded and that's practically what's happened to some of them. And then I thought what is the alternative to this program so that I might vote intelligently.

The alternative seemed to me—I knew these dentists, I knew these doctors, I knew the businessmen and I knew the judges and so forth, all up and down the valley. I knew they were sound people, not loud, or you know what I mean, pretentious people. But quietly they are sound men. For two hundred years those mountains have built up the system of operating their own way. The majority of the people have, operating their own way. And it's built up an establishment, if you please, and it's been good. Those mountains have gone on when other areas have actually suffered a lot more than the mountains have. It's a one industry system up there. When it came back, mechanization had done away with a lot of jobs and tremendous poverty has been a result of that. And they'll never get out of it unless they unify the area, the whole area.

There are only two classes in that valley, they're either very poor or they're very rich. And unless we work it all together, into the hospitals, into the dentist's office, into the headstart of the schools, instead of segregating them off into the hollers . . . we've defeated the purpose of these comprehensive health programs. So that's the reason I voted to maintain the board. And the new hospital going up at Prestonsburg will make it just as possible for a poor person in Floyd County, or Johnson or Martin or the others to go to that hospital and become part of that, as I see it. . . . But if you isolate and segregate and subject them to a minority of cells, of professional persons whose business it is to tear down

the establishment, you defeat the purpose of America itself. . . . The only thing that keeps wearing us down is
the continual harassment from organizations whose professional business it is to tear down the establishment.

Pope invited the people of OHA to come down and "to walk the
paths with us." He was sure they would then find

that the establishment is the one that will integrate the
people into one and the one that will save the program
in the mountains. And God knows we need that program
in the mountains.

Contrasted with the past efforts and the present potential of
existing arrangements was the transient nature of many government
programs. Year-by-year funding for these programs created job
insecurity and oftentimes provided positions for less than a year.
"Who would take a job for six months?" one doctor asked. Even if
a satisfactory answer to that question might be given, the larger
question remains: can a program financed year by year or even
biannually ever gain the confidence necessary to concentrate on the
achievement of its task rather than on satisfying perceived requirements to achieve renewed funding?[10] The immediate concern of the
doctors of the county was that such short-term positions and funding
would attract unqualified outsiders or at best qualified outsiders,
but outsiders in any event. One official stated:

My attitude was this basically: What is Floyd County
going to be like when Uncle Sam, and he's rather fickle,
when he decides he's going to pull out his dollars from
the FCCHSP if we have established fourteen or fifteen
drugstores and have put our own boys out of business
and if we have brought in some doctors that will compete
—and Floyd County already has better medical services
than most any Eastern Kentucky county—my question
was, if all these pharmacies are started which obviously
will compete with pharmacies that have been struggling
for an existence here for thirty years, if we put them
out of business and Uncle Sam pulls out his dollars,
then we may have to go to Huntington to get pills. . . .
The same thing with medical services.
    I wasn't carrying the ball for doctors . . . they
can carry their own load and the pharmacies, I don't
patronize those people much. I'm not a pill-taker so
I don't patronize those people much. So with me the

question was, will Floyd County be better off or worse off —the poor people as well as Floyd County generally. And that is the reason I took the attitude I did.

When coupled together, these two factors—the pride the civic and social leaders had in their past and present achievements and the distrust of outside intrusion, even in government form—generated an implicit sense of self-sufficiency, but not the rugged individualism form of self-sufficiency. Outside aid was welcomed when it could be channeled and controlled by those already in power and for purposes they approved. FCCHSP had been welcomed within the county until it came under the direction of Schecter. Up until that time FCCHSP had taken its place among the recently constructed third-party payment mechanisms. Records of the Kentucky Department of Economic Assistance show that the medical payments for Floyd County averaged $1,216,133 annually from 1968 to 1972. Payments to physicians, pharmacies, and dentists averaged $286,460, $280,138, and $32,036, respectively.[11] Records of FCCHSP, though sketchy, indicate that nine physicians received $47,440 in 1969 and $62,212 in 1970, while the five pharmacies received payments from FCCHSP of $37,937 and $69,624 for the same two years. When change of the control and nature of portions of the county's health services became the cost of the continuation of FCCHSP, the program did not seem worth the price, especially in the light of existing medical arrangements— including the new hospital, constructed with federal funds, and state and federal medical payment arrangements. In fact, all that health providers stood to lose if the program was ended was OEO subsidization of transportation and health care payments on a last-dollar basis.

The belief in the sufficiency of Floyd County to care for its own problems grew weaker the farther one traveled from the center of power and wealth in the county. Correspondingly, this distance made Schecter's proposals appear more and more attractive. Not a single consumer interviewed—including those who voted to approve the budget and to dismiss Schecter, and even eventually to end the program—failed to mention that physician-staffed outposts and/or greater provision of care at the outposts were among the improvements they would like to have seen occur.

> I'dve like to seen outposts with a practical nurse. There's no use to go to a doctor for a runny nose and he sends you to a drug store and you pay him double or triple. ... The nurse can take care of you and have the medicine right there where you can buy cheap instead of paying twenty-five cents for a two-cent pill. The drugstores could've done better by the people. They made double

and triple, everyone knows it. They give you one hundred pills and you ask them why so many and they tell you we can't call up the doctor everytime to find out if you're really that sick.

Contrasting Views of Participation

The dissatisfaction of consumers was the second point of Bryant's memo. Particularly upsetting to OHA was the reaction of the board to this dissatisfaction.

There are indications that many low-income residents of Floyd County, whom the OEO grant was designed to serve, are dissatisfied with the sporadic, inefficient health services the FCCHSP has provided. I have been informed that the reaction of the board to this dissatisfaction has been an attempt to suppress and stifle dissent rather than make meaningful reforms in the program. In violation of OEO instructions . . . the low-income residents of Floyd County have not been provided with an adequate voice in the direction and management of the program.[12]

Two consumer critics of the program could recall the velvet fist of parliamentary procedure that left them at a distinct disadvantage and often out of order.

Poor people didn't have the chance to speak up to say what they felt. I did speak up once, it was about Helen Wells. We were talking if she should be hired again and when I asked why Helen Wells resigned, I was ruled out of order by Judge Stumbo.
They rehearsed every damn thing. Sometimes I would raise my hand to ask a question or express a point, I'd never be recognized. One night in particular, over at the Lodge . . . that colored guy from Wheelwright he's sitting right there and Judge Stumbo was sitting close enough to him to elbow him and like a robot, up would go his arm.
I asked if the meeting was being run by Robert's Rules of Order and I was told yes they were. Then I made a motion that all votes be taken in secret ballot. At the time I had the floor . . . then two politicians and a medical man stood up and they started shouting no, no, no, no, no. Finally Mrs. Robinson looked at me

and said, "Mr. N___ you're out of order." I had the floor
and these sons of a gun interrupted me. That there
proves it, that the person who is trying to get a point
across, if he is a poor person, ain't got a chance.

Another consumer member, who was neither a member of EKWRO
nor part of the dissenting bloc, likewise complained about rehearsed
meetings. Referring to the meeting in January when Adams took
his seat on the board, this consumer recalled:

I believe a lot went on, you couldn't prove. I do. A
group of three or four fallutin' people would leave and
go to a closed room and one would make a motion to
adjourn and that would kill it. You see what they'd
done is go to that room and talk, "I don't want this
passed or brought up," you see. Then they'd figure
up and come out and do it. But it wasn't anything you
could prove. I brought it up to one of them once. I told
him right out and his face grew red, and he looked like
a man, you know when he's been hit by something. He
told me, they could've been talking about fishing. I said
they could've been, but I don't believe they was. But
there's nothing you can prove, see.

EKWRO members charged that intimidation discouraged participation in the program as well as parliamentary maneuvers.

Judge Stumbo threatened to lock me and Jay and several
of the other welfare rights people in jail, just for speaking up at a meeting. We're supposed to sit there and
listen to Judge Stumbo. . . . They checked out the education of Frank Daniels and they spread it around. "Frank
Daniels," they said, "he don't have much education, he
can't really represent the poor." Frank said they did
every consumer on the board like that, you know, that
kind of stuff. They made fun of the consumers on the
board and ridicule them in every way they can. That's
what bothers them so much about the welfare rights
group cause they don't stand for that, and they brand
them as loudmouths and radicals and all that. They're
the radicals and the loudmouths. But, you know people
don't think about that. When you shout back you're
called or branded with something. They held a comprehensive health board meeting at Johnson County
Country Club. Can you imagine a poor person meeting

in the country club of Johnson County with the bankers
and the lawyers and the doctors and the superintendent
of schools and the county judge? Can you imagine how
the poor person felt?

Even distance and weather were factors used to discourage participation according to EKWRO members.

They called meetings when it was so slick and bad you
had to slide out of here in order to get to a meeting.
Yea, God-damn. They had that meeting once in
Johnson County. I know there was three foot of snow
and I was in a Volkswagen and the windshield wiper it
wouldn't move, it froze up on us. And they wouldn't
call it off cause they thought we wouldn't get there.
We finally made it but we were late. It was a meeting
to reform the program. It was the only meeting held
that night in Eastern Kentucky. Everything else had
been called off . . . even bowling clubs had been called
off. Yet they figured we couldn't get there so they had
it.
That's the way they treat the people. They don't
want no consumer input. They won't have a program if
it got consumer input. They don't want to hear the consumer's side.

As might be expected, these events as well as EKWRO's participation had widely different interpretations. In contradistinction
to charges of stifling dissent, board members placed the blame on
EKWRO.

That's the damnedest mixed up bunch. The one they
pushed out front is a woman, Mrs. Eula Hall, and everytime something popped up she had a written statement.
Now she isn't qualified to make those statements. Everytime I saw them they had three or four attorneys with
them and somebody was putting words in their mouth.
I don't know who it was, but I know damn well it wasn't
Eula Hall.
I never saw them add anything. All that they caused
was confusion. They went to tear down everything. Anything that was said they were all ready to hit the floor
and disagree with it. The judge would call a meeting,
when he was acting as chairman, with the understanding
that it was a closed meeting, and here comes EKWRO.
They had to put a guard on the door to keep them away.

134

Even some consumer members of the board had trouble sympathizing with EKWRO's participatory role. One consumer board member complained that because of Eula Hall's part in the program, the board was powerless to do anything. This consumer likewise complained about EKWRO following the board "all the way to Paintsville." What she saw of EKWRO convinced her that "if they listen to them, they'll never have a program. They wouldn't listen to anything. It's a shame. They ought to put everyone of them in jail." Another consumer board member tried to put EKWRO's participation in perspective.

> EKWRO did the best they knew how. If the people from Big Mud were fiery, it was because they have so many sick people and so little money up there. I didn't like the meetings where the people had to keep quiet. Especially when it's their program and they should be listened to with dignity.

Participation and the Poor

Several cultural and political influences were converging to make the problem of participation of the poor a very difficult one, not only in Floyd County but in OEO in general. Maximum feasible participation of the poor in decision making was premised on a political equality not found in Lockian liberalism. In the civil society of Locke, all persons were equal before the law, but only those with vested interest were permitted to make the law.[13]

If one believes in a direct relation between the capacity to make sound political decisions and social position, as Madison did, much of the conflict over participation of the poor becomes understandable, especially if the problems of poverty are viewed as administrative and technical ones. In Floyd County the problem was not only poverty but also health, an area long ago ceded to "experts." Doctors particularly are experts with specialized knowledge, and this sets them apart—especially since modern medicine can be classified as a science.[14] In many ways, then, participation of the poor should have resembled a doctor-patient relationship: "Those who understand, follow, respond to and are grateful for treatment are good patients."[15] Clark and Hopkins state that this was in fact the most prevalent attitude toward the participating poor throughout OEO.

> The total context of deprivation tends to lead to passivity among many who, when chosen to represent the poor, are pleased to be accepted by middle-class leadership and function with docility.[16]

135

Such docility is easily taken for wisdom by the middle-class experts and professionals, who take it to be agreement with their "sophisticated judgements." Through the docility of the poor, stratification, competence in decision making, participation of the poor, and unanimity are all spontaneously blended and no contradiction appears between social structure and political goals. Rather,

> Policy is built into the social structure of an organization
> . . . official aims and methods are spontaneously protected
> or advanced. The aspirations of individuals are so stim-
> ulated and controlled and so ordered in their mutual rela-
> tions, as to produce the desired balance of forces.[17]

It has been pointed out that this was especially true of Appalachia.

> In such a society the reinforcement system sufficiently
> rewards dependent and unaggressive behavior in the
> subordinate class member. Members of the controlling
> class, however, are rewarded for aggressive, independ-
> ent behavior. The rewards are continued and increased
> as the institutions' requirements are satisfied. By defi-
> nition, the controlling class manipulates the conditions
> for both reward and punishment as related to the be-
> havior of the subordinate class members.[18]

This manipulation forms part of a socialization system "which essentially suppresses the pro-social aggressive techniques that are necessary for the lower strata to take part in the more normal distribution of resources."[19]

These considerations of the social origins of the competency to make decisions had important implications for both sides of the conflict in interpreting dissent and agreement among board members; where EKWRO saw rehearsed meetings and robot, mechanical cooperation, one middle-class participant saw significant cooperation.

> The consumers on the board were an excellent group.
> . . . They had very intelligent people. It amazed me
> frankly that the poor could think and reason far better
> than I expected them to, knowing their background and
> so on. . . . There was no one that told them what to do.
> But you can't comprise a whole board of people like that.
> People who never had over $100 in their lives can't handle
> a program with $1,000,000.

I was pleased . . . some of them really took a stand
on the issues and some of them, you didn't know how they
were going to stand on it. You really got the idea they
were their own people, and they were speaking for those
they represented. I felt good about that.

Professionals, both on and off the board, expressed concern
that consumer participation remain genuine and not become the manipulation of the poor by others.

I think when you establish representation of the poor, it
should be the poor people. They should speak for the
poor people and not for someone else pushing their own
ideology, or their particular hang-ups or problems and
trying to get the poor to voice that for them. In other
words, they ought not to be used from a moral standpoint, a philosophy of life standpoint, a political standpoint or any other way.

A medical facility administrator expressed the same caution.

Poor people are not capable of directing such a medical
program. They need direction and leadership, but it has
to be selective and not a hearing to the noisiest. Poor
people are too easily manipulated. Coal companies, for
example, manipulated the poor for years. That's one
reason they're still poor. What's needed is checks and
balances, consumers and providers.

Some concern was expressed that too much participation of
the poor could be easily turned to the communists' advantage.*
The red scare aside, the majority of board members believed
that EKWRO was a "passionate movement" not only unnecessary
but also manipulated by outsiders. One county official felt very
strongly about this.

One of the difficulties we've had recently in the participation of the poor is that many of these outside groups

―――――――――――――

*This board member was the only one interviewed who had a
conception of participation as use of the facilities or services of the
program. Despite the ambiguity within OEO, maximum feasible participation was accepted in Floyd County as meaning some part in
decision making.

. . . were concerned with using the poor and I'm the fellow
who knows because I had some of those people come to me
from the valley [Mud Creek] with obviously legal docu-
ments, a list of ten demands, obviously written by an attorney, or a learned person, and when I asked these four
or five people from this area what number one is, they said
they didn't know, they got it out here at the Appalachian
Volunteer office. Using those people—now I would say,
if those outside groups had been able to gain the support
and participation of a wider group of those in the lower
income level instead of those who were obviously willing
to be used, they would sign any document as long as they
were told to do it by these wild-eyed, fuzzy-headed out-
landers who had looked at our area here and decided the
only thing wrong with this county was the present leadership. Remember they had only been here a matter of two
weeks. . . . I'm firmly convinced that poor people, a cross
section of poor people now, not these who have an educational achievement level of grade one—I would certainly
hope that when we have a delegation of poor people that
we would have an overwhelming majority of those people
who could read and write—those people are less likely
to be led by these dreamers, you see, from the outside.

When asked if he thought EKWRO was representative of the
poor of Floyd County, this same county official replied: "I do not!
I do not! I do not! I would have to say that EKWRO was and is still,
as far as I know, made up of those people who are willing to be used."
Matching this concern of the professionals that EKWRO members were being manipulated was the concern of consumer critics
of the program, including EKWRO, that the politicians and doctors
were manipulating the poor of the county into apparent support. Doctors were criticized for profiteering and abusing their medical service
by giving it free to board members who supported them and withholding it from poor persons who supported EKWRO. Politicians
were likewise criticized.

The politicians know there are poor people. What they
do is use them like a chess board. You set your chess
board up there and you set all your kings and your pieces,
you set them all up. If one of the pieces falls over, all
the politician does is set him up in the same environment
he was in before. They just set him up and they use him
right on.

Particularly appalling to EKWRO members was the appearance local politicians gave that federally financed and supervised programs were coming from them.

But the recognition of the use of federal programs to enhance the power and prestige of local politicians extended beyond EKWRO, as another consumer member of the board indicated.

> You see we've had the Nelson gang [Operation Mainstream], the dropout gang [Neighborhood Youth Corps], and OEO and the judge, he wants two-thirds of the people to think he gets it all. Anyone with sense about government knows there are higher-ups than him, but he has some poor fooled. They think he gets them a job or gets the program for the county. I can't blame him. If I, or you, were in power and all that money was up for grabs, you'd try to get some of it for your county, wouldn't you? And make people think you were getting it for them, wouldn't you?

The consequent dependence incurred in receiving political favors also was described by this consumer board member.

> Let me tell you buddy, Floyd County is no poorer than anywhere else. You got poor everywhere and Floyd County's no poorer than any other county and Kentucky's no poorer than any other state. Let me tell you something else. There's a lot of rich ones in this county, some of them have enough money to burn a wet mule. But as far as poor peoples, it's a lack of jobs. I had a job with the state, an easy job, just drive a truck, had it four years. It paid good but they took it all out in taxes anyway. But some of it was worth it, I had good medical coverage with it. I have a job now cutting weeds round the powerlines, you know that run through here. Well, I'll tell you, I work harder on this job in one day than I did in two weeks with the state. But I like it. If something better comes along, well, I'll take it. It's no great job but it's better than working for the state. I'll tell you, I just never got used to being under a thumbnail. I figures this way, your life ain't but a short time anyway, what's the use of your not being satisfied. You know what I mean? What's the good? It's no good, that's what. I've been North and West, I've been all over but I love this place. Had some good jobs in Michigan but I wasn't satisfied.

That's the way it is with a lot of folks. They try here and there, there just ain't no jobs. I'll tell you one thing about jobs though. If you use your own free rights to be your own man you get nowheres. If you swallow everything those politicians tells you, you'll get a job. When something is right or wrong, I'll speak for myself—I'll stay poor.

A COUNTY DIVIDED

Traditional Values Become "Unstuck"

In a sense the everyday common sense beliefs of a community were challenged as a result of the conflict over FCCHSP. The doctors, politicians, and other professionals had been rewarded by this belief system and achieved prominence and success through it and within it. Many of the poor shared these very same beliefs and accepted the views of prominent officials as their own. One consumer acknowledged, "I never knowed it [FCCHSP] was political if it was," but yet criticized some board members who "took with the other side." Her role seemed easy and, if it came to a choice of sides, that choice was simplified by trusting those in authority. "No one knows poor people better than Charles Clark and Judge Stumbo know the poor and what they would need. He's superintendent of schools, he ought to know, shouldn't he?"

This trust contrasted sharply with those groups who were accusing the professionals and the politicians of willfully withholding the benefits of a poor people's program and using them to enhance themselves. This was only part of a wide-ranging distrust of the people of prominence and success.

They've [the poor] finally figured out that the coal mine operators, and the politicians and the doctors are all one and the same. I mean you tackle one and you have to tackle the whole bunch of them again.

They all know now that when they stand up to ask one question they'll be attacked everytime, by the coal mine operators, the county officials, the medical society, everyone of them.

I'd be ashamed if I did to mountain people like they do to Mud Creek people. They come out to campaign and everything and people give them vegetables out of their garden, they give them apples, and they give them everything

140

they got and they try to work with them. Then, when they
raise one question, you know, they get chopped down.
Then when elections come on, they're right out here,
because District Four's the biggest district, they're
right out here and they're ready to go see everybody.
. . . But the next week, after the election's over they're
not allowed to speak with them, ask questions or anything.[20]

I used to laugh at people up North, used to talk
about coming in and organizing Appalachia. . . . It's
been organized for a hundred years, each holler has
a person to carry the votes of that holler and he turns
around and hands out the jobs and all the favors to that
holler. People are scared to death to vote the wrong
way for fear that they'll be found out and lose food stamps.

Some pressure was brought to bear by and on members of
both sides to resolve the contrasting interpretations of events and
political arrangements. This was the grounds of Thomas E. Bryant's
third criticism of the program.

Various members of the FCCHSP have sought to intimidate other members of the board or patients of the program, who desire to restructure the comprehensive
health care needs of Floyd County. According to these
reports patients who are actively involved in community
affairs have been intimidated as to their employment and
the employment of their relatives. These individuals have
also been warned they would have difficulty in attaining
health, social, and municipal services to which they are
entitled. In addition, we have been informed that staff
members of the project who have been actively involved
in community affairs have reported that their files have
been rifled, and that they have received telephone calls
from board members warning about adverse personal
action against them.[21]

Floyd County was experiencing one of those rare moments in
American political experience when the consensus of values enters
uneasy times. What the "given" appearance of American political
values disguises is that liberal democratic government exists to
maintain the power relations among individuals and groups.[22] Those
power relations are hidden further by the conformity required for
the cohesion of a liberal society that dissipates community in pursuit
of individual liberty.[23] When the "given" appearance of social and

political arrangements is questioned by the articulate alienation of nonconformists, "the dynamite which normally lies concealed beneath the appearance of freedom and equality of the American liberal community"24 may be ignited. In the months from February to August 1971, the cost of nonconformity to prevailing attitudes and arrangements became abundantly clear in the form of a variety of intimidations.

One form of intimidation was felt by those desiring to stay on neutral ground in the controversy but who were torn by the gains and losses of such a stance.

> I suffered by the time it was over. I'm not a political
> person. I'm just interested in people. I don't know how
> people are pulled this way and that. I just know I was
> in the middle of it and I didn't like it and I don't want to
> be there again.

Those board members who felt this way simply stopped attending the meetings.

Others who opposed the program felt the intimidation that comes with opposing those who they rely on for specialized services. County officials can affect children in very many ways, it was pointed out: lunch programs, their relationship with teachers, and even grading the road leading to the house. Without graded roads—the responsibility of the county judge—the school bus will not travel to a home to pick up children. Thus, if a road into a holler is left ungraded for a period of time, the children in that holler must walk to the road where the bus does travel. This may mean a walk of more than a mile both ways and a period of waiting. On the other hand, conformity with the expectations of county officials could mean a crew of Nelson Mainstream men to paint a consumers' house, as was the case in one instance.

The primary, informal, and personal nature of social relations with doctors and public officials was sacrificed by those who opposed their direction of the program. One board member used an out-of-county doctor rather than continue with one to whom he often was opposed. This alteration of the nature of social relationships requires the courage to face that which is unfamiliar and unknown. Moreover, EKWRO members realized that their opposition to the county judge entailed the possibility of direct reprisal.

> Judge Stumbo is the head of a very powerful political
> machine. No consumer in Floyd County dares to oppose
> him. Judge Stumbo control thousands of jobs and is the
> judge before whom members of consumer families

frequently come. Frequently, board meetings are held in
Prestonsburg in the Judge's chambers—no doubt to remind
all of his power in the county.[25]

Finally, even OEO could be intimidated. In the excellent class-
room that this program was, some board members learned the hard
realities of politics.

OEO was caught between Perkins and a desire for change.
It did its best, but there were too many county politicians
with a direct line to Perkins.

Perkins' position of influence in the very life and death of OEO was
bound to lead that agency to anticipate his preferences and to try
to meet them. When the first unfavorable staff reports on FCCHSP
were made, they quickly were stifled. The first disclosure of the
1968 medical audit came only in late 1970 when an OHA official who
was leaving the agency gave Schecter a copy.

It is difficult to verify or deny that one form of intimidation
felt or exercised by some board members; the closer one gets to the
center of influence the less intimidation is seen or is even imaginable.
One pharmacist thought the county judge was incapable of intimidating.

These officials get out and have to be elected. They're
a friend to everybody. A lot more poor people vote than
there are any other kind in this county, so this isn't a
problem at all. As a matter of fact, they probably had
more voice than anyone else, especially in a program
like this.

Nevertheless, violence and threats of violence emerged from
the existing divisions. Two consumer critics of the program, who
had attended the January meeting with OHA, found that their eligibility
for the program was challenged shortly after returning from that
meeting, and one was declared ineligible without a hearing. Several
board members as well as staff and several OHA staff members
independently arrived at the conclusion that some phones were tapped.
While this might be dismissed as paranoia, the evidence was substantial enough for the several people involved to be real in its consequences; thus, calls were made to and from public phones.

The comings and goings of anyone connected with the program,
or strangers inquiring about it, were quickly reported to all interested
parties, as each faction had informants within or around the program. (In such an atmosphere, biosomatic indicators of the tensions
people felt also became evident. One administrator broke out in hives,

and a nurse, even a year after leaving the project, still had an alarming and measurable increase in blood pressure at the mere mention of the program.) There were even rumors of the planned assassinations of EKWRO members. Such rumors are generated by an atmosphere of tension and suspicion and in turn contribute to that climate. But it would be grossly naive to dismiss them as groundless or as without consequence in the conflict; they stem directly from the challenge to traditional values that the conflict over FCCHSP represented. As one member of the OHA staff described it, her dealings with the FCCHSP were "very upsetting for me as a human being to live through." Leon Cooper, director of Comprehensive Health for OHA during this period, dismissed any personal sense of fear or intimidation. However, one health professional within the county saw it quite differently.

> They tried to set a program up in Washington never having
> been here. . . . Now take for instance Dr. Cooper, he's an
> intelligent man. He came to Prestonsburg went down to
> Wheelwright and went back to Prestonsburg. He made
> one or two trips like that. He told me himself that it
> was not wise for him to stay up here that he might get
> killed. Hell if a man is going to worry about being killed,
> he can't make very important decisions. I know damn well
> I couldn't. I'd be like the old westerns. I'd want to bolt
> the door and have my old six-shooter in my hand.

Authority Reassessed and Challenged

The charges of intimidation and manipulation, and the criticism levied by and on each group, placed the county's soul on public view. This view was valuable and instructive for many county residents. One board member had this advice for any program.

> I believe the medical people if good qualified and for the
> people should be on the board. But politics should be kept
> out. Anytime you got a program for the poor you got to
> keep the rich and the middle class out. Don't you think?
> Otherwise the ones that don't need it, get it and the ones
> who do, can't get it. If I was running it I'd screen out
> the people pretty good. I'd come out and see what they
> owned, how much they made, and the like. But instead,
> they was employing wives making $400 or $500 a month
> whose husbands were making $600 or $700 a month in-
> stead of giving it to someone who needed it, a poor man's
> wife or a widow. If you check into it, you'd see local

politicians and officials run it. I asked the women at Allen
who gave them their job. I didn't know if it was my business but I thought I'd ask. They told me they didn't know.
"Now," I said, "why I had a state job and I know who gave
me that job." They knew, you see, but he told them not
to say. But I knew as soon as they said they didn't know.
But this program was used too bad by the people who had
a hold of it. When you help the poor you have to get away
from that.

Aside from this lesson, little was gained for or by the poor in
the program. A great deal of frustation was in evidence among the
board members, which stemmed from the realization that a program
greatly needed in the county and greatly desired could be at a hair
breadth's distance but never implemented, because control of the
program was of prime importance to everyone concerned. The service of the poor was inextricably linked to the program's control,
and this service was jeopardized because the conflict over control
was not resolved.

Everyone said they were for the poor but they didn't
show it. One official said, "I'm for the poor," but that
same man wouldn't let them speak, and I say actions
speak louder than words.

For some board members the inability to compromise over control
was a mystery.

I believe with all my heart that the politicians and all
of them were all in cahoots. But I asked myself very
often what they had to gain, but I couldn't answer it.

Control of the health needs of Floyd County had important
tangible benefits that provide an answer to what was to be gained.
Few groups could better exemplify the Lockian belief of abundance
as the reward of effort than the doctors of Floyd County. Not only
did their profession reward them financially but also the service
they provided ingratiated them with the population. They stood out
in startling contrast in a county with a median income of $4,878 and
a median educational level of 8.4 grades. Traditionally their education
and wealth meant prestige and respect for doctors in the mountains
and indeed elsewhere. But now the doctors found themselves criticized
for profiteering from third-party payment mechanisms and a "glorified
taxi service" that they controlled to bring in hundreds of newly created
paying customers.26

145

EKWRO, and other poor people, were motivated by their resentment of the influence that doctors had in the management and administration of the program to challenge that influence. This was partially because, ironically enough, doctors were "outsiders" to the poor. As one consumer member, a non-EKWRO member stated,

> Our doctors are not poor and they can't understand what it means to be poor. Some can, but the doctors in this county don't want to. The only way to get results with a health program for the poor is by having greater consumer participation. Only the man making $3,000 knows how it feels to be poor, not a $20,000 man, like our doctors.

Some consumer critics found the charity of the medical providers to be less than total and far from sufficient and often cited Marilyn Osborne as a case in point. Osborne was in intense labor when her husband brought her to Prestonsburg General Hospital, which refused to admit her without proof of the ability to pay. Her husband's insurance coverage was questioned, and a check from his aunt for $250 was unacceptable as proof of payment. Further, the hospital had a policy of not accepting maternity cases as emergencies, since the woman had had nine months to make financial arrangements. The police were called to escort the couple from the hospital. Shortly after returning home, Marilyn Osborne gave birth to a baby girl. She soon developed severe headaches and died two weeks later, November 30, 1970.[27]

A consumer board member cited Marilyn Osborne as only one of many examples of the tragic cost of lives. Within her own family a mother had not been able to get her infant child admitted to the hospital for lack of funds. When the child died its mother developed signs of mental illness. The only group satisfied with the provision of health care in the county, this consumer board member explained, was the medical society—and their satisfaction was uncritical and self-serving. It was a commonplace observation that the wealthier class of people do not "doctor" in Floyd County. Indeed, the wives of the doctors, it was alleged by critics of the program, go outside the county for their medical attention.[28] The satisfaction of this group just added to the frustration of their critics, whose experience belied the contentment of the doctors. "Unless you see the waste of life in Floyd County you just can't understand, you just can't understand."

The program's critics soon realized they were faced with a choice of opposing the program wholeheartedly and perhaps fostering its demise or moderating their criticism and working for reforms, which, even if inadequate, would at least assure the program's future. It was decided that a program the size of FCCHSP was too much power to leave in the hands of the politicians and the doctors.

> If you went into Prestonsburg and said now look we'll go along with you. If the poor people were to say, we'll go along with you there's no doubt in two months they'll be a comprehensive health program in here. But we can't go along with them because we are poor. We know what we need, we know what our people want and if we were to go along with them we wouldn't have a damn thing except what the politicians want.

A decision to leave the program in their hands, with minor modifications, would only guarantee the perpetuation of a system already viewed as intolerable. The destruction of the program would at least elicit the hope that a new program could be started on the razed site of the old program.

EKWRO, working together with Schecter, sought to embarrass, or perhaps intimidate, the board by a high-powered publicity campaign as well as by active participation of its members at meetings. Hearings sponsored by EKWRO were held in Allen, Kentucky on March 28, 1971 that probed into the nature of health care in the county. The meeting produced a Bill of Health Rights and publicity concerning the abuses of the county's medical system.[29]

Previously, on February 23, 1971, EKWRO members had gained statewide publicity by picketing the program's central office in Wheelwright and, then moving on, the Floyd County Courthouse, the Prestonsburg General Hospital, and the program's office in Prestonsburg. In addition to the publicity, this picketing set off a chain reaction from Floyd County to Carl Perkins and finally to OHA. In the words of one OHA staff member, "the building shook." Newspaper articles concerning the conflict over the program had appeared regularly in the local and statewide newspapers, but now articles generally sympathetic to Schecter and EKWRO appeared in Science, Medical World News, and The New York Times; Articles in the Washington Star linked OEO and Perkins to the failure of the program.[30] Judith Randall, who wrote these latter articles, visited the county for several days and attended a board meeting on April 28, 1971. She asked a question of the board and was told that the board had no use for "Northern outsiders," whether from OEO or the press. Here resentment was small compared to that of county officials to her article, which was reprinted in the Huntington Herald-Dispatch with wide circulation in Floyd County.

She visited this valley where these people live [Mud Creek], as far as I know that young lady never visited a single professional member of the Comprehensive Health Board in Floyd County, and she wrote a very scathing article of the comprehensive health program.

Such scathing articles were exactly the purpose of the publicity campaign; namely, to demonstrate to OEO and Representative Perkins, at the very least, that unbiased outside observers considered the FCCHSP a scandal.[31]

Reaction to publicity was uniform among the professionals. They resented it because it was biased and quotes were taken out of context; moreover, while they were busy taking care of the county's medical needs, the people of EKWRO had ample time to engage in such activities. "Physicians look bad answering a lot of petty things and that's what the complaints came down to, a lot of petty silly stuff." Local officials were protected somewhat from the criticism by established ties and the existing consensus. OEO did not enjoy the same type of insulation and could not as easily dismiss the criticisms levied at the program as petty and silly stuff. While it is impossible to trace a causal relationship between the publicity and the ensuing events, certainly, at the very least, it is safe to say that OEO was made more resolute in the stand taken by Bryant and received some relief from the pressure it might otherwise have felt from Perkins' office. Members of both Perkins' office and the staff of OHA realized that it was to Perkins' advantage to "keep them as clean as a hound's tooth down there," especially because of the increasing publicity.

A PROGRAM LOST, A PROGRAM GAINED

Show Cause and Showdown

There is little doubt of the significance of Leon Cooper's role in the firm stand that OHA took. Representing OHA as the director of the Division of Comprehensive Health, Cooper, the first black to hold his post, came to Floyd County on March 3, 1971 to meet for two days with the board. Just two weeks later Bryant's memorandum arrived to express the most serious concern OHA had yet shown toward FCCHSP. In the ensuing months, board members flew to Washington to meet with Cooper and OHA officials to arrange funding for the new program. Cooper's last visit to the county came on May 6, 1971, just two days after the first appearance of the Judith Randall article.

The meeting of May 6 was a culmination in several respects.
It evidenced the frustration of OHA in establishing a comprehensive
health program according to its guidelines in Floyd County and the
board's frustration in its dealings with OHA, which would not fund a
program satisfactory to them. Schecter's strategy of public embarrassment also culminated that night in the Floyd County courthouse;
newsmen from several area and state newspapers were present as
well as a camera crew from a Pittsburgh television station.

The meeting did not abide by parliamentary amenities. Board
members wanted to know what "federal troubleshooter," cited by
Judith Randall, had labeled FCCHSP "totally corrupt." Several board
members complained of one-sided publicity, socialistic medicine,
Schecter's contribution to the ruin of the program, and favored treatment from OHA. Why, it was questioned, was Schecter ever approved, since he had had trouble achieving certification in "other
states?" The fact that Schecter and Cooper attended Howard Medical
School at approximately the same time provided further evidence of
collusion between the two men—to the detriment of the county and its
health program. This alleged collusion confirmed the opinion of many
that OEO was "a black man's program" first and foremost.

The anger over past events and experiences paled in the light
of Cooper's business at hand: the board was given the choice of
turning FCCHSP over to an interim board—made up of representatives
of the Kentucky Medical Association, the Council of the Southern
Mountains, the University of Kentucky, and the State Health Department—or lose the program. The board, as might be anticipated,
reacted strongly. Adams took it as an insult.

> What the Office of Health Affairs has done is, to me,
> as a member of the board, an insult. I have done my very
> best to implement a program that will serve the people.
> . . . It is difficult to carry on a health program without
> funds.[32]

Another county official gave perhaps the strongest reaction of all.
He, like Adams, took it as a personal insult and a year later was
still upset with OHA.

> It was most difficult, as I understood it, for anyone on
> our board to work with the Office of Health Affairs in
> Washington because it was obvious to me, as well as
> to others, that EKWRO had their ear and they didn't
> seek any help or advice from others. All we got were
> ultimatums. After the young lady wrote the story for
> the Washington Evening Star, or whatever, and some

of the people came from the Office of Health Affairs to
investigate the thing, I never saw any of them. They
were evidently met at the airport by EKWRO people.
They never visited the county judge, as far as I know;
they never visited the health officer here in Floyd County,
Dr. Hall. They never saw anybody except EKWRO.

So when Dr. Cooper came down and just told us to
vote ourselves out of existence, it was a direct insult to
me. And I practically said so. . . . I stood up at a much
publicized meeting over here at the courthouse and told
him that I felt insulted that we had been charged with incompetence, negligence, and several other outlandish
charges . . . and that we had to vote ourselves out of
existence as a board or the money was gone, wiped out,
just like that. I said at that meeting that I took it as a
personal affront, the ultimatum, and that I positively refused to vote myself out of existence and I wanted to find
out if that man right there from Washington had the power
to do what he threatened to do.

To test this suspicion concerning the actual power of Cooper,
Charles Clark moved that Cooper's motion be tabled. A voice vote
passed the resolution. After the vote, Cooper announced that as of
that date the funds of the program, promised on April 5, 1971, were
frozen. His staff and he immediately left for Lexington, partly because
they felt that in light of the tempers shown at the meeting Lexington
would be safer than Floyd County for their overnight stay.

The day after Cooper's meeting with the board, Paul Stark,
Deputy Project Director for Administration, was fired, along with
Robert Titzler, project physician and acting medical director. This
latter firing precipitated the resignation of the two remaining nurses.
While the board accelerated its own efforts of local control of a local
issue, OHA toned down its opposition to the program. Cooper was
not, in fact, empowered to suspend the program with the suddenness
he had indicated at the meeting of May 6, as had been suspected.
Upon Cooper's recommendation, OHA had begun suspension proceedings
and a letter of the intent to suspend had been sent to Judge Stumbo and
Eleanor Robinson. Both boards of FCCHSP and the Big Sandy CAP
were instructed to "show cause," on June 1, 1971 in Washington, as
to why the program should not be suspended. Harry Eastburn called
a closed session in Johnson County to answer the charges of OHA,
which included the lack of consumer participation and the suppression
of dissent. Members of the press were allowed into the closed meeting; but when Eula Hall—representing EKWRO—and John Rosenberg—
counsel for EKWRO in the show-cause proceedings—attempted to

enter the meeting, they were turned away by a member of the Paintsville police. The Paintsville meeting gave both boards and administrators of the program the opportunity to prepare their defense. The show-cause hearing gave them the opportunity to address themselves to the allegations of their critics and OHA. It was the opportunity to offer the other side of the publicity and to offer the rationale for the program's preference and past performance.

The show-cause meeting of June 1 in Washington covered the familiar criticisms and elicited justifications equally familiar. Adams did voice one board grievance previously unemphasized.

> There are a group of people who have been employed
> with this program, and I know I'm a board member, who
> are very insubordinate. Now if you can run Health Affairs
> with people not obeying a line of command, then I bet you,
> prove it. We can't do this with our program either. We
> would direct our so-called professionals to perform a
> duty and it would not be done. Instead, these particular
> people who voided our program attempted to polarize
> our other professionals. A good example of this, this
> is my opinion, was the manner in which the seven health
> nurses resigned. This sir, is polarization. . . . The
> reasoning behind the resignation of these nurses was
> that we re-employed two persons, Mr. Wells and Mr.
> Compton. We re-employed them upon their dismissal
> by Dr. Schecter. They went through the procedure of
> a grievance committee. They had a meeting and the
> vote was two to two, and the board rehired them. And
> so far as people employed by the program telling the
> board what to do, I don't think this is good. I think if
> people given directions carry them out, then maybe
> we could get something done.

At the conclusions of Adams' remarks, John Burton pointed out the shortcomings and inadequacy of the role that OHA had played in the FCCHSP up to the present. This seemed to be the only point that EKWRO, consumer critics, doctors, and board members agreed upon. Burton detailed these shortcomings, which included the failure to be present at meetings and the failure to provide technical assistance or directives.

The meeting was subdued, since EKWRO's lawyers did not present their evidence in the belief that the board had the burden of proof. This disappointed some critics of the FCCHSP because the newsmen present offered the program's opponents their finest opportunity to "embarrass the hell out of Perkins and OEO" as well as the boards of FCCHSP and the Big Sandy CAP. But others felt it would do more good to show OHA that EKWRO was an alternative group with a health plan that could be used to keep the program in Floyd County than to achieve a Pyrrhic victory. Hall hoped to make it clear that EKWRO was not opposed to the health program.

> We do not want to destroy the hopes for a health program.
> We want a comprehensive health program in our area.
> We do, however, want to see the program structure al-
> tered in such a way that it will be responsive to the poor
> for whom the program exists. We know this is also the
> desire of the announced reason that four board members
> have decided to resign from the board as of June 5,
> 1971.

These board members, including three consumers, believed their resignation and the resignation of other board members was the only way to save a feasible health program for the poor of Floyd County. But, on the other hand, Joe Hyden felt that with what he had learned at the show-cause meeting combined with similar expe- riences of other members, the board was ready to start again.

New Beginnings

OHA's deliberation was short, and on June 4, 1971 Carl Smith, acting director of the OHA, notified Judge Stumbo and Eleanor Robinson that any continued assistance to the FCCHSP would have to be pre- ceded by the actions previously proposed by Cooper.[33] The board, now without the four resigned dissenters, reacted predictably and voted 12 to 1 not to reorganize.

Judge Stumbo went on record as the one person who favored a reorganization.

> Technically I had no vote unless it was a tie vote. But I
> did not go along, as County Judge, with a vote that may
> lose medical services for the poor and employment for
> many people.[34]

At least one consumer regretted voting not to reorganize.

> The only thing I ever hated to do was to vote against the
> program. After I studied it, I didn't care who ran the
> program, even if up in Washington, as long as it helped
> the poor people. It don't make a lot of difference who

152

runs it. They should've give more time to understanding. But I looked around and saw they had the votes and I didn't see no good fighting those odds. That's the only thing I'm sorry about.

There was little doubt in Judge Stumbo's mind of the cause for this unhappy state of affairs.

The health program was affording good service to the poor until the employment of Dr. Arnold Schecter as Director. Our treatment by Health Affairs has been ridiculous, many people don't know how bad it has been.[35]

Other board members claimed that OHA had prejudged the program before the hearing of June 1. Communicating with OHA, in their estimation, was like "talking to a blank wall," because evidently the issue was cut and dry with them.[36] Joe Hyden, speaking for the county's dentists, felt that "unless we can run our own program and be satisfied with it, we'd rather have none."[37] Adams cited the statements of the consumers at the meeting of June 1 as evidence of consumer satisfaction with the program and opinioned that the program had nothing wrong with it that more money and less outside interference would not cure.[38] Probably because of this conviction, Adams called for a congressional investigation into the reasons for OEO requirements and the suspension of funds.[39]

But hope was still within the suspended program. Eula Hall announced that EKWRO soon would submit a proposal for a multi-county medical program (which it did in fact submit but which like its predecessor was neither acknowledged by OHA nor acted upon). On July 10, 1971 Judge Stumbo and Eleanor Robinson applied for a last defense of the program and arranged for a termination hearing on August 10. Between the time of this request and August 10, secret and successful negotiations among OEO, the Big Sandy CAP, and members of the suspended FCCHSP board were conducted; consequently, the termination hearing was canceled, a planning board was established, and a planning grant was provided to begin a new program.

Opponents of the old FCCHSP were bitter. Not only had they lost the chance to publicly air their criticisms and grievances but also the very same machinations that they resented in the old program had been utilized to bring about this new arrangement. Consumers and critics had not taken part in the negotiations, and, instead of cutting itself off from the past, the new program deliberately maintained ties with it. The county judge and the two remaining and acquiesing consumer board members were named members of the planning board.

OHA felt that no program in Floyd County would be possible without Judge Stumbo's cooperation; therefore, he was included on the planning board. It was argued that consumers from the old board should be continued on the planning board for the sake of their experience; importantly, not one of the remaining consumers had ever cast a dissenting vote.

The earliest actions of the planning board were to publicize and conduct elections for the remaining consumer representatives to the board. The arrangements made were not satisfactory to EKWRO, who successfully sought a court injunction until reasonable notice of the elections could be made and the court could specify procedures and eligibility for the elections. Despite these efforts the elections held on October 29, 1971 resulted in not a single EKWRO member's election.

EKWRO members recounted the election and the campaign in dissatisfied terms.

> Where you got five people on the Board and seven consumers, hell they'll spend all kinds of money to make sure that the true representatives of the poor don't get elected. That was proven in this last Comprehensive Health election. They went all out. . . . They had a slate of consumers, you know. They ran a slate, you know, to make sure those consumers got elected.
> They used money, they used jobs, they used Nelson Mainstream men, qualified everyone of them, to go out and work against their own people.

One OHA staff member claimed the office was bitterly disappointed by the failure of EKWRO to seat representatives on the new interim board. Leon Cooper, who became director of OHA, was not as disappointed and took a more philosophical position invoking the principles of opportunity and market mechanism of elections.

> The local people have to decide that. In our position in including EKWRO as a member of the planning board, we would assure that there would be opportunity for the people of Floyd County to seat EKWRO or for EKWRO to seat themselves, if in fact they were that kind of force. But we couldn't come down, and wouldn't come down, and say you've got to include EKWRO simply because there is an EKWRO. We got viewed as an adversary with EKWRO about that, but this time it was from a position of absolute neutrality about who was representative of the poor in Floyd County. . . We felt that our responsibility was to provide a forum whereby EKWRO could

154

gain a seat on the Board, if indeed EKWRO was the force which it described itself as.[40]

The elections were significant because, in the estimation of some, they allowed a democratic measure of EKWRO's support and strength. The lack of success in the election confirmed critics in their doubts concerning EKWRO's constituency. This was certainly true of one critic of EKWRO who was on the interim planning board.

They weren't advocating, you know, reasonable, practically attainable means. Eula Hall stood and raised hell for two hours over the type of vehicle, in most abusive language. . . . I don't want to ride in a goddamn International Bronco, I want a Cadillac just like the County Judge. She has been presented as a "spokesman," as a "leader" and has generally been rejected. Whether she was associated with EKWRO, or had she been associated with the establishment gang and done the same type of mouthing she would have been rejected.

Most important, the election results influenced the views of new members of the interim board.

EKWRO could have been [represented] but the poor people didn't elect them. They had the chance to elect them, they didn't. Why? In the consumer group there seems to be some substantial antagonism towards EKWRO. Many of these people, inadequate as these services were, they were at least getting something. They tend to point the finger and say, "Well EKWRO, they may have recognized all the problems but now we ain't got nothing." . . . There is a division within that community, you ask one of these fellas and they say, "Well, they only represent four hundred families."

The election taken as a measure of the democratic strength of EKWRO led at least one new planning board member to view EKWRO as a manipulated group of poor persons.

Eula Hall is a lady who actually is a pretty well-meaning person but is the front for other persons in that operation.[41]

The VISTA lawyers were pointed out as being the brain power behind EKWRO. "I don't think that particular group [EKWRO] would have come to surface without them." The role of EKWRO toward the planning board continued as it had been, that of an outside critical observer.

In addition to its critical observance of the dealings of the planning board, EKWRO has pursued several other health-related matters. In the summer of 1971, EKWRO sponsored a health fair in Mud Creek in conjunction with medical students from Vanderbilt University. In one week, 481 Mud Creek residents underwent a complete diagnosic checkup for over 70 specified or general ailments and conditions. Of the number diagnosed, 345 were found with some ailment and 102 of them were found with a diagnosed condition requiring follow-up examination and treatment—which was provided.[42]

In the summer of 1972, EKWRO organized a summer health project that sent young local residents—trained, and sometines accompanied, by voluntary health professionals from out of the county— into the homes of Mud Creek residents. These health teams conducted tests for tuberculosis, anemia, worms, high blood pressure, diabetes, and pregnancy. In addition, they arranged for immunization for diphtheria, measles, mumps, and polio from Public Health nurses and provided further preventive measures by teaching residents how to test and purify water, by educating them about drugs and their usage, and by distributing a first aid manual dealing with problems of burns, poisoning, and other accidents. Provision also was made for the collection, testing, and reporting of home cures and herbs.

EKWRO also continued advocate services for Mud Creek residents, such as follow-up care for persons the health teams found seriously ill and without health services. In addition, EKWRO has failed and successfully contested a suit against the Internal Revenue Service for granting tax-exempt status to several proprietory hospitals of the area, including the new Highlands Hospital, even though their provision of charitable care was insufficient for that status. Highlands for example, claimed 32 out of 3,634 patients as charitable cases in fiscal 1973.[43] EKWRO also has succeeded in gaining from the McDowell Hospital a policy of treatment for all sick persons regardless of their ability to pay. Its one attempt to start its own federally funded health program under the auspices of the National Health Service Corps of the Department of Health, Education and Welfare (HEW) failed because the required approval of state-local medical societies and local political officials was not forthcoming.

EKWRO did establish its own health clinic in April 1973 with the aid of loans from the Kentucky Welfare Rights Organization, fund-raising efforts of Mud Creek residents, and the medical supplies donated by hospitals outside the county. Another large contribution to the clinic came from the husband and wife team of physicians who staffed the clinic for an annual salary of one dollar. EKWRO has tried to separate the clinic from its organization in order to present the clinic as a Mud Creek citizens' project. The board of directors of the clinic are all local residents, EKWRO members as well as non-members. The clinic handles from 30 to 50 patients a day and provides for some house care by a nurse practitioner formerly with both FCCHSP and the McDowell Hospital. Transportation is provided and charges for service are on a sliding scale according to the ability to pay. Third-party payments have made the clinic self-supporting in the first year of its operation. Medicine is provided free, whenever possible, from donated stocks; and, when it must be purchased, it is purchased under contract with a pharmacy in Martin and delivered to the house of the person. Follow-up care is available, since both clinic physicians also practice at Our Lady of the Way Hospital in Martin. The clinic is yet unable to provide emergency care, and, while it has employed and trained local residents for some positions in the clinic, other positions have educational requirements that have precluded the hiring of poor people. EKWRO members take great satisfaction in the operation of the Mud Creek Citizens' Project and feel the greatest challenge remaining is to keep the project out of the control of county political, medical, and even antipoverty officials. If successful, the clinic will be, in Eula Hall's estimation, a demonstration to the community and the medical people as well of how people can organize to meet their own real health needs.[44]

After its first full year of operation the clinic has been moved to a new location which is both more accessible and spacious. The finances of the clinic have enabled the board to increase the salaries of the staff and to institute an annual salary of $10,000 for each physician. In the summer of 1974, plans were being made to recruit an additional physician, additional nurses, and a dentist. In addition to innovating a much needed dental program, thought has been given to programs of day care and therapy for the mentally ill.

In contrast with EKWRO's successes, the interim board seemed unable to surmount some initial hurdles including formulating a job description for the project director. The first description was rejected by OHA because requirements were set so low that local nonprofessional persons previously associated with FCCHSP would be eligible to become project director.

The board later succeeded, in July 1973, in gaining OHA approval for the newly hired project director, Quentin Allen. Allen, a native of Floyd County, is the son of the Floyd County Times editor and graduate of the University of Cincinnati, with a master's degree in community health. OHA after extending the original planning grant period approved funding for the new comprehensive health program in July 1974. The problems of the new project director are obvious to the professionals on the board. The program's future funding is an immediate problem, with OHA's future so tenuous and HEW's role uncertain. The program's relationship with the Big Sandy CAP has not been specified; although, as one professional pointed out, it is doubtful that OEO will give any further power to any CAP. EKWRO must be reckoned with by the new program as the one group in the county with experience in alternative health systems but past experience has made EKWRO members skeptical of government-funded programs and determined to protect the Mud Creek clinic from outside encroachments. Further, EKWRO's place in any new program might resurrect the animosities of the medical society. One professional on the interim board noted that the medical society had not raised objections to the board's dealings thus far, although the limited activity of the board did not really test the attitude of the medical society. Moreover, George Archer, in July 1972, expressed strong opposition, "I know of not a doctor or pharmacist who will cooperate." But it was believed that the attitude of the medical society was very likely to be modified because of the new young physicians in the county in independent and innovative practice and because of the influence of the new doctors recruited for the new hospital. The death of Archer also left a very serious leadership vacuum that will perhaps lessen resistance to change within the medical society. Last, the new project director must devise a plan that accommodates existing facilities—including the new Highlands Hospital, and the Mud Creek Clinic—and the goals of a comprehensive health program.

Other problems await to be resolved as well, the chief of which is the participation of consumers. The interim board has approximated quite exactly the administered spontaneity of a socially stratified group, and decision making has been relegated to the professionals, except for the hiring of a director—which was greatly influenced by Judge Stumbo. It remains to be seen if consumer participation can achieve any real meaning in a program marked with serious conflict over participation in the past, yet so little of it in its reorganization.

The necessity of consumer participation points to another problem: that is, the "arm-tying" regulations and conditions that OHA often imposes on local programs. OHA, in the estimation of one outside professional on the interim board, still resembles the "shadow government" tactic of some CAP's prior to the Green Amendment whereby some "resources of the system were employed to confront other aspects of the system." It is not at all certain that the special conditions of OHA can be met and, at the same time, local medical approval still gained for any new FCCHSP. OHA, moreover, has reflected its own tenuous future by changes in its own administrators and neglect of meetings and communication with the interim board and the new project director.

Despite these remaining and important problems, the interim board has succeeded in cooling the passions surrounding FCCHSP and in reducing the program's dimensions to administrative and technical questions. In this sense it is a "new beginning" in devising a nonconstant-sum game and very representative of the essence of liberal reform.

A consumer member of the former board holds out only conditional hope for a new program, however.

> I would do it again, even though it is nerve-wracking. But I want no part of it unless some of the old board members would keep their hands off. . . . Washington should train the poor people and let the consumers run it. Poor people may not have much in books, but they have lots of common sense. . . . You have to know how obligated people are to the Judge. He'll have to go to have a good program.

Echoing this sentiment was the remark of another consumer board member who was associated neither with EKWRO nor the dissenting bloc on the board. After recalling the efforts of the "experts," the doctors, the educated representatives of other groups, OHA, and the elected officials, she could not help but feel, "If they'd let common sense poor people plan that and do that, that would be the finest program in the world."

NOTES

1. Letter of Harry Eastburn to Eleanor Robinson, Chairperson FCCHSP, January 28, 1971.

2. Kenneth B. Clark and Jeannette Hopkins, A Relevant War Against Poverty: A Study of Community Action Programs and Observable Social Change (New York: Harper & Row, 1968), p. 242.

3. Thomas E. Bryant, Memorandum to the Director (no date), p. 1.

4. J. D. Adams in Courier-Journal, February 12, 1971, p. B-1.

5. Idem.

6. EKWRO, "Proposals for Changing the Floyd County Comprehensive Health Program," mimeographed, no date, p. 1.

7. There was ample precedent for Adams' position. A political campaign poster from the 1930s pictured an operation in progress with a caption, "Vote for the common man's friend, Dr. W. L. Stumbo for Sheriff of Floyd County." An appeal below the caption struck the theme of Adams:

Above is a picture of an operation in progress in the operating room of one of Dr. Stumbo's hospitals, where
thousands of penniless men, women and children have
been given medical and surgical care regardless of
their station in life.

He has been a friend to you and your loved ones —
you can now return the friendship by voting for him for
Sheriff at the Democratic Primary Election August 2.

8. The implication of this record of effort was like Franklin's
observation of a similar accounting: "Surely, there is some gratitude
due for so many instances of goodness." Benjamin Franklin, The
Political Thought of Benjamin Franklin, edited by Ralph L. Ketcham
(New York: Bobbs-Merrill Company, 1965), p. 221.

9. This material and other material from the show-cause
hearing was taken from a tape provided by Arnold Schecter. Eula
Hall's statement was taken from materials provided by Appalred
attorneys.

10. Huey Perry, "They'll Cut Off Your Project": A Mingo
County Chronicle (New York: Praeger Publishers, 1972), gives a
name to this syndrome of insecurity caused by precarious funding.

11. Kentucky Department of Economic Security, Annual Reports,
1968-72 Frankfort, Ky: 1969-73 Floyd County's self-sufficiency is
woefully belied by the $6 million annually received from the state wel-
fare and federal relief programs, which amounts to 10.7 percent of
the annual personal income of the county. For a discussion of Clay
County's reliance on welfare, see Bill Peterson, Coaltown Revisited:
An Appalachian Notebook (Chicago: Henry Regnery Co., 1972), pp.
123-32.

12. Bryant, Memorandum, pp. 1-2.

13. C. B. Macpherson, The Political Theory of Possessive
Individualism: Hobbes to Locke (New York: Oxford University Press,
1962), p. 248.

14. Hans Peter Dreitzel, ed., The Social Organization of Health:
Recent Sociology No. 3 (New York: Macmillan, 1971), pp. xiv-xv.

15. Roger Hurley, "The Health Crisis of the Poor," in
Dreitzel, The Social Organization of Health," p. 109.

16. Clark and Hopkins, Relevant War Against Poverty, p. 246.

17. Philip Selznick cited in Sheldon S. Wolin, Politics and
Vision: Continuity and Innovation in Western Political Thought (Boston: Little, Brown and Company, 1960), p. 413.

18. Roman Aquizao and Ernest Vargas, "Technology, Power
and Socialization in Appalachia," in Peoples' Appalachian Research
Collective (PARC), ed., Appalachia's People, Problems, Alternatives,
vol. 1 (Morgantown, W. Va.: PARC, 1971), p. 126.

19. Ibid., p. 127.

20. See also Tony Dunbar, Our Land Too (New York: Vintage Books, 1971), pp. 169 and 178.

21. Bryant, Memorandum, p. 2.

22. C. B. Macpherson, The Real World of Democracy (New York: Oxford University Press, 1972), p. 39.

23. Wolin, Politics and Vision, pp. 343-51.

24. Louis Hartz, The Liberal Tradition in America: An Interpretation of American Political Thought Since the Revolution (New York: Harcourt, Brace and World, 1955), p. 59.

25. EKWRO letter to Frank Carlucci, April 16, 1971.

26. Interestingly enough, critics of the doctors did not castigate them for their alleged profiteering. "The doctors had a good thing going, I don't blame them. The doctors and the pharmacists both had a good thing going." They pointed out that the federal government could have saved money with a comprehensive health program but "you know it's hard to disregard a county association like that of professional people." Indeed, the history of eastern Kentucky is replete with efforts of amelioration that resulted in fabulous amounts for some professionals. We have seen Caudill's report of the profits accrued to doctors by means of UMW efforts to improve health. He points out also that morticians found the fund a lucrative sponsor of otherwise unavailable expensive funerals. Harry M. Caudill, Night Comes to the Cumberlands: A Biography of a Depressed Area (Boston: Little, Brown and Co., 1962), p. 301. Medicaid provided a bonanza for some eastern Kentucky doctors; See T. N. Bethell, "Ill Wind in Appalachia: The Medicaid Mess," in Peoples' Appalachian Research Collective, Appalachia's People, pp. 148-49. Only recently black lung has proven the largest money-maker of all with lawyers awarded up to 20 percent of the settlement their clients receive. This maximum fee is awarded by the state compensation board 80 percent of the time and has meant more than $1 million to one Pike County lawyer (chairman of the senate committee that wrote the bill) and an average of $4,679 per successful case in 1973. A General Accounting Office study found that in 1972 the average attorney fee per successful black lung claim in Kentucky was $4,277, compared with $300 in Pennsylvania and $456 in Virginia. Louisville Courier-Journal, October 8, 1973, p. A-1. Like other payment mechanisms, the escalation of costs have led to charges of fraud and calls for a cutback in benefits. Courier-Journal, Louisville, Ky., June 6, 1973, p. 1; and June 8, 1973, p. B-1. Black lung also has increased the importance and earnings of mountain doctors as their depositions are requiried to certify the pneumoconiosis of a man and may cost $100 to $225. Kyle Vance, "Physicians Fatten Purses with Pay for Black Lung Medical Tests," Courier-Journal, July 29, 1973, p. A-1.

It should be noted that this experience adds another dimension to the colonial analogy as applied to eastern Kentucky; that is, a native professional class benefits by its area's relation with the dominant area.

27. Courier-Journal, December 4, 1970, p. B-1.

28. Lewis cites the use of services and facilities outside the area by the managerial class as an indication of colonialism. Helen Lewis "Fatalism of the Coal Industry? Contrasting Views of Appalachian Problems," Mountain Life and Work 46, no. 11 (December 1970): 12.

29. Maxine Kenny, "Mountain Health Care: Politics, Power and Profits," Mountain Life and Work 47, no. 4 (April 1971): 14-17. See Appendix A for Health Bill of Rights.

30. Robert J. Bazell, "Health Care: What the Poor People Didn't Get from Kentucky Project," Science 172, (April 30, 1971): 458-60, "OEO Hedges on Kentucky Program," Science 172 (October 1, 1971): 45, "OEO Program: What did Millions Buy?" Medical World News, May 14, 1971. Pratt's reply appeared in Medical World News, June 11, 1971, p. 12. Homer Bigart, "Anti-Poverty Programs Imperiled in Appalachia," The New York Times, June 15, 1971, p. 36. Bigart is given credit with bringing the problems of Appalachia to the attention of Kennedy almost a decade before. Judith Randall, "Poor Rap OEO Health Project: Perkins Hit," in the Washington Evening Star, May 4, 1971, p. 1. Also Judith Randall, "OEO Project Blessing for Whom?" the Washington Evening Star, May 6, 1971, editorial page. The Louisville Courier-Journal's extensive coverage of the program's trouble culminated in a mildy sympathetic editorial on July 10, 1971.

31. Letter to Leon Cooper, April 15, 1971, from Woodrow Rogers, President of EKWRO.

32. Floyd County Times, May 13, 1971, p. 12.

33. Letter of June 4, 1971 from Carl Smith to Judge Stumbo and Eleanor Robinson.

34. Floyd County Times, June 17, 1971, p. 1.

35. Idem.

36. The Louisville Courier-Journal, June 17, 1971, p. B-1.

37. Idem.

38. The Louisville Courier-Journal, June 13, 1971, p. B-1.

39. Floyd County Times, June 17, 1971, p. 1.

40. Interview with Leon Cooper, Washington, D.C., March 31, 1972.

41. This view is also presented in a study of Floyd County by a University of Kentucky medical student. EKWRO is said to epitomize "the illiterate, impoverished culturally bankrupt Floyd County residents" whose real brain and voice is Maxine Kenney, "a highly effective, behind-the-scenes agitator and manipulator." The report

correctly summarized the political nature of the program but criticized OEO and project critics for not recognizing—or perhaps better, not accepting—this fact of life as "an endemic, essential, and effective means of administration." James R. Stivers, "Floyd County Comprehensive Health Services Program," unpublished paper, College of Medicine, University of Kentucky, June 1971. It is significant of how far the politics of FCCHSP extended that this report—the most sympathetic review of the program; critical of OEO, EKWRO, and Schecter; and critical of the excessive demands of consumers while defending the "medical establishment"—won honors among the reports submitted by senior medical students. Reports critical of the study were actively discouraged.

42. Statistics provided by Louis Lefkowitz, M.D., Vanderbilt Coordinator of the Floyd County Health Fair.

43. "EKWRO Wins Healthcare Suit," Mountain Life and Work, (March 1974): 20-21.

44. "Why a Health Fair?" Mountain Life and Work 47, nos. 7-8 (July/August 1971): 11-12.

6

FORESTALLING CHANGE

Nondecisions and Legitimations

The way in which common sense poor people were not allowed control of the health program has been depicted in detail by the narration of events. What remains now is to explain, as well as possible, why the poor were denied control. The primary conclusion of this study is that the poor could not be left alone to their own antipoverty devices in Floyd County, or elsewhere, because poverty, politics, and even health are circumscribed by cultural values that have a bearing on the differences among people and the maintenance of those differences. The interrelation of elite opposition to FCCHSP and their socioeconomic position, as well as existing cultural values, is a factor important to any attempt at change and one that allows us to generalize beyond Floyd County.

To understand the full implications of this opposition it may be helpful to examine the controversy as a nondecision, in the terms of Bachrach and Baratz, involving the board of directors of FCCHSP, OEO, EKWRO, and Arnold Schecter. It is hoped that this examination will bring a new dimension to the events of Floyd County and, moreover, reveal the explicit relationship of the events there with other battles in the War on Poverty and the skirmishes of other groups of powerless people when they attempt to organize and act.

The comprehensive health controversy evidenced many of the characteristics of a nondecision making process, which Bachrach and Baratz define as:

> A decision that results in the suppression or thwarting
> of a latent or manifest challenge to the values or interests
> of the decision-maker. To be more nearly explicit,
> nondecision-making is a means by which demands for
> change in the existing allocation of benefits and priv-
> ileges in the community can be suffocated before they
> are even voiced; or kept covert; or killed before they
> gain access to the relevant decision-making arena;
> or failing all these things, maimed or destroyed in the
> decision-implementing stage of the policy process.[1]

The changes inherent in a truly comprehensive health program, as
envisioned by OHA, were "suffocated" during the first three years of
FCCHSP's existence. However, the opposition of EKWRO and Schecter
forced the controversy to the decision making arena, where, more
plainly, the changes were destroyed. The threat that EKWRO represented was not merely to the allocation of benefits and power as
it existed but also as a process; EKWRO was attempting, along with
Schecter, to establish a new system of health care delivery that would
have contended with the existing system. Their very attempt was a
threat, since it was action outside of the traditional channels of power
and, if successful, meant a substantial change in the management of
jobs, money, and services.

This more than anything else provoked the FCCHSP conflict.
Neither the professionals and acquiescent consumers of the FCCHSP
board, nor the members of EKWRO and other consumer critics, nor
the "new class" representatives—Schecter and OHA—were fighting
a defensive battle; rather, all of them were asserting and furthering
a set of values, a world view, which gave identity and meaning to themselves as well as their opponents.

The conflict over FCCHSP makes clear that the force, power,
influence, and authority of the Floyd County elites were insufficient
to contain the opposition of EKWRO, Schecter, and OHA. This insufficiency necessitated the explication of the elites' views of themselves, their world, and their opponents and affords us the rare view
of the elements of socialization that often are taken for granted within
a traditional society—which by definition is one that is imbued with
the world view of its elites. In other words, the elite-dominated
and -sustaining network of meanings in which the threat to FCCHSP
took place was not sufficient to dissipate the threat, prevent a crit-
ically reflective examination of the adequacy of that network of shared
meanings, and therefore forestall change. Instead, the ontological
appearance of elite beliefs and consequent socioeconomic and political
arrangements as just, right, and necessary was altered.

Myths, Hegemony, and Legitimations

An understanding of the interaction and interpenetration of the FCCHSP conflict and the network of elite beliefs and structures within which it took place adds an important dimension to the controversy, as well as to other studies of decision making and community power. However, such an understanding requires that we suspend the reified appearance of the existing institutional arrangements and view the conflict as an attempt to re-establish a network of cultural meanings and the political and social arrangement they supported and from which they stemmed. The professional members of the FCCHSP board and its acquiescent consumer representatives, in this view, were acting to preserve a system of beliefs of great significance in that it served as the secondary legitimations of the existing distribution of power and benefits—"things as they are," which represented everything in its right place. This attempt to preserve "things as they are" entailed mobilizing the bias or beliefs within them. In this it resembled a nondecision that squelches a threatening demand or incipient issue by invoking the existing bias that approximates what Edelman terms socially cued myths: "a belief held in common by a large group of people that gives events and actions a particular meaning."[2]

It is important to note that we are not talking about the manipulation of myth by elites nor the deliberate deception of others by them; rather, we are speaking of a process in which myth is presented as fact. But facts, as Georg Lukacs has pointed out, "can only become facts within the framework of a system."[3] The system of Floyd County legitimated the beliefs and actions of at least two professional members of the board who could recall boyhood experiences of bitter poverty that taught one of them, "you'll either root hog or die." Their success was biographical and existential evidence of the ability of the system, which they now represented, to reward efforts and characteristics like their own. The great success of a few created a "fact" out of a belief with no better expression than the comment, "If I could do it, anyone could do it."

In a study of elites in the Kentucky mountains, H. Dudley Plunkett and Mary Jean Bowman concluded with an observation pertinent to the belief-system-as-fact of the Floyd County professionals.

> They do have strong commitments, both cultural and
> political; their attitudes are not simple defense-mechan-
> isms to deny an unwelcome reality. Their attitudes have
> positive connotations also, and they reflect phenomenolog-
> ical realities of the mountain heritage: the characteristics
> of the pioneer of the nineteenth century entrepreneur
> are still held up to be admired; a man's virtue is still

evident in his worldly success and the ambitious man
need not stay poor.[4]

The myths within a belief system are not necessarily manipulated,
then; rather, they may have the nature of ontological fact for those
in power whose experience has proven them true. Plunkett and
Bowman found, for example, that over 90 percent of the public officials, bankers, lawyers, Baptist clergy, physicians, and manufacturing
entrepreneurs they interviewed ascribed to the belief that a young man
with real ambition can make a success of his life no matter how poor
or ignorant his family background.[5] It seems only "natural" that this
would appear as true to successful men. This is of immense importance because it is constitutive of the relationship of the elites, as
legitimators of myth, and those less fortunate or less privileged or
powerless and the reconciliation of their differences.

The array of myths invoked on behalf of "things as they are"
in Floyd County served one of two related functions, both of which
implied no need for change; they either enhanced or explained the
existing privilege of some or they explained the position of the poor.
Among the former legitimations was the function of elections to
guarantee that public officials represent the best interest of the poor.
As a pharmacist of the county explained:

> These officials get out and have to be elected. They're a
> friend to everybody. A lot more poor people vote than
> there are any other kind in this county. [Intimidation]
> isn't a problem at all.

This belief has endured despite a history of voting irregularities, so
that even the chairman of the interim planning committee believed
with confidence that the county judge could speak for all poor people.

Another belief that enhanced existing arrangements was the
privatization of the forms of relief; among these were effort and
medicine. The belief was common among the professionals on the
board that poor people still had bootstraps but some refused to use
them.

> It's my own conviction, perhaps it's Victorian, perhaps
> it's been indelibly stamped on my character by virtue of
> having been a Depression youngster, that any program
> that isn't directly related to some work, certainly has
> its shortcomings. One of the pitfalls I have observed in
> most of these federal programs to eliminate poverty
> seems to be there's always a lack of proper supervision.
> There are a great many people who won't work without

proper supervision. When I say supervision, I mean
perhaps talking to them and explaining the fact, that if
you don't work, you don't eat.

Effort appeared as a moral test and individual success as a proof of
worth.

> I can cite you an example, my father was a coal miner,
> between a little town right over here . . . between there
> and a little farm outside of Prestonsburg I grew up until
> I got my family out of there when I was twenty-two years
> old. I stood in lines during depression times with my
> mother and we got what they called commodities, give-
> away groceries. I wanted something better. I was the
> oldest child so I went to school and then I put my brothers
> and sisters through school. We had all a desire to get
> ahead. We now in turn have helped others. I have a son
> who is a dentist; another son who shortly will be a physi-
> cian; a daughter who is a dental hygenist; a son-in-law
> and daughter in pharmacy school. . . . If we could do it,
> anyone could do it.

This privatization of relief removed the necessity of explaining the
serious unemployment chronic to Floyd County and enhanced the
stature of those who had achieved considerable material improvement
over the conditions they knew as children. Contrasted with this is
the stark appraisal of Tom Gish, "The capitalistic system which
made America great has failed in eastern Kentucky."[6] But the privatization of relief through effort was not unique to Floyd County. In a
very insightful article John Schaar points out that this privatization
could be easily accommodated within the early ambiguity of OEO.

> No policy formula is better designed to fortify the dom-
> inant institutions, values, and ends of the American social
> order than the formula of equality of opportunity, for it
> offers everyone a fair and equal chance to find a place
> within that order. In principle, it excludes no man from
> the system if his abilities can be put to use within the
> system.[7]

In addition to the privatization of effort for relief, the narration
of events of the FCCHSP conflict makes obvious the ascription of the
private nature of medicine. The inability of the program to advance
beyond fee-for-service and third-party payment schemes evidenced
the same entrepreneurial mentality that supported the proprietary

hospitals, noted by the Boone Report, and the profiteering from the UMW Fund that is described by Harry M. Caudill. In cases where payment was not possible, medical care was termed charity, clearly indicating it was the largesse of the provider and not the right of the sick person. The privatization of medicine was the equivalent of including it under the Lockian rubric of property and thus legitimizing the existing monopolization of health care and the opposition to outside doctors, nursing practitioners, and additional pharmacies.

Besides all these social, political, and economic implications, the scientistic mantle of medicine has greatly enhanced the authority of the doctor so that, more than any other group, the medical profession determines the social definitions of health and illness.[8] Cognizant of their place apart, it is not surprising to find that the legitimations of enhancement have fostered elitist attitudes. Plunkett and Bowman found the physicians of their study to be among those elites

> who retain an individualistic rationale, but who oppose active involvement of the poor (or the young) in affairs they have come to regard as their particular preserve, or who have a very low opinion generally of the competence of the less-favored members of the local society.[9]

In Floyd County the educational attainment of the poor or the illiteracy of EKWRO members often was alluded to as if they had bearing on participation in civil and political society. The views expressed by two medical professionals on sterilization of the poor best depict the Social Darwinism implicit in the legitimations of enhancement (see p. 127).

The other set of myths, attributed identity, served the reciprocal purpose of enhancement: to explain the position of the less-privileged and to portray the concern of the privileged without risk to their position. Those who legitimate "things as they are" and represent them help shape the identity of others by shaping their relationships with the prevailing institutions. In Paulo Freire's terms, the oppressed find in the oppressor the model of manhood[10] and come to accept the world that the oppressor has shaped for them. Insofar as ascribed identity or oppressed consciouness serves to legitimate existing institutions by explaining the relationship of privileged and less-privileged persons, it approximates the cultural hegemony written of by Antonio Gramsci.

> Hegemony is "an order in which a certain way of life and thought is dominant, in which one concept of reality is diffused throughout society in all its institutions and

private manifestations, informing with its spirit all taste, morality, customs, religious and political principles, and all social regulations, particularly in their intellectual and moral connotations.[11]

Thus, the poor were manipulated or thoughtful; the victims of mechanization and difficult times or professionals at the art of handouts; rude and aggressive or apathetic; depending on their relation with existing institutions, their demands on them, and their conformity to the reciprocal typification of poor and elites.

One consumer representative of the FCCHSP board was told by a professional that she had been the best consumer representative on the board, even though she had never cast a vote different from the majority of the board and, as far as any one could tell, had never spoken at a meeting. This same consumer was explicit in her recognition that the superintendent of schools and the county judge understood the poor. Such acceptance of one's attributed identity instills myth with its greatest power, the power to go unquestioned.[12]

The dependence of the poor on their attributed identity is an important part of the satiric accuracy Louis Hartz spoke of, by which history fulfills the American dream. Poverty has become an industry for large numbers of bureaucrats whose job it is to enforce the social definition of poverty, a definition construed more in terms of cost than need: when Medicaid or Medicare costs soar, more stringent criteria for eligibility and benefits are imposed; when the numbers of poor are to be counted and programs for them devised, scarcity is the measure of poverty; when poor groups organize themselves for action, cost efficiency replaces maximum feasible participation as the guiding spirit of OEO; whenever meeting the needs of the poor seem to require the modification or redistribution of wealth and power, the latter are avoided by denying the extent of the need of the poor. Nothing illustrates this quite so concisely as the incident related by an EKWRO member concerning the removal of a sign that warned a bridge was unsafe for more than cars and pickup trucks so that the bridge could continue to be used by schoolchildren and the school bus. The consequence of this acceptance of their attributed identity has been, as Edelman notes, that

the American poor have required less coercion and less in social security guarantees to maintain their quiescence than has been true in other developed countries, even authoritarian ones like Germany and notably poor ones like Italy; for guilt and self-concepts of the poor have kept them docile.[13]

The apparent "naturalness" of some of the beliefs within Floyd County were subject to doubt before the FCCHSP conflict. It was recognized by poor and professional that a person might be willing to work but yet be poor because of the inability to find work. But by far the most serious threat to "things as they are" was the alienation of some people from the existing set of objectivated institutions and beliefs. Alienation represents not only a dissatisfaction with the integration of personal biography and social history and arrangements offered by "things as they are" but also may lead to the construction of alternative beliefs, a new set of initial conditions,[14] which, if consensus for them is gained, may become myths and sponsor political action to objectivate an alternative set of meanings.

An articulate alienation represents both a critique of "things as they are" and the need for either new legitimations to be provided by the elites or new institutions that would entail real change in existing objectivations. The reaction of Floyd County professionals to certain kinds of outsiders is pertinent to this point. The outsiders most objected to are those who dealt in a counterdefinition of reality, which permitted a new theoretical understanding of existing institutions.[15] With the aid of outsiders, alienated groups within the county, of which EKWRO was the most organized, could come to a new theoretical understanding of "things as they are." Outsiders' criticisms were blunted by attributing characteristics to them. OEO was, for example, a black man's program and not directly applicable to "things as they are" in Floyd County.

It may be a case of people trying to conceive grandiose schemes on a theoretical basis without knowing the type of people they are working with. . . . Now quite often, in fact always, legislation written by congress, someone takes and writes guidelines; and there it seems to reflect to us . . . that they [guideline writers] are ghetto-bred people, and are hipped to urban ghetto situations. Ghetto legislation would fit our situation here like a hole in my head would fit. It's almost impossible, it appears to me, to write legislation for Watts or Hough or some of the other ghetto areas that doesn't permit a little bit of flexibility that isn't ridiculous when it gets to us.

An articulate alienation is a real threat to "things as they are" not only because a new set of legitimations contends with prevailing legitimations but also because it exemplifies what reified objectivations and legitimations deny; namely, that a given set of institutions and meanings is not inevitable.[16] The beliefs of elites become

171

vulnerable, and the elites themselves become accountable to the ideas of others. This is the sense in which EKWRO members feel poor people are beginning "to wake up" and to insist that officials abide by the rules by which they are bound, and by the purposes programs were intended to serve, whether it be the administration of a school lunch program or a health program. What appeared to many professionals in Floyd County as government waste was explained as elite mismanagement by one consumer representative not associated with EKWRO.

> If I'd knowed the mess it was in, I would never got in it. They fooled around with the money till it was gone and no one knew where it went. I can't figure out why someone didn't holler before it got into that mess. I wouldn't astood around and watched that mess agrowing without speaking up, would you? The Prestonsburg bunch just got that program and ran it for themselves and it was the awfulest mess you ever did see.

EKWRO undoubtedly is cognizant of the liberal tenets of contractual arrangements in society and government and has been uniquely successful in promoting the enforcement of them. The instances of the termination of an antipoverty program because of its failure to serve poor people are few; it may be that FCCHSP is the only such instance. In any event, it is no small achievement to have wrested a program of such dimensions from elite control. More important, however, EKWRO's opposition stemmed not just from shared liberal principles but from a vision of alternatives that "destroyed the social fact" of "things as they are." The events and conditions of Floyd County, like the market system of the 19th century, have produced a group of persons of the same class, as well as some allies, who can envision and realize alternatives to the meanings and arrangements they are asked to accept.[17] The tangible instances of the articulation of this vision is the Health Bill of Rights and the Mud Creek Citizens' Health Project. It also can be heard in the defense of their vision against legitimations of attributed pejorative identity: "If that's communism, Floyd County could do with a little more of it."[18]

The change in the relationship between the elites and the alienated poor is felt by the elites and was articulated very clearly.

> I think the attacks made on the establishment here in Floyd County have really done more harm than they have done good. Because now I think we're much more suspicious of people with a foreign accent than we were before

we had the influx of people. I predicted then, to those
young people, "If you don't use your heads, you're going
to sow dissension and when you leave here—and I can
tell you I'm going to be here, if I live, while you're going
back home—it's conceivable then, if you don't handle your
contact with our people here most wisely, when you leave
here the people with whom you've had contact are
going to be worse off. They'll have no faith in anyone."

That's somewhat come to pass as in the case of
EKWRO and its leaders and so forth. There is no bridge
as I can see it. There is absolutely no meaningful
communication at all between the leadership of EKWRO
and the establishment of Floyd County. We used to be
able to talk to those people and they used to be able to
talk with us. They don't come to see me anymore; they
don't ask me for help and advice.

ACCOMMODATING CHANGE

Determining the Limits of Feasible Change

What we have termed legitimations of enhancement and attributed
identity were attempts to maintain arrangements and beliefs that
could no longer be taken for granted. Definitions of reality were contending with each other; which definitions would prevail was a question
of power. The elites enjoyed a certain consensus for the beliefs they
represented and sought to reinvoke these beliefs and to reify them.

The first form of maintaining "things as they are" is therapy,
which is designed to prevent the inhabitants of one set of beliefs and
socioeconomic arrangements from emigrating to another. Thus, the
legitimating apparatus is used selectively, and a pathology is ascribed
to deviants that accounts for their alienation or disaffection: EKWRO
was the "manipulated poor," or made up of loafers who had time to
dissent, or victims of a culture of poverty. Along with the pathology
came such curative procedures as the reawakening of drive, motivation, and patriotism and the breaking down of the culture of poverty
and isolation.

The second form of maintaining "things as they are" is what Peter
Berger and Thomas Luckman term nihilation, which has two manifestations. The first is to accord an inferior status, a "not-to-be-taken-
seriously" status, to all definitions existing outside of elite values
and arrangements. Thus, definitions take on the characteristics of
those who offer them; the worthy poor, unworthy poor, and outsiders,

173

which include not only Schecter but officials from Washington who did not realize the uniqueness of Floyd County. The second form of nihilation is to account for the deviant definitions of reality in terms of "things as they are."

> The final goal of this procedure is to incorporate the deviant conceptions within one's own universe, and thereby liquidate them ultimately. The deviant concepts must, therefore, be translated into concepts derived from one's own universe. In this manner, the negation of one's universe is subtly changed into an affirmation of it. The presupposition is always that the negator does not really know what he is saying.19

This form of nihilation approximates the second form of non-decision making offered by Bachrach and Baratz, which "involves reshaping or strengthening the mobilization of bias in order to block challenges to the prevailing allocation of values."20 This is a non-decision by which elites accommodate themselves to changes that are required by the pressures of the alienated and to those for whom "things as they are" is no longer relevant or satisfactory. Unable to forestall change completely by the mobilization of existing bias, elites appropriate those changes to their views, in order to forestall changes that would either do violence to "things as they are," which undergirds their own position, or legitimate an opponent's view. Jurgen Habermas typifies this phenomenon as rationalization from above; new legitimations replace fragile old ones, and existing distributions of privilege and power are legitimated by their display of vitality and their ability to reorganize tradition in the face of changing times.21

Legitimations of nihilation define the limits of feasible change and in this way reconstruct and reaffirm "things as they are" and its social structural correlatives. The thoughts of change that remain are, in the words of Freire, "a reflection of the director society"22 and construct the limits for action while assigning other thoughts to the margins of untested feasibility.23

The origins of OEO as well as its history make clear that there never was any serious consideration given to the probability that the federal government would sponsor conflict for the sake of institutional or political change. The myths OEO ascribed to, including the opportunity theory, precluded such consideration. Moreover, John H. Schaar points out that OEO perpetuated "things as they are" by its subscription to equality of opportunity.

> [Equality of Opportunity] is the perfect embodiment of the Liberal conception of reform. It breaks up

solidaristic opposition to existing conditions of inequality
by holding out to the ablest and most ambitious members
of the disadvantaged groups the enticing prospect of rising
from their lowly state into a more prosperous condition.
The rules of the game remain the same: the fundamental
character of the social-economic system is unaltered.
All that happens is that individuals are given the chance
to struggle up the social ladder, change their position
on it, and step on the fingers of those beneath them.[24]

It should not be surprising, then, that the elites of Floyd County,
when change could not be forestalled, expressed caution and took
steps to see that change would be "within channels"—even if that meant
the Big Sandy CAP—because confusion would result "as to authority
and everything else, if it was not." Likewise it was often heard that
EKWRO had, or probably had, some good points but that their means
were all wrong; they were going too fast; or they were too aggressive.[25] It may be that their aggressiveness was upsetting because,
as one study of Appalachian culture shows, the Floyd County elites
were likely to reward dependent and unaggressive behavior in the sub-
ordinate class, while rewarding independent and aggressive behavior
in the "controlling class."[26] Thus, Eula Hall was disparaged while
George Archer was praised as the "go-gettingest man in Eastern
Kentucky."
One important difference between the aggressiveness of EKWRO
and the aggressiveness of two professional board members of FCCHSP
who had been poor in childhood was that the latter's aggressiveness
was the action of the rugged atomist individual, while EKWRO was
acting as a group and supposedly as representative of a class. It
should not be forgotten that atomist individualism was one of the proper
channels of change and part of "things as they are." Furthermore,
"legitimate" group action, when undertaken, is to achieve or protect
individual benefits and liberty, not class goals related to equality.
Thus, there was a very large difference between the formation of the
Floyd County Pharmaceutical Association and the action of the medical
society, on the one hand, and the intervention of EKWRO, on the other.
EKWRO apparently had no interest to protect or power to contribute
that could not be done by the elected representatives of the poor and
hence was officially excluded from the Board of Directors.
The efforts of the elites were to embody the necessary changes
within traditional, albeit modified, institutions and legitimations.
OHA, on the other hand, along with EKWRO and Arnold Schecter,
appeared as the "outsider," pressing elites to increase the area of
tolerable change or lose not only control of the program but even the
program itself. As one professional put it:

They [OHA] wanted control over it without the intervention of local people. It's pretty hard to cram a program
like that down the throats of people who've lived all their
lives in Eastern Kentucky.

It is important to realize, however, that OEO from its beginnings
to its present demise has been instrumental and not autonomous in
nature. Those who provided cues for OEO may have varied from
professional reformers to purveyors of the puritan ethic, but in every
case OEO was expected to perform as any other administrative agency
which is

to create and sustain an impression that induces acquiescence of the public in the face of private tactics that
might otherwise be expected to produce resentment,
protest, and resistance.27

OEO, in other words, was not free to determine the initial conditions
of an antipoverty strategy but functioned within, and was expected to
contribute to, a political and social context based on "given" networks
of meanings, which included: a tolerance for inequality; confidence
in the free market mechanism as a model of human relations; and
the importance of social and political stability for the proper function
of the market mechanism.

The consequence of OEO's dependence most often was to force
the agency to make concessions within "things as they are" of local
elites.28 In this way OEO came to be a legitimation of those elites
as it devised antipoverty strategies with greater feasibility in relation
to existing institutions and, on the other hand, seriously compromised
groups of organized and articulate alienated poor by pushing them to
the margin of infeasibility. The result was a situation that was far
less threatening to local elites, as participation became "responsible
collaboration"29 within limits far more greatly influenced by elites
than by the organized and articulate alienated poor—as illustrated
by the CDGM controversy.

Thus, while OEO has provided a step in awakening the consciousness of the poor by providing a challenge to local elites and
even to itself by introducing a demand for change, at best, the extent
of this demand was the equitable enforcement of contractural relations.
The successful pursuit of these demands diverts the attention of the
poor from larger questions of equality and validates the system's
capacity to perform, on its own terms, for the poor. Thus, the poor
were socialized to accept a better functioning set of legitimations
and institutions rather than allowed to create their own, as exemplified
by the lack of response to EKWRO's proposals for new programs.
The poor were still "beings for another," and although some traditional
legitimations of power could be challenged, others could not.30

OHA's action in Floyd County was both a threat and an accommodation to "things as they are" there. While it is true that the physicians of the county did not achieve representation on the interim committee, there is little doubt that their views toward participation and the nature of comprehensive care were shared by the beneficient outsiders on the board much more than those of EKWRO. One health professional on the interim board from outside the county held views toward the new hospital very similar to those that prevailed among the physicians.

> That thing [hospital] is going to turn that whole thing [health care] around. Eleven doctors are going into that area. . . . It will provide an environment that is attractive to doctors to practice, which has been missing.
> OEO will have an impact, but the presence of that facility and new professional opportunity will have a much greater impact on what really happens down there.

Equally important, this interim committee seriously compromised EKWRO's influence on any subsequent health program. This is primarily because of EKWRO's failure to have a representative elected to the new board and because of the symbiotic relationship between a belief in popular control and popular elections. No less than three outside professionals on the new board expressed confidence, "If there was substantial support of EKWRO one of them would have been elected." The election results made far more easy the typification of EKWRO, given by one outside professional, as a group that "will probably be most difficult no matter what's the plan" and whose brainpower was in fact the "VISTA lawyers."

Despite the objections of the elites, OHA's efforts are representative of reforms that make change a new beginning of a nonconstant-sum game that costs no one anything and leaves "things as they are" fundamentally unaltered. It represents the leveling up spoken of by David Potter.

> In order to raise the lower without reducing the higher, to level up, it is necessary to increase the total of all the incomes—that is, to introduce new factors instead of solving the problem with the factors originally given. And it is by this stratagem of refusing to accept the factors given, of drawing on nature's surplus and on technology's tricks, that America has often dealt with her problems of social reform.[31]

177

The Margin of Infeasible Change

Several important aspects of the infeasibility of some change remain to be discussed. First, there are the problems related to eliminating the single greatest disadvantage of the poor—their powerlessness. As C.B. Macpherson pointed out, the privatization of means of production excluded some from access to the means of labor without a transfer of power—that is, the ability of the laborer to produce excess value or profit. The poor of Floyd County, Appalachia, and the United States no longer have that power. They are not poor because their power is exploited; if that was so they could rebel and withdraw their power until better terms of the transfer of power are set. They are poor because they have no relation to the production of market value. If they are exploited it is by being maintained at the position that past exploitation has brought them and then blamed for their condition. Government-sponsored community organizing did not change this powerlessness. EKWRO and Schecter gained little power by their dependency on OHA. After his dismissal Schecter had no power except as an ally of EKWRO and the power that they both had been given by OHA, that is the limited power to hold OHA to its own regulations.

EKWRO's experience has made possible a greater realization of some of its other powers. The theoretical understanding it gained in having alternative plans fall on deaf ears has imparted a further understanding of maximum feasible participation of the poor and made it more conscious of the limitations of agents of secondary socialization and less likely to swap one set of other-dominated legitimations for the set it finds itself presently alienated from. This new realization is manifest in its operation of the Mud Creek health clinic.

The ability of Mud Creek citizens to operate their own measures by their own power is not simply a matter of their strength. Also to be tested is their power to overcome elite opposition. The two are not separable, for power and powerlessness stem from the same social, economic, and political values and arrangements that establish the legitimations for inequality and its redress. The acceptance of socially structured inequality by both the poor and the nonpoor is an important determinant of feasible change.

It is important to recall that this acceptance of inequality is related to, and supports, the American liberal political culture. The outstanding characteristic of this culture is consensus. Conflict within this consensus is moderate and on relatively high authority levels. Even differences between liberals and conservatives are differences of degree, rather than kind, with the essential contentions between them being: first, the extent of the conditions warranting change; second, the ability of unchanged political social and economic conditions to meet the needs prompting demands for change; and third, the extent of change feasible without endangering consensual values such as property, liberty, ambition, and other characteristics of the entrepreneur.[32] Even the most "radical" liberal interpretation of maximum feasible participation was related to a prerequisite of entrepreneurship, that is, opportunity. The conflict between OHA and FCCHSP centered around these three foci and was aggravated by OHA's apparent ambiguity on the extent of feasible change within existing arrangements. The interim board has shown less ambiguity toward existing arrangements in their views of the judge, the new hospital, and the need of taking present conditions into account in a new program. Thus, conflict has been "elevated" to a relatively high level of authority and moderated by a more apparent consensus. The liberal consensus on degrees of inequality is an important demarcation of feasible power for the articulate alienated poor because their class demands for change extends beyond the cleavage of liberal and conservative contentions.

Another important and related determinant of the feasibility of change is the liberal conception of man as an infinite appropriator, the possessive individual. This conception of man may explain the recurrence of new beginnings of nonconstant-sum games, the leveling up spoken of by Potter. As long as the capacity to produce more is present, the validity of unlimited acquisition will not be jeopardized by the inequality of some. If, however, a fixed set of goods is posited, the market mechanisms of enforcing inequality are imperiled and redistribution necessarily becomes the social and political policy of equality.[33]

It has been argued that the market model for society and human beings is no longer sufficient.[34] Bred by a fear of scarcity, the liberal tenet of man as infinite appropriator now justifies excess wealth and imposed scarcity and hinders egalitarian thought as long as a human being's ultimate good is seen as "the indefinite increase of the aggregate of material goods."[35]

The FCCHSP conflict brought into question the sufficiency of the market model by positing health care as a right, with all the implications for equality and social responsibility for the needs of others that health care asserted as a right conveys. Richard Lichtman asserts, "The argument that would make health a communal value is a revolutionary contention."[36] It is revolutionary because it is premised on the view that health is a fundamental constituent of a fully realized human life; that each of us is responsible to the other for the development of life; and that the economic system radically maldistributes wealth, making human beings radically unequal in obtaining health care.[37]

The FCCHSP conflict leaves two important questions unanswered: Is it possible to reduce our tolerance for inequality and is it possible to grant equal access to all persons to means of full human development, such as health care? What the events in Floyd County do make clear is that consensus need not be democracy and that while the acceptance of the premises of prevailing values and their legitimating institutions may ensure change without conflict they also may continue the prejudices and inequalities of the present into the future.

The events also portray the difficulty of regaining human control of the socially constructed forms, such as medical care and participation, that now confront us in an alien and reified fashion with correlates of power. What is happening in Floyd County makes clear that democratic control hinges upon the ability of people to reach a new theoretical understanding of the "obvious" and then to act to reshape the social, economic, and political constructions of the past according to the newly realized needs of the present.

NOTES

1. Peter Bachrach and Morton S. Baratz, Power and Poverty: Theory and Practice (New York: Oxford University Press, 1970), p. 44.

2. Murray Edelman, Politics as Symbolic Action: Mass Arousal and Quiescence (Chicago: Markham Publishing Co., 1971), p. 14. See also Richard Parker, The Myth of the Middle Class: Notes on Affluence and Equality (New York: Liveright, 1972), pp. 168-69.

3. Georg Lukacs, History and Class Consciousness, translated by Rodney Livingston (London: Merlin Press, 1971), p. 5.

4. H. Dudley Plunkett and Mary Jean Bowman, Elites and Change in the Kentucky Mountains (Lexington: University of Kentucky Press, 1973), p. 87.

5. Ibid., Table 32A, p. 127.

6. Cited in James L. Sundquist, Politics and Policy: The Eisenhower, Kennedy and Johnson Years (Washington, D.C.: The Brookings Institution, 1968), p. 97.

7. John H. Schaar, "Equality of Opportunity and Beyond," in Up the Mainstream: A Critique of Ideology in American Politics and Everyday Life, edited by Herbert G. Reid (New York: David McKay Co., 1974), p. 235.

8. Hans Peter Dreitzel, ed., The Social Organization of Health: Recent Sociology No. 3 (New York: Macmillan, 1971), p. vii.

9. Plunkett and Bowman, Elites and Change, p. 43.

10. Paulo Freire, Pedagogy of the Oppressed (New York: Herder and Herder, 1970), pp. 30-32 and 144.

11. Gramsci in John M. Cammett, Antonio Gramsci and the Origins of Italian Communism (Stanford, Calif.: Stanford University Press, 1967), p. 204.

12. Murray Edelman, The Symbolic Uses of Politics (Urbana: University of Illinois Press, 1967), p. 4.

13. Edelman, Politics as Symbolic Action, p. 56.

14. Richard Lichtman, "Symbolic Interactionism and Social Reality: Some Marxist Queries," Berkeley Journal of Sociology 15 (1970): 91.

15. For county and state governments' reactions to outsiders and counterdefinitions, see Gene L. Mason, "Stripping Kentucky: The Subversive Poor," The Nation 207 (December 30, 1968); and Paul Good, "Kentucky's Coal Beds of Sedition," The Nation 205 (September 4, 1967).

16. Peter Berger and Thomas Luckman, The Social Construction of Reality: A Treatise in the Sociology of Knowledge (Garden City, N.Y.: Doubleday Anchor Books, 1967), p. 108.

17. Macpherson points out the challenge to liberal beliefs that the labor class represented. C. B. Macpherson, The Political Theory of Possessive Individualism: Hobbes to Locke (New York: Oxford University Press, 1962), pp. 271-72.

18. The dismemberment of "things as they are" is graphically portrayed by the experience and alienation of Appalachian migrants to Chicago. See Todd Gitlin and Nanci Hollander, Uptown: Poor Whites in Chicago (New York: Harper Colophon Books, 1970).

19. Berger and Luckman, Social Construction of Reality, p. 115. Their discussion on universe maintenance commences on p. 112.

20. Bachrach and Baratz, Power and Poverty, pp. 45-46.

21. Jurgen Habermas, Toward a Rational Society: Student Protest, Science and Politics, translated by Jeremy Shapiro (Boston: Beacon Press, 1968), p. 98.

22. Paulo Freire, Cultural Action for Freedom (Cambridge, Mass.: Harvard Educational Review, 1970), pp. 2 and 21.

23. Freire, Pedagogy of the Oppressed, pp. 92-94.

24. Schaar, "Equality of Opportunity and Beyond," p. 240.

25. Fanon writes: "So they say that the natives want to go quickly. Now, let us never forget that only a very short time ago they complained of their slowness, their laziness and their fatalism." Again, "For the native, objectivity is always directed against him." Frantz Fanon, The Wretched of the Earth (New York: Grove Press, 1968), pp. 75 and 77.

26. Roman Aquizao and Ernest Vargas, "Technology, Power and Socialization in Appalachia," in Peoples' Appalachian Research Collective (PARC), ed., Appalachia's People, Problems, Alternatives, vol. 1 (Morgantown, W. Va.: PARC, 1971), p. 126.

27. Edelman, Symbolic Uses of Politics, p. 56.

28. Much of the following discussion stems from Gramsci's insight: "The trade union was limited in freedom of action by its increasing observance of strict legality in relations with the propertied class." Cammett, Antonio Gramsci, p. 84.

29. This phrase is taken from Theodore Roszak, The Making of a Counter Culture (New York: Anchor Books, 1969), p. 206. The idea is central to Kenneth B. Clark and Jeannette Hopkins, A Relevant War Against Poverty: A Study of Community Action Programs and Observable Social Change (New York: Harper & Row, 1968).

30. In this sense OEO was not instrumental in constructing what Freire terms a developed society in which all persons are beings for themselves or the similar condition of a modern society, which, according to Habermas, is the questioning of traditional legitimations of power. Freire, Pedagogy of the Oppressed, p. 160; Habermas, Toward a Rational Society, p. 96. See also C. B. Macpherson, The Real World of Democracy (New York: Oxford University Press, 1966), pp. 10-11; and Donald J. Devine, The Political Culture of the United States: The Influence of Member Values on Regime Maintenance (Boston: Little, Brown and Company, 1972), pp. 61-62, for further discussion of the transformation of demands into support by liberal society.

31. David M. Potter, People of Plenty: Economic Abundance and the American Character (Chicago: University of Chicago Press, 1954), p. 121. This leveling up approach is now apparent in the forms of national health insurance that approximate new payment mechanisms with reform of the health care system.

32. Devine, The Political Culture of the United States, pp. 255-60.

33. C. B. Macpherson, "Democratic Theory: Ontology and Technology," in Political Theory and Social Change, edited by David Spitz (New York: Atherton Press, 1967), p. 213.

34. Macpherson, The Real World of Democracy, pp. 57-67.

35. Macpherson, "Democratic Theory: Ontology and Technology," p. 206.

36. Richard Lichtman, "The Political Economy of Medical Care," in Dreitzel, The Social Organization of Health, p. 276.

37. Ibid., p. 267.

BILL OF HEALTH RIGHTS

1. In Floyd County last year over $2 million in Federal money was paid to four local hospitals for treating poor people, at least another $1 million went directly to the county doctors for seeing poor patients. About $1,500,000 was promised to the Prestonsburg Hospital for building the new Highlands Hospital. These so-called "private" hospitals continue to receive most of their funds from tax-payers' money. They are not "private" at all, they are public.

   WE DEMAND THAT A PUBLIC BOARD OF DIRECTORS BE ELECTED TO SET POLICY FOR EACH OF THESE HOSPITALS. A MAJORITY OF THE BOARD MEMBERS MUST BE PEOPLE WHO ARE SERVED BY THE HOSPITALS—THIS INCLUDES POOR PEOPLE WHO GET THE SICKEST AND HAVE TO GO TO THE HOSPITAL THE MOST.

2. Every day people die because they are turned away from the hospital emergency rooms for lack of money. We believe health care is a right, not a privilege for those who happen to have money.

   WE DEMAND THAT HOSPITALS END THIS MURDEROUS PRACTICE, OR LOSE THEIR ACCREDITATION AND THEIR LICENSE TO OPERATE.

3. Most poor people's homes in Eastern Kentucky are crammed full of prescription drugs they got from their doctors. They are not told by their doctors that many of the drugs are dangerous and could be addicting. Many of our doctors have part ownership in the local drugstores, or often the drugstores are owned by the doctors' kin.

   WE DEMAND THAT DOCTORS STOP PROFITING FROM POOR PEOPLE'S SICKNESS. THAT ALL DOCTORS WHO HAVE FINANCIAL INTERESTS IN DRUGSTORES GET OUT OF THE DRUGSTORE BUSINESS. THAT DOCTORS WRITE PRESCRIPTIONS (instead of phoning them) SO THAT PEOPLE HAVE THEIR LAWFUL RIGHT TO CHOOSE THE DRUGSTORE THEY WISH TO TRADE AT. THAT DOCTORS DIRECT THE DRUGGISTS TO LABEL EACH

PILL BOTTLE WITH THE NAME OF THE DRUG INSIDE, SO THE PATIENT CAN FIND OUT WHAT ITS SIDE EFFECTS ARE.

4. There are not enough doctors in Floyd County to give medical care to all the people who need it. Yet, the Floyd County Medical Society which claims to care about people's health, has worked hard to keep doctors out of the County. They are afraid they will lose some of their patients and some of their profits.

    WE DEMAND THAT THE COUNTY DOCTORS STOP OBSTRUCT-ING OTHER DOCTORS FROM COMING INTO THE COUNTY TO PRACTICE.

5. There are few doctors in Eastern Kentucky and even fewer specialists. (There is only one specialist in Floyd County.) To receive specialist care a person must hire a private ambulance ($85) and travel 125 miles to the University of Kentucky Medical Center. Very few poor people can afford this, and even if they could find the money, many won't go because they are discrimi-nated against as "hillbillys" at the University Hospital.

    WE DEMAND THAT THE UNIVERSITY OF KENTUCKY MEDICAL CENTER—WHICH HAS A MONOPOLY ON ALL THE TRAINING, HAS ALL THE SPECIALISTS, AND MOST OF THE ADVANCED MEDICAL EQUIPMENT IN THE STATE STOP RUNNING "TOKEN" PROGRAMS FOR EASTERN KENTUCKY AND ASSIGN 500 DOC-TORS AND OTHER MEDICAL PERSONNEL TO WORK IN EAST-ERN KENTUCKY.

6   In order to begin to meet the doctor shortage in Eastern Kentucky with doctors who understand and respect the poor and the disabled and in order to compensate for the history of keeping Eastern Kentucky's poor out of the University of Kentucky Medical School.

    WE DEMAND THAT UNIVERSITY OF KENTUCKY MEDICAL SCHOOL RECRUIT AND GIVE SCHOLARSHIPS TO MINERS' AND POOR PEOPLE'S SONS AND DAUGHTERS. SINCE EASTERN KENTUCKY MAKES UP ONE THIRD OF KENTUCKY AND SINCE THE SONS AND DAUGHTERS OF POOR PEOPLE HAVE BEEN KEPT OUT OF THE UNIVERSITY OF KENTUCKY MEDICAL SCHOOL IN THE PAST, AT LEAST ONE THIRD OF ITS MEDICAL STUDENTS SHOULD COME FROM EASTERN KENTUCKY.

184

7. The OEO Comprehensive Health program of Floyd County has
cost the public over $4 million in the last four years. In that time
the doctors, dentists, druggists and politicians have gotten rich
and health services for poor people have not improved one bit.
Now OEO has threatened to cut off the funds. We are tired of
the doctors and politicians playing football with our health and
our lives. We have written and submitted a proposal to OEO for
the funds to be given directly to an all-consumer board of directors and that a community-controlled comprehensive health service
be set up.

WE DEMAND THAT OEO AND CONGRESSMAN CARL D. PERKINS
TURN THE OEO MONEY OVER TO POOR PEOPLE SO THAT WE
CAN HIRE OUR OWN DOCTORS AND SET UP OUR OWN CLINICS.
WE ARE THE PEOPLE WHO CARE ABOUT GOOD HEALTH SER-
VICES FOR THE POOR, AND ARE THE ONLY PEOPLE WHO
WOULD SEE THAT THE PUBLIC MONEY IS SPENT IN THE
RIGHT WAY.

The Eastern Kentucky Welfare Rights Organization pledges to
fight for decent health care for all people in Eastern Kentucky.
We believe all patients should be treated with respect and dignity
and should receive quality services in well-equipped hospitals
and clinics near their home.

APPALACHIA

Axelrod, Jim, ed. Growin' up Country. Clintwood, Va.: Council of
the Southern Mountains, 1973.

Bazell, Robert J. "Health Care: What the Poor People Didn't Get
from Kentucky Project." Science 172 (April 30, 1971): 458-60.

_____. "OEO Hedges on Kentucky Program." Science 172 (October
1, 1971): 45.

Bethell, Thomas N. Conspiracy in Coal. Huntington, W. Va.: Appalachian Movement Press, 1971.

_____. The Hurricane Creek Massacre. New York: Harper &
Row, 1972.

Branscome, James. Annihilating the Hillbilly: The Appalachians'
Struggle with America's Institutions. Huntington, W. Va.:
Appalachian Movement Press, 1971.

Caudill, Harry M. Night Comes to the Cumberlands: A Biography
of a Depressed Area. Boston: Little, Brown and Co., 1962.

Dudley, H., and Mary Jean Bowman. Elites and Change in the Kentucky
Mountains. Lexington: University of Kentucky Press, 1973.

Dunbar, Tony. Our Land Too. New York: Vintage Books, 1971.

Ford, Thomas R., ed. The Southern Appalachian Region: A Survey.
Lexington: University of Kentucky Press, 1962.

Gitlin, Todd, and Nanci Hollander. Uptown: Poor Whites in Chicago.
New York: Harper Colophon Books, 1970.

Good, Paul. "Kentucky's Coal Beds of Sedition." The Nation 205
(September 4, 1967): 166-69.

Jewell, Malcolm E., and Everett W. Cunningham. Kentucky Politics.
Lexington: University of Kentucky Press, 1968.

Kenny, Maxine. "Mountain Health Care: Politics, Power and Profits."
Mountain Life and Work 47 (April 1971): 14-17.

Lewis, Helen. "Fatalism or the Coal Industry? Contrasting Views
of Appalachian Problems." Mountain Life and Work 46, no. 11
(December 1970): 4-15.

Maloney, Mike, and Ben Huelsman. "Humanism, Scientism and Southern Mountaineers: A Review." People's Appalachia 2, no. 3
(July 1972): 24-27.

Mason, Gene L. 'Stripping Kentucky: The Subversive Poor." The
Nation 207 (December 30, 1968): 721-24.

Peoples' Appalachian Research Collective (PARC), ed. Appalachia's
People, Problems, Alternatives, vol. 1. Morgantown, W. Va.:
PARC, 1971.

Perry, Huey. "They'll Cut Off Your Project": A Mingo County
Chronicle. New York: Praeger Publishers, 1972.

Peterson, Bill. Coaltown Revisited: An Appalachian Notebook.
Chicago: Henry Regnery Co., 1972.

Schwarzweller, Harry K., James S. Brown, and J. J. Mangalam.
Mountain Families in Transition: A Case Study of Appalachian
Migration. University Park: Pennsylvania State University
Press, 1971.

Stephenson, John B. Shiloh: A Mountain Community. Lexington:
University of Kentucky Press, 1968.

Stivers, James R. "Floyd County Comprehensive Health Services
Program." Unpublished paper, College of Medicine, University
of Kentucky, June 1971

U.S. Department of Interior. Coal Mines Administration. A Medical
Survey of the Bituminous Coal Industry. Washington, D.C.:
U.S. Government Printing Office, 1947.

Vry, John. "The Floyd County Comprehensive Health Service: A
Rural Health Program in Eastern Kentucky." Unpublished paper,
College of Medicine, University of Kentucky, 1969.

Walls, David S., and John B. Stephenson. Appalachia in the Sixties: Decade of Reawakening. Lexington: University of Kentucky Press, 1972.

Weller, Jack. Yesterday's People: Life of Contemporary Appalachia. Lexington: University of Kentucky Press, 1965.

HEALTH

Anderson, Odin W. Health Care: Can There Be Equity? The United States, Sweden and England. New York: John Wiley and Sons, 1972.

Coles, Robert. "Psychiatrists and the Poor." Man Against Poverty. Edited by Arthur I. Blaustein and Robert R. Woock. New York: Random House, 1968.

Dreitzel, Hans Peter, ed. The Social Organization of Health: Recent Sociology No. 3. New York: Macmillan,1971.

Fortune, Editors of. Our Ailing Medical Society: It's Time to Operate. New York: Harper & Row, 1969.

Glazer, Nathan. "Paradoxes of Health Care." The Public Interest 22 (Winter 1971): 62-77.

Health Policy Advisory Center. The American Health Empire: A Report from the Health Policy Advisory Center. New York: Vintage Books, 1971.

Illich, Ivan. "Two Watersheds: The American Public Health System." Social Policy 3, no. 6. (March/April 1973): 46-50.

Kennedy, Edward M. In Critical Condition: The Crisis in America's Health Care. New York: Pocket Books, 1973.

Klarman, Herbert. The Economics of Health. New York: Columbia University Press, 1965.

Marmor, Theodore R. The Politics of Medicare. Chicago: Aldine Publishing Company, 1973.

Office of Economic Opportunity. Guideline: Healthright Programs. Washington, D.C.: U.S. Government Printing Office, 1970.

_____. Healthright Programs: The Neighborhood Health Center. Washington, D.C.: U.S. Government Printing Office, 1970.

Report of the National Advisory Commission on Health Manpower. 2 vols. Washington, D.C.: U.S. Government Printing Office, 1967.

Rosen, Sumner N. "Health Issue: Change and Resistance to Change." Social Policy 1 no. 5 (January/February 1971).

Yerby, Alonzo S. "The Disadvantaged and Health Care." American Journal of Public Health 6, no. 1 (January 1966): 5-9.

POLITICAL AND SOCIAL THEORY

Aronowitz, Stanley. "The Trap of Environmentalism." Social Policy 3, no. 3 (September/October 1972): 34-38.

Ash, Roberta. Social Movements in the United States. Chicago: Markham Publishing Co., 1972.

Bachrach, Peter. The Theory of Democratic Elitism: A Critique. Boston: Little, Brown and Company, 1967.

_____, and Morton S. Baratz. Power and Poverty: Theory and Practice. New York: Oxford University Press, 1970.

Banfield, Edward C. The Unheavenly City: The Nature and Future of Our Urban Crisis. Boston: Little, Brown and Company, 1968.

Baskin, Darryl. American Pluralist Democracy: A Critique. New York: Van Nostrand Reinhold Co., 1971.

Berger, Peter, and Thomas Luckman. The Social Construction of Reality: A Treatise in the Sociology of Knowledge. Garden City, N.Y.: Doubleday Anchor Books, 1967.

_____, Stanley Pullberg, and Ben Brewster. "Reification and the Sociological Critique of Consciousness: Comment and Response." New Left Review 35 (January/February 1966): 56-77.

Boorstin, Daniel J. The Genius of American Politics. Chicago: Phoenix Books, 1958.

189

Cammett, John M. Antonio Gramsci and the Origins of Italian Communism. Stanford, Calif.: Stanford University Press, 1967.

Cloward, Richard, and Lloyd Ohlin. Delinquency and Opportunity. New York: The Free Press, 1960.

Devine, Donald J. The Political Culture of the United States: The Influence of Member Values on Regime Maintenance. Boston: Little, Brown and Company, 1972.

Dreitzel, Hans Peter, ed. Recent Sociology No. 1: On The Social Basis of Politics. New York: Macmillan, 1969.

_____. Recent Sociology No. 2: Patterns of Communicative Behavior. New York: Macmillan Company, 1970.

Edelman, Murray. Politics as Symbolic Action: Mass Arousal and Quiescence. Chicago: Markham Publishing Co., 1971.

_____. The Symbolic Uses of Politics. Urbana: University of Illinois Press, 1967.

Fanon, Frantz. The Wretched of the Earth. New York: Grove Press, 1968.

Franklin, Benjamin. The Political Thought of Benjamin Franklin. Edited by Ralph L. Ketcham. New York: Bobbs-Merrill Com- 1965.

Freire, Paulo. Cultural Action for Freedom. Cambridge, Mass.: Harvard Educational Review, 1970.

_____. Pedagogy of the Oppressed. New York: Herder and Herder, 1970.

Galbraith, John Kenneth. The Affluent Society. New York: New American Library, 1958.

Goffman, Erving. Stigma: Notes on the Management of Spoiled Identity. Englewood Cliffs, N.J.: Prentice-Hall, 1963.

Habermas, Jurgen. Toward a Rational Society: Student Protest, Science and Politics. Translated by Jeremy Shapiro. Boston: Beacon Press, 1968.

190

Hartz, Louis. The Liberal Tradition in America: An Interpretation of American Political Thought Since the Revolution. New York: Harcourt, Brace and World, 1955.

Hofstadter, Richard. Social Darwinism in American Thought. New York: George Braziller, 1959.

Lichtman, Richard. "Symbolic Interactionism and Social Reality: Some Marxist Queries." Berkeley Journal of Sociology 15 (1970): 75-94.

Light, Ivan H. "The Social Construction of Uncertainty." Berkeley Journal of Sociology 14 (1969): 189-99.

Lukacs, Georg. History and Class Consciousness. Translated by Rodney Livingston. London: Merlin Press, 1971.

Macpherson, C. B. The Political Theory of Possessive Individualism: Hobbes to Locke. New York: Oxford University Press, 1962.

_____. The Real World of Democracy. New York: Oxford University Press, 1972.

Miliband, Ralph. The State in Capitalist Society. New York: Basic Books, 1969.

Miller, S. M., and Ronnie Steinberg Ratner. "The American Resignation: The New Assault on Equality." Social Policy 3 no. 1 (May/June 1972): 5-15.

Mills, C. Wright. "The Professional Ideology of Social Pathologists." American Journal of Sociology 49, no. 2 (September 1943): 165-80.

_____. The Sociological Imagination. New York: Oxford University Press, 1959.

Natanson, Maurice. "Alfred Schutz on Social Reality and Social Science." Social Research 35 no. 2 (1968): 217-45.

Olson, Mancur, Jr. "Orthodox Theories of Pressure Groups" and "By Product and Special Interest Theories." Interest Group Politics in America. Compiled by Robert H. Salisbury. New York: Harper & Row, 1970.

Paine, Thomas. The Complete Writings of Thomas Paine. Edited
by Philip S. Foner. 2 vols. New York: Citadel Press, 1945.

Parker, Richard. The Myth of the Middle Class: Notes on Affluence
and Equality. New York: Liveright, 1972.

Potter, David M. People of Plenty: Economic Abundance and the
American Character. Chicago: University of Chicago Press,
1954.

Psathas, George. "Ethnomethodology and Phenomenology." Social
Research 35, no. 3 (1968): 500-17.

Reid, Herbert G., ed. Up the Mainstream: a Critique of Ideology in
American Politics and Everyday Life. New York: David
McKay Company, 1974

Roszak, Theodore. The Making of a Counter Culture. New York:
Anchor Books, 1969.

Rule, James B. "The Problem with Social Problems." Politics and
Society 2, no. 1 (1971): 47-56.

Schroyer, Trent. "Toward a Critical Theory for Advanced Industrial
Society." Recent Sociology: No. 2. Edited by Hans Peter
Dreitzel. New York: Macmillan Company, 1970.

Schutz, Alfred. The Phenomenology of the Social World. Evanston,
Ill.: Northwestern University Press, 1967.

Selznick, Philip. TVA and the Grass Roots: A Study in the Sociology
of Formal Organization. New York: Harper & Row, 1966.

Sundquist, James L. Politics and Policy: The Eisenhower, Kennedy
and Johnson Years. Washington, D.C.: The Brookings Institution, 1968.

Weber, Max. The Methodology of the Social Sciences. Translated by
Edward A. Shils and Henry A. Finch. New York: The Free
Press, 1949.

Wolin, Sheldon S. "Political Theory as a Vocation." American
Political Science Review 63, no. 4 (December 1969): 1062-82.

_____. Politics and Vision: Continuity and Innovation in Western Political Thought. Boston: Little, Brown and Company, 1960.

POVERTY AND ANTIPOVERTY

Anderson, W. H. Locke. "Trickling Down: The Relationship Between Economic Growth and the Extent of Poverty Among American Families." The Quarterly Journal of Economics 78, no. 4 (November 1964): 511-24.

Boone, Richard. "Reflections on Citizen Participation and the Economic Opportunity Act." Paper presented at the National Academy of Public Administration's Conference on Crisis, Conflict, and Creativity, Washington, D.C., May 7, 1970.

Bremner, Robert H. American Philanthropy. Chicago: University of Chicago Press, 1960.

_____. From the Depths: The Discovery of Poverty in America. New York: New York University Press, 1965.

Caplovitz, David. The Poor Pay More: Consumer Practices of Low Income Families. London: Free Press of Glencoe, 1963.

Clark, Kenneth B., and Jeannette Hopkins. A Relevant War Against Poverty: A Study of Community Action Programs and Observable Social Change. New York: Harper & Row, 1968.

Cloward, Richard, and Richard M. Elman. "Poverty, Injustice, and the Welfare State." The Nation 202 (February 28, 1966): 230-35.

Coles, Robert. Still Hungry in America. New York: World Publishing Co., 1969.

Donovan, John C. The Politics of Poverty. 2d ed. New York: Pegasus Press, 1967.

Dorfman, Robert, ed. Measuring Benefits of Government Investments. Washington, D.C.: The Brookings Institution, 1965.

Duhl, Leonard J. "Are We Mentally Prepared for the Elimination of Poverty?" The Social Welfare Forum, 1961. New York: Columbia University Press, 1961.

Gans Herbert J. More Equality. New York: Pantheon Books, 1973.

Gladwin, Thomas. "The Anthropologist's View of Poverty." The Social Welfare Forum, 1961. New York: Columbia University Press, 1961.

_____, Poverty U.S.A. Boston: Little, Brown and Co., 1967.

Greenberg, Polly. The Devil Has Slippery Shoes: A Biased Biography of the Child Development Group of Mississippi. London: Macmillan, 1969.

Harrington, Michael. The Other America: Poverty in the United States. Baltimore: Penguin Books, 1964.

James, Dorothy B. Poverty, Politics and Change. Englewood Cliffs, N.J.: Prentice-Hall, 1972.

Kershaw, Joseph A. Government Against Poverty. Chicago: Markham Publishing Co., 1970.

Kristol, Irving. "Poverty and Pechaniff." The New Leader 47 (March 30, 1964): 220-23.

Leacock, Eleanor Burke, ed. The Culture of Poverty: A Critique. New York: Simon and Schuster, 1971.

Levitan, Sar A. The Great Society's Poor Law. Baltimore: Johns Hopkins University Press, 1969.

Lewis, Oscar. "The Culture of Poverty." Scientific American 215, no. 4 (October 1966): 19-25.

Marris, Peter, and Martin Rein. Dilemmas of Social Reform: Poverty and Community Action in the United States. New York: Atherton Press, 1967.

McDonald, Dwight. "Our Invisible Poor." New Yorker, January 19, 1963, pp. 82ff.

Melville, Herman. "Poor Man's Pudding and Rich Man's Crumbs," in Great Short Works of Herman Melville. Edited by Warner Berthoff. New York: Harper & Row, 1970.

Miller, Herman P. "Is the Income Gap Closed? No!" New York Times Magazine, November 11, 1962, pp. 50.

Moynihan, Daniel P. Maximum Feasible Misunderstanding: Community Action in the War on Poverty. New York: The Free Press, 1970.

_____, ed. On Understanding Poverty: Perspectives from the Social Sciences. New York: Basic Books, 1969.

Office of Economic Opportunity. Dimensions of Poverty in 1964. Washington, D.C.: U.S. Government Printing Office, 1965.

Ornati, Oscar. Poverty Amid Affluence. New York: Twentieth Century Fund, 1966.

Orshansky, Mollie. "Counting the Poor: Another Look at the Poverty Profile." Social Security Bulletin 28, no. 1 (January 1965): 3-29.

_____. "The Shape of Poverty in 1966." Social Security Bulletin 31 (March 1968): 3-32.

_____. "Who's Who Among the Poor: A Demographic View of Poverty." Social Security Bulletin 28 (July 1965): 3-33.

Piven, Frances Fox, and Richard Cloward. "Nathan Glazer's Retroactive Wisdom on Welfare." Social Policy 3, no. 1 (May/June, 1972): 26-27.

_____. Regulating the Poor: The Functions of Public Welfare. New York: Random House, 1971.

Ryan, William. Blaming the Victim. New York: Random House, 1971.

Seligman, Ben B. Permanent Poverty: An American Syndrome. Chicago: Quadrangle Books, 1968.

Sundquist, James L., ed. On Fighting Poverty: Perspectives from Experience. New York: Basic Books, 1969.

Thernstrom, Stephan. "The Myth of American Affluence." Commentary 48, no. 4 (October 1969): 74-78.

Thurow, Lester C. Poverty and Discrimination. Washington, D.C.: The Brookings Institution, 1969.

_____, and Robert E. B. Lucas. The American Distribution of Income: A Structural Problem. A study prepared for the use of the Joint Economic Committee, Congress of the United States. Washington, D.C.: U.S. Government Printing Office, 1972.

U.S. Congress. House Committee on Education and Labor. Administration and Conduct of Antipoverty Programs. Hearings. 91st Cong., 1st sess., November 6 and 13, 1969.

_____. Economic Opportunities Amendments of 1967, Hearings before an ad hoc task force of the Committee on Education and Labor, House of Representatives, on H.R. 513, 90th Cong., 1st sess., 1967.

Valentine, Charles. Culture and Poverty: Critique and Counter-Proposals. Chicago: University of Chicago Press, 1968.

Wiley, George. "Masking Repression as Reform." Social Policy 3, no. 1 (May/June 1972): 16-19.

GENERAL

Jewell, Malcolm. Kentucky Votes. 3 Vols. Lexington: University of Kentucky Press, 1963.

Johnson, Lyndon Baines. The Vantage Point: Perspectives of the Presidency, 1963-1969. New York: Holt, Rinehart and Winston, 1971.

Kentucky Department of Health. Vital Statistics, 1971. Kentucky Department of Health, Frankfort, Ky, 1973.

Sorauf, Frank. "State Patronage in a Rural County." American Political Science Review 50, no. 4 (1956): 1046-56.

U.S. Department of Commerce. Bureau of the Census. Current Population Reports, series P-60 No. 81 "Characteristics of the Low-Income Population, 1970." Washington, D.C.: U.S. Government Printing Office, 1971. vol 1, pt. 19.

_____. Revision in Poverty Statistics, 1959-68. Washington, D.C.: U.S. Government Printing Office, 1969.

_____. Statistical Abstract of the United States, 1972. 93rd ed. Washington, D.C.: U.S. Government Printing Office, 1972.

U.S. Department of Labor. Bureau of Labor Statistics. 3 Standards of Living for an Urban Family of Four Persons Spring 1967 Washington, D.C.: U.S Government Printing Office, 1969.

White, Theodore H. The Making of the President: 1960. New York: Atheneum Publishing Company, 1961.

RICHARD A. COUTO is Assistant Professor of Political Science at Northern Kentucky State College, Highland Heights, Kentucky. He has been associated with a number of antipoverty efforts in Eastern Kentucky since 1966.

Dr. Couto earned his B.A. from Marist College in Poughkeepsie; his M.A. from Boston College; and his Ph.D. from the University of Kentucky.

AMERICAN HEALTH: Professional Privilege
vs. Public Need

>Tom Levin

CHANGING THE MEDICAL CARE SYSTEM: A
Controlled Experiment in Comprehensive Care

>Leon S. Robertson, John Kosa,
>Margaret C. Heagarty, Robert J.
>Haggerty, and Joel J. Alpert.
>Foreword by Charles A. Janeway

COAL MINE HEALTH AND SAFETY:
The Case of West Virginia

>J. Davitt

THE HEALTH-IMPAIRED MINER UNDER
THE BLACK LUNG LEGISLATION

>edited by Leo Kramer, Inc. and
>Ewan Clague

HOSPITAL EFFICIENCY AND PUBLIC POLICY

>Harry I. Greenfield

THE ORGANIZATION AND DELIVERY OF
MENTAL HEALTH SERVICES IN THE GHETTO:
The Lincoln Hospital Experience

>Seymour R. Kaplan and Melvin Roman

THE POLITICS OF HEALTH CARE: Nine
Case Studies of Innovative Planning in New
York City

>edited by Herbert Harvey Hyman